THE COMPLETE IN TO

REC
COLLECTING

Published in the United Kingdom 1995

by Diamond Publishing Group Limited,
45 St. Mary's Road, Ealing, London W5 5RQ

Printed in England

ISBN No. 0 9515553 6 7

The Complete Introduction To
Record Collecting

PUBLISHED BY
RECORD COLLECTOR
The world's leading publication for
collectors of rare records and memorabilia

PUBLISHER
Sean O'Mahony

MANAGING EDITOR
Johnny Dean

EXECUTIVE EDITOR
Peter Doggett

EDITOR
Pat Gilbert

CONTRIBUTORS
Pat Gilbert
Peter Doggett
Mark Paytress
John Reed
Andy Davis

ART DIRECTOR
Ian Gray

PRODUCTION MANAGER
Nicholas Barfield

THANKS TO
Barry Plummer, Esprit Mail Order, Key Mail Order, Daren Butler, Ian Peel, Lewis Gilbert, Paul Pelletier.

CONTENTS

INTRODUCTION

When you start collecting records, you're joining a very large and exclusive band of top stars, including Noel Gallagher of Oasis, Peter Buck of R.E.M., Paul Weller, John Peel, Paul McCartney and Elton John. They're just a few of the celebrities who've discovered the fascination of acquiring the great recordings of the past few decades.

Record collecting is one of the world's fastest-growing pastimes, but for newcomers, it can seem a bit complicated to begin with. Identifying which kinds of records are likely to sell for hundreds of pounds, and which are virtually worthless, isn't always easy, and the expressions and jargon used by experienced collectors need some explaining. That's what this book is all about. It explains everything simply and easily, and tells you exactly how to go about finding the rare records in a pile of old 45s, or a stack of new CDs.

We've also included advice about buying and selling rare records, plus handy hints on everything from looking after your collection to purchasing records by mail-order. There are also sections which look in detail at the Top 10 collectable artists, and the rarest records in every type of music over the past 40 years.

MILLION POUND INDUSTRY

Over the last decade, the record collecting scene has grown from a back-street business into a multi-million pound industry. Today, more people than ever are buying secondhand singles and albums, and the prices being paid for rare releases by bands like the Beatles and the Rolling Stones continue to rise every year.

As the market has expanded, so too have the number of people discovering the pleasures of searching car boot sales and cupboards in the hope of finding a clutch of juicy rarities. While doing just that, a retired Liverpool policeman stumbled across a tape he made in the late 1950s of a local skiffle group called the Quarry Men. As you may know, one of the teenagers on that recording — John Lennon — later found fame and fortune with the Beatles. The tape became the star attraction when it was put up for sale at Sotheby's auction house in September 1994, and sold for an incredible £78,000.

Of course, very few of us are going to find a rare pre-Beatles recording in our attic, but there are literally thousands of other rare records, tapes and CDs to look out for, ranging from vintage rock'n'roll singles by Elvis Presley and Bill Haley to recent rarities by Blur, Oasis, Pulp and Nirvana. In fact, our *Rare Record Price Guide*, which is now in its third edition, lists no fewer than 75,000 collectable U.K. releases, and that figure is increasing all the time.

EXPERT GUIDANCE

Record collecting is a complex subject. You only need to look at a copy of our monthly magazine, *Record Collector* — the 'bible' of the scene with its comprehensive discographies, in-depth features and cutting-edge news stories — to realise that the

Blur made a massive impact on the collecting scene after the success of "Parklife" in 1994.

collecting market keeps on growing faster every year. But it's not difficult to get into it once you know how it works.

One basic rule is that you can't generalise about the kinds of records that are worth money. A rule that holds true in one area of collecting often doesn't apply in another. Couple this with the fact that each individual music fan has their own idea about what's worth buying, and you're left with a situation where expert guidance is essential.

For instance, take the simple matter of promotional records, which are free discs given away to DJs and journalists to publicise a new release. Are they collectable or not? Well, this book will tell you that fans of modern pop and indie groups like Blur and East 17 tend to prize them highly, paying two or three times the value of the normal issue for them, while 50s enthusiasts don't usually bother with promos at all. Dance, hip-hop and rap collecting, however, is dominated by promos distributed to select club DJs.

It's that kind of inside information that this book provides.

DETAILS

In collecting, the details are always important. What the papers often don't point out when they break a story about a record selling for hundreds of pounds is that it's often only a small difference that identifies it as a rarity. As the value of two almost identical versions of the same record can be very big indeed, you need to know the difference

Pulp's commercial breakthrough in the mid-'90s increased interest in their early releases.

between an acetate, a test pressing, a reissue and a white label, so you can tell the rarities from the rest.

Many people have been misled into thinking they owned a rarity. For example, after *Record Collector* wrote about the very scarce U.S. version of Bob Dylan's *Freewheelin'* album with a different tracklisting to the U.K. edition, it was wrongly reported elsewhere in the media that *all* copies of the album were extremely valuable.

Of course, that was ridiculous. Hundreds of thousands of copies of the U.K. edition exist, and in perfect condition, they still only sell for around £15 apiece. It's only the American stereo version with the unique sequence of tracks that collectors are prepared to pay upwards of £10,000 for. But inaccurate reporting in the press meant that thousands of people had their hopes raised, and then quickly dashed.

COLLECTABLE

Of course, the vast majority of records, tapes, LPs, EPs and CDs that people buy on the collector's market aren't worth thousands, or even hundreds, of pounds. For the most part, collectors want to track down the music by their favourite groups that is no longer available in the high street stores, or to buy albums and singles in their original form — which often means on vinyl.

Remember, a classic secondhand LP from the 1970s, like Led Zeppelin's *Four Symbols*, will often only set you back around £15 (and that's for a perfect or 'Mint' copy), and many people regard these originals, with their full-sized artwork and 'first edition' feel, as an attractive alternative to buying a new CD version.

REWARDING

The Complete Introduction To Record Collecting is the key to discovering a rich and rewarding world. Once you've read it, you'll be armed with all the knowledge you need to recognise the rarities from the rubbish!

MAKING A START

What exactly distinguishes a collector from a 'normal' record buyer? If you've ever been a big fan of an artist, you'll already know part of the answer, because fans usually want everything they can find by, and about, their heroes. Most collectors tend to share the desire to delve deep into the recording history of the bands or the music they like. Rather than having just a handful of LPs, for example, they'll usually want a copy of every record the artist made, plus anything else that includes exclusive material.

WHERE TO START

But how do people start a collection? One 16-year-old Blur fan from Basingstoke recently wrote to *Record Collector*, with a typical tale about how he got into the collecting scene. "I went to see Blur at the Alexandra Palace in North London and didn't recognise several of the songs they played," he confided. "At that point, I was bitten by the bug, and I went out the next day to a specialist shop off Oxford Street and bought all the Blur records I could find.

"When I paid at the counter, the owner told me about 'The Wassailing Song', a one-sided record the band gave away to fans at a gig. As there are only 500, they're worth about £15 each, but I'm going to get it when I can afford it!"

It's a story that is probably familiar to most collectors. In fact, every member of the *Record Collector* staff started off as a teenage fan of one group or another, before widening their interests to include different genres like psychedelia, punk and folk-rock, as well as famous record labels like Apple and Creation.

Nirvana, whose early recordings for American labels like Sub Pop are highly sought-after.

BEYOND THE HIGH STREET SHOPS...

Once you started collecting, it's not long before you realise that some of the choicest rarities are the releases that don't appear in the shops, or are items that are produced in limited numbers. This brings you into contact with terms that you may have never across before, like 'acetate', 'white label', 'promo', 'flexidisc', 'die-cut sleeve' and 'reissue', which refer to different types of record or their packaging.

An acetate, for example, is a record made from aluminium, which is then coated with a special soft covering called laquer. Before cassette tapes were common, recording studios used to use these discs to give the artists an idea of what the finished single or album would sound like, or as a reference of the work they'd completed that day. This sometimes means that they include different music to that commercially released — thus making them highly-prized by many fans.

WIDE SCOPE

Because the scope for collecting any one artist can be enormous — especially when you consider that there are overseas releases to think about, and that singles are normally issued on several different formats — most fans restrict themselves to certain areas. Some collectors don't bother with foreign releases and only buy one version of any single — usually the one with the most tracks on it. As this is usually the CD, this can sometimes present a dilemma for people who still want everything on vinyl.

However, there is one group of collectors called 'completists' who, as their name suggests, will buy everything that a band releases, even when tracks or artwork are duplicated. Usually, such fans build up an invaluable archive of recordings, and they sometimes even find themselves helping the artist to put together compilations and reissues of their material.

RARE AND COLLECTABLE

As you might expect, the 'collectability' of a record depends on the popularity of the band who made it, and the number of copies in circulation. The most collected group at present are the Beatles, whose '60s recordings still hold an immense fascination for thousands of fans around the world. Most collectors want to get hold of original copies of their albums, EPs and singles, so this pushes up their price. Competition is fierce for very scarce items like the stereo version of their first album, *Please Please Me* — that's why it sells for around £700.

The demand for that album demonstrates another point — that collectors usually value the very first edition of any record more highly than any subsequent pressings or reissues (though there are exceptions). It's a way of saying 'I got there first!', and it can also have other benefits, as first issues often come with extras like lyric sheets, inner sleeves, inserts and posters which later reissues miss out on.

Of course, there are literally thousands of collectable groups. Many of them are quite obscure outfits with a cult following or one rare record that is sought after for some special reason.

But don't forget, there some records you can't give away: items by flash-in-the-pan chart acts like '80s wannabes Johnny Hates Jazz, Curiosity Killed The Cat or Bros aren't worth more than a nominal price. Things can change, though — ten years ago, almost no one collected '70s glam rock, but now it has become a major genre in the market.

When Elton John sold his valuable collection of antiques and stage costumes at Sotheby's, he was careful to hang on to his most precious possession — his record collection!

A WORD ABOUT CDs...

Finally, a word about CDs. Their arrival has, as many people predicted, all but killed off vinyl. But it certainly hasn't dented the enthusiasm for record collecting. Interest in collectable secondhand vinyl albums is as great as ever, and prices for famous vinyl rarities by everyone from the Rolling Stones to Nirvana continue to rise.

At the same time, though, CDs are in themselves becoming collectable, and an increasing number are winging their way into our *Rare Record Price Guide* every year. If they are nicely packaged or include exclusive material, collectors want them!

Throughout this book, song titles are printed in single quotation marks (for example: 'She Loves You', 'Anarchy In The U.K.', etc.).

Titles of LPs and albums are printed in italics (for example: *Sgt. Pepper, Automatic For The People,* etc.).

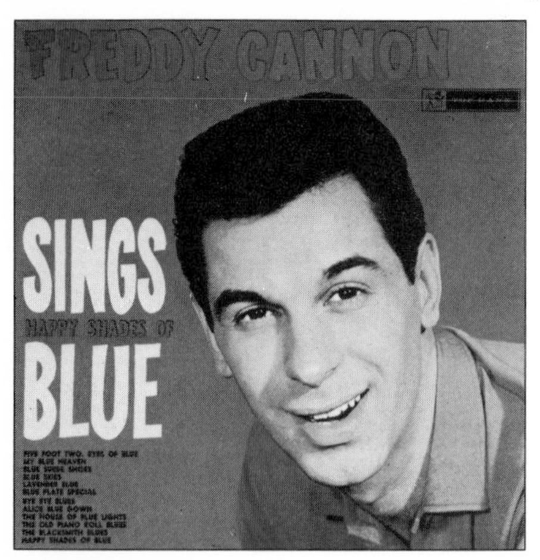

"Happy Shades Of Blue" was the second of three Freddy Cannon LPs for Top Rank.

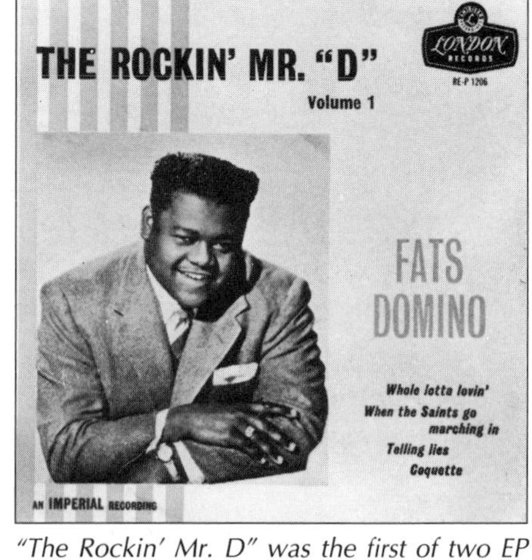

"The Rockin' Mr. D" was the first of two EP volumes from piano wizard Fats Domino.

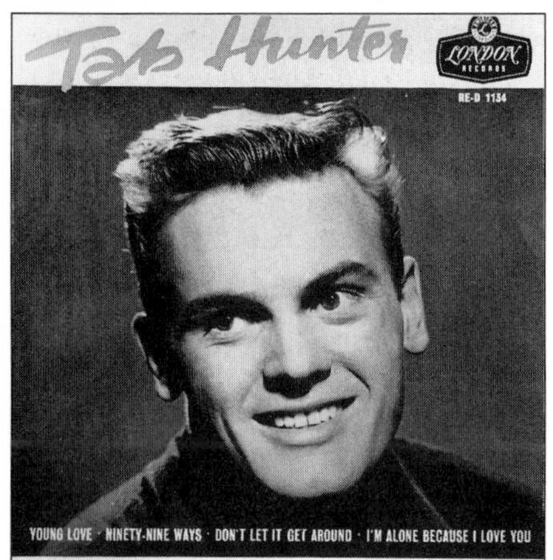

Tab Hunter's self-titled 1958 EP on London kicked off with his first U.K. 45, "Young Love".

Jane Morgan's first extended play record was Part 1 of "All The Way" on London.

R&B vocal group Ruby & the Romantics, with the scarce "Hey There Lonely Boy" EP.

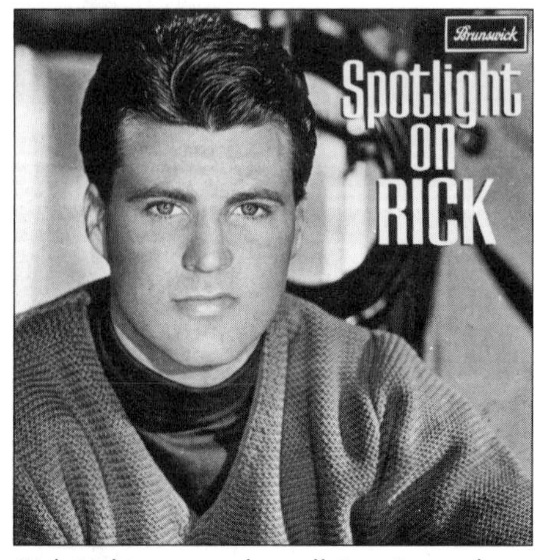

Rick Nelson sported an all-American, clean-cut look for his "Spotlight On Rick" album.

HISTORY OF RECORD COLLECTING

"From the day that the first record got deleted, people felt proud about owning them. Other people saw this, and off they went to collect their own." *(Paul Jones, Manfred Mann/Blues Band)*

"A world of matrix numbers and 'rare black wax', Cobra 78s and deleted Sun recordings of priceless worth — rock'n'roll is of the essence!" *(Sleevenote to the Deviants' "Social Deviants" LP, 1968)*

ALL THAT JAZZ

Although music fans have always had a love affair with records, the collecting scene as we now know it didn't really take shape until the early 1950s, when modern jazz from America began to make an impact in Britain.

Prior to that, lovers of classical music had swapped rare recordings and occasionally advertised in journals for obscure items. But it was jazz that first inspired interest in the records themselves and encouraged people to pay substantial sums for scarce discs and rare first pressings.

As far back as the '40s, collectors were hunting down rare jazz 78s by artists like Ella Fitzgerald.

The psychedelic 3-D sleeve for the Rolling Stones' "Their Satanic Majesties Request" LP.

"Nashville Skyline", the title of Bob Dylan's country-influenced album from the late '60s.

Many modern jazz recordings were issued in America long before they appeared elsewhere and, as a result, British fans wanting the latest 78s by artists like Charlie Parker, Miles Davis and John Coltrane often had to order them from specialist outlets. These were usually based in large cities, and had developed from shops which had imported jazz, swing, blues and country recordings for U.S. servicemen and women during the war.

With all these jazz lovers chasing scarce American recordings, some releases achieved a certain celebrity among fans, and a collecting scene quickly developed. People began to take notice of a record's label, catalogue number and country of origin — all of which could affect its value.

ROCK'N'ROLL & VINYL

In 1956, rock'n'roll hit Britain in a big way, and with it came vast improvements in record manufacturing. Up until then, most singles took the form of 78rpm 10" discs, made from a brittle material called shellac. However, these gradually began to be replaced by 45rpm 7" vinyl discs, which were far more durable and, despite what many 78 enthuasists claimed, sounded better if they were played on suitable equipment. 33⅓rpm LPs with advanced 'microgrooves' were also introduced in the '50s, giving fans the opportunity to hear more of their favourite music at one sitting.

BRITISH R&B

Rock'n'roll ushered in the modern 'pop' era, and record-buying quickly became an essential part of the teenage lifestyle. But tastes were changing, and by the beginning of the 1960s, people were looking elsewhere for their musical kicks. Across the country, a small but dedicated group of enthusiasts started picking up on the earthy R&B and blues sounds coming out of America, and particularly Chicago.

Just as jazz buffs had been forced to buy expensive U.S. imports ten years earlier, R&B fans relied on specialist outlets to supply them with records by Howlin' Wolf, Muddy Waters and Big Bill Broonzy.

Dick Taylor, a Rolling Stone for a short period, and later bassist with the Pretty Things, once said: "We thought we were the only people in England who'd ever heard

R.G. Jones Of Morden — this is what a mobile sound system looked like back in the 1940s!

of R&B." Of course, by 'we', he meant himself, Mick Jagger, Keith Richards and the father-figure of the British blues scene, Alexis Korner — all of whom were bowled over by the raw R&B they heard on American labels like OKeh, Modern, Imperial and Chess.

Legend has it that a passion for collecting brought Jagger and Richards together on the platform of Dartford railway station in 1961. Apparently, it was the American Chuck Berry album under Richards' arm that caught Mick's eye, and which resulted in the fateful renewing of their boyhood friendship.

COLLECTOR'S SHOPS

In London, blues and folk collectors could buy rare records in specialist shops like Dobells at 77 Charing Cross Road, which became a major stopping-off place for music enthusiasts from all over the world — including a young Bob Dylan, who recorded some songs in the basement there in 1963.

Another regular was Paul Jones, former lead singer with Manfred Mann. "I used to buy Leadbelly and Big Bill Broonzy records there," he remembers. "And also at Pete Russell's Hot Record Store. Pete turned me on to T-Bone Walker and electric blues. I was aware even then that there was a vibrant collecting scene among jazz and blues

Throughout this book, song titles are printed in single quotation marks (for example: 'She Loves You', 'Anarchy In The U.K.', etc.).

Titles of LPs and albums are printed in italics (for example: *Sgt. Pepper, Automatic For The People,* etc.).

fans, although it wasn't as big as in the States. Here, people were buying Broonzy recordings on Bluebird Records and old bluesmen like Charlie Patton on labels like Paramount."

"I remember that Chris Barber, the jazz musician, bought half a warehouse full of stuff when Savoy Records went out of business. He didn't even know what some of it was. He had a vast collection that even included a flexidisc from the 1920s, which featured a brief but rather wonderful solo from Louis Armstrong. There was some serious collecting going on."

GUY STEVENS

In the early '60s, as the Beatles were preparing to dominate the pop world, a new wave of collectors began to gain a cult profile. Among them was the late Guy Stevens, boss of Sue Records and sometime record producer, who DJ'ed regularly at the hip London hang-out, the Scene Club. Although groups played there, most people went to hear the latest U.S. soul and R&B titles he'd shipped in from the States.

Stevens' passions included rockabilly and rock'n'roll, and in the mid-1960s, he organised Saturday sales of imported singles, which took place in a room above a brothel in Lisle Street, in London's Soho district.

London was entering its 'swinging' phase, and many fans of original rock'n'roll were getting dewy-eyed about the halcyon days of Elvis, Jerry Lee Lewis and ripping up the seats in their local Odeon. This nostalgic yearning reawakened interest in vintage rock'n'roll records, many of which were already recognised as classics. It was at this point that collecting really took off, with enthusiasts buying vintage singles and LPs at well above the usual retail price.

One particular area of interest was the Sun label, which had issued the first recordings by Elvis, Jerry Lee and Carl Perkins. In 1965, a British dealer visited the Sun warehouse in Memphis, Tennessee, where he found thousands of unsold singles that he knew he could sell to enthusiasts in Britain. At first, he had about a dozen customers, who met regularly in a cafe off Petticoat Lane in London's East End. Soon, however, the circle swelled to more than 30, and their rendezvous switched to the Black Raven pub.

Some of the most expensive U.K. rarities stem from '50s rock'n'rollers like Carl 'Blue Suede Shoes' Perkins.

Continued on page 21

As all of Blur's singles have charted, their rarest release is a one-sided single, "The Wassailing Song", given away at a gig.

John Lennon pictured in 1967, just before he began his relationship with Yoko Ono. Their early avant-garde releases, like "Two Virgins", are particularly in demand.

ORIGINAL BEATLES LPs

The rarest pressings of "Please Please Me" came with a gold and black label.

The group's second album, "With The Beatles", appeared in December 1963.

"A Hard Day's Night" included seven songs featured in the Beatles' first movie.

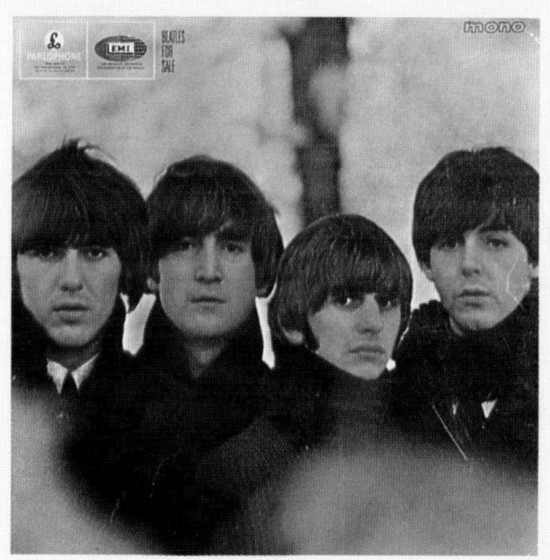

"Beatles For Sale" was the first album by the group to be issued in a gatefold sleeve.

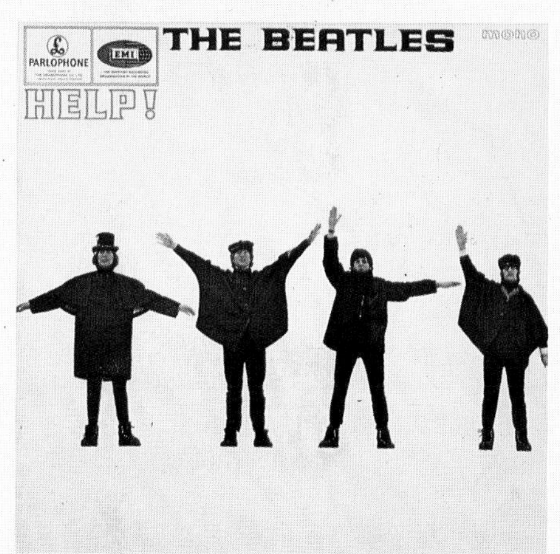

"Help!" followed the "A Hard Day's Night" format, devoting one side to film songs.

"Revolver", issued in August 1966, featured artwork by session bassist Klaus Voorman.

60s SINGLES IN COMPANY SLEEVES

The Brunswick label issued all the early singles by the Who, like "I Can't Explain".

The Byrds and Bob Dylan were among the acts who appeared on the orange CBS label.

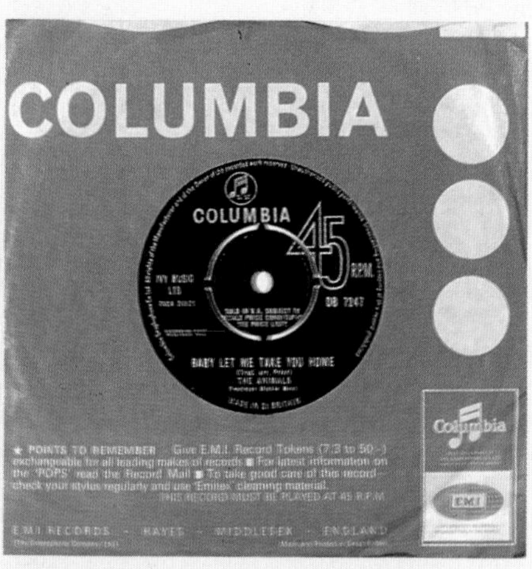

Columbia was EMI's most successful 60s label, thanks to groups like the Animals.

The Immediate label was founded by Andrew Oldham, the Rolling Stones' manager.

60s Decca singles by artists like the Rolling Stones came in this orange company sleeve.

United Artists was one of EMI's labels, and issued 45s by artists like Bobby Goldsboro.

It isn't just old records which are valuable. The Lemonheads' first single currently fetches £40.

BOOM TIME

"The market really began to boom in 1968," remembers Paul Sanford, a Sun devotee and a regular at the Black Raven and Guy Stevens' sales. "Several friends and I started to talk about travelling over to the Sun warehouse and selling the stuff across the counter over here." However, Sanford and his friends didn't make the journey until 1971, when they bought up 5,000 singles for as little as 5 cents each. These they sold off to fellow enthusiasts, via the London-based fanzine, *Rock'n'Roll Collector.*

At this time, mail-order was the chief way of buying rare discs, and adverts regularly appeared in publications like *Record Mart, Record Mirror* and *Melody Maker.*

"The best place to get stuff back then was junk shops," recalls discographer Paul Pelletier. "There were a couple in Catford where I lived which bought records in for a shilling, and sold them at two shillings. There was also a shop run by James Azman in the City. He sold deletions — left-over stock that the shops didn't want — which could be bought at a reasonable price. It was mainly classic vocal stuff and crooners."

As the early '70s arrived, so did a number of new collector's shops and market stalls, which specialised in vintage rock'n'roll records, but also occasionally supplied rare U.S. psychedelic and garage rock albums. Among the most first and most celebrated outlets were the stall run by Ted Carroll (later the man behind the Chiswick and Ace labels) in Portobello Market, and the Vintage Record Centre, off the Caledonian Road in north London.

At that time, many records that are now worth hundreds of pounds could be picked up for relatively small sums. Even so, a celebrated collectable like the original 1956 Coral pressing of Johnny Burnette's 10" LP, *Rock And Roll Trio,* would have set you back around £40, which is roughly equivalent to the £500 it sells for today. The idea that old records could actually be valuable in the same way as rare stamps or cigarette cards was starting to take hold.

Other early '70s collectables included psychedelic band Kaleidoscope's 1969 album, *Faintly Blowing,* and the legendary *Glastonbury Fayre* triple album from 1971. There was also a growing market in bootlegs — unofficial records and tapes that featured live performances or unissued studio material.

TAKING OFF

The quiet revolution of the late '60s and early '70s got a boost during the mid-1970s, when antipathy towards AOR artists and manufactured glam pop heightened interest in '60s American West Coast music, Northern Soul, garage rock and U.S. punk bands like the Ramones, Patti Smith, Television and Pere Ubu.

Around the same time, Chiswick began reissuing vintage rock'n'roll singles for those enthusiasts unable to find or afford the originals. With its chief rival, Stiff, releasing records with picture sleeves as standard, the 7" single soon became an attractive artefact in its own right, like the EPs of the '60s.

When British punk rock hit the streets in late 1976, its D.I.Y. ethic inspired hundreds of bands to release their own singles. Because of their shoestring budgets, they had little

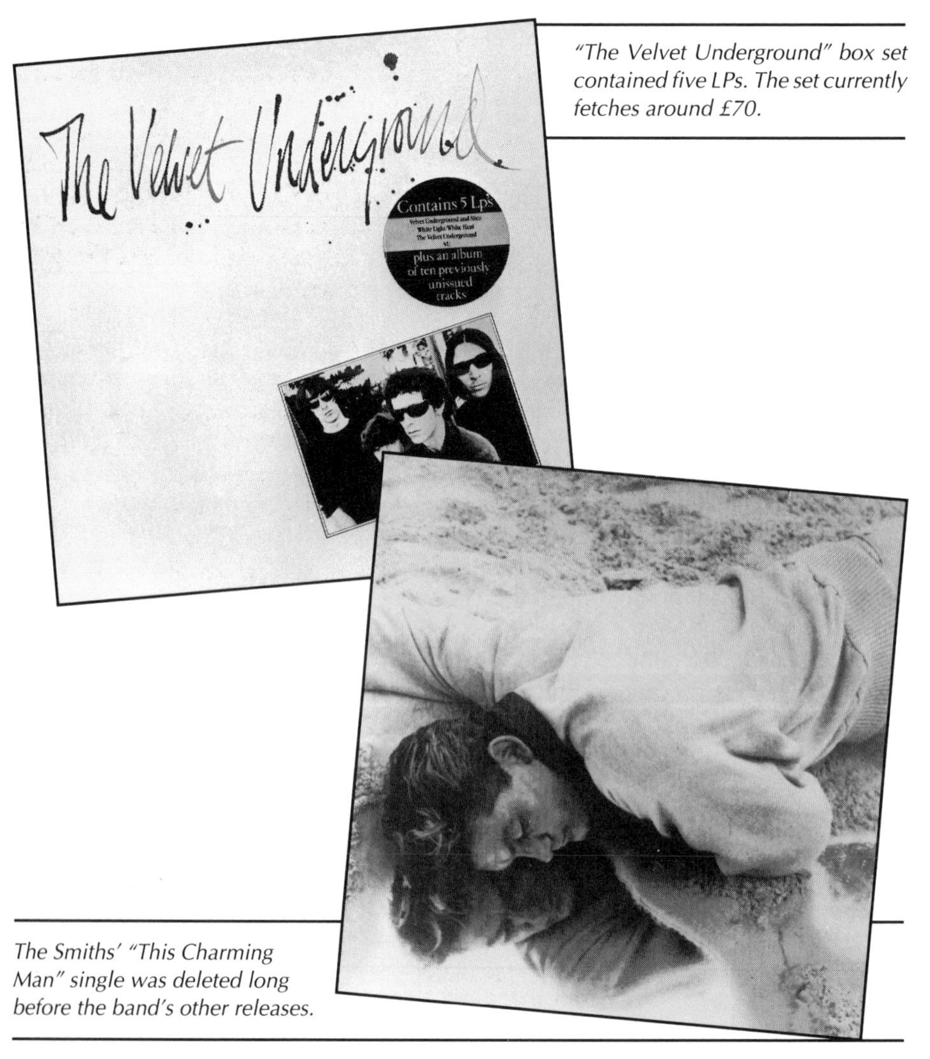

"The Velvet Underground" box set contained five LPs. The set currently fetches around £70.

The Smiths' "This Charming Man" single was deleted long before the band's other releases.

option but to press their releases in small quantities. This in-built exclusivity went a long way, and soon punk collectors were paying £10-£20 for rarities.

In fact, the punk era was probably the first time when record companies issued product with the knowledge that a collector's market existed and, as a result, singles and albums often appeared on different coloured vinyl, or with variations of packaging, to entice buyers.

RIPPED OFF

At first, collectable editions benefited both the record companies and collectors — the labels gaining higher sales and the fans an exclusive item. But as the '80s wore on, music fans increasingly felt they were being ripped off, as singles started to appear on five or more different formats, each with different tracks. Sometimes, the standard 7", cassette, 12" and CD were supplemented with a second 12" and CD, plus a picture disc, coloured vinyl pressing and poster sleeve! Among the worse offenders were the Cure, who in 1990 issued 'Pictures Of You' on no fewer than twelve formats, stretching their fans' pockets to bursting point.

The madness had to stop, and the following year chart compilers Gallup ruled that only sales of four formats would count towards a chart placing — though some labels have got round this ruling by releasing a second 12" or CD with different tracks and a different catalogue number two or three weeks after the initial release date.

Throughout the 1980s, the idea of the 'record collector', hell-bent on scouring the shops and adverts for rare records and CDs, became firmly established in people's minds, fuelled by the success of our own *Record Collector* magazine, launched in 1979, which provided the scene with a central focus. Record fairs — large indoor markets that brought together scores of small stall-holders — also began to flourish, providing people with more outlets to buy deleted records and collectables.

CDs

With the introduction of CDs in 1984, some enthusiasts worried that the death of vinyl was imminent, and that CDs wouldn't excite the same interest among collectors as 7"s and LPs. As a result, there was concern that collecting would become an increasingly retrospective activity, with the market centring around the records issued between the mid-1950s and the mid-1980s.

Now, ten years later, we can see that it was a false alarm. CDs have superseded vinyl albums and singles for new releases, yet most records still enjoy limited runs on these formats, while in some areas of collecting, like indie, vinyl still thrives. Just how long vinyl can hang on is open to debate, but it's safe to say that we'll probably be able to buy 7"s, 12"s and LPs up until the year 2000.

However, many record collectors now value CDs just as much as they do vinyl products, especially as CD packaging has become more imaginative over the years, with the introduction of formats like cardboard 'digipaks'. It all goes to prove that record collecting goes hand in hand with the music industry, and that as long as music is being released in a tangible form, enthusiasts will be rushing out and buying it.

In stark contrast to the days when discs were traded for a couple of pounds in rooms above pubs, record collecting is a multi-million pound industry today, with individuals interested in releases from every area — from dance to reggae, punk to indie, psychedelia to folk, jazz to blues, kitsch to classical, and film soundtracks to big bands. In the 90s, there's a flourishing market for almost everything — even (or perhaps especially) records ignored by the general public when they were originally issued.

TYPES OF RECORDS

From the 78rpm singles of the 1950s to today's CD-ROMs and DATs, music has been available on an enormous variety of formats in the last 40 years. Over the next 50 pages, we explain the history of all those different records, tapes and discs — starting with normal commercial editions, and then moving on to look at all the special formats and promotional items which have been produced over the past four decades.

78 rpm RECORDS

Before 7" vinyl records were introduced in the mid-1950s, singles were usually pressed as 10" discs which played at 78rpm. Made from a brittle material called shellac, they were the format on which most rock'n'roll classics by Elvis Presley, Bill Haley and Jerry Lee Lewis were sold. Contrary to popular belief, most of them aren't worth much — though there is a specialist market for some rock'n'roll, doo-wop and jazz titles.

In Britain, sales of 78s dropped rapidly after 1958, and the format was abandoned around 1960. As a result, the rarest examples tend to date from the late '50s,

Eddie Cochran, one of the undisputed rock'n'roll greats. His later 78s are the most valuable.

when far fewer were manufactured. This is one reason why Elvis Presley's 1960 'A Mess Of Blues' 78 is worth £400, while its 7" counterpart changes hands for just £7.

Because rock'n'roll peaked in 1956, most of the early hits like Bill Haley's 'Rock Around The Clock' and Elvis's 'Heartbreak Hotel' are actually much harder to find on 45 — and values reflect this.

"Leaning On A Lamp Post" by George Formby — the typical kind of vintage 78 you'll find in junk shops and jumble sales.

Since its demise, the 78 has been revived from time to time as a promotional gimmick, though in almost every case, the records have been pressed on vinyl, not shellac. Examples include the Sundown Playboys' 'Saturday Nite Special' (1971) and 999's 'Nasty Nasty' (1978), which change hands for around £175 and £30, respectively.

There are interesting parallels between the demise of the 78 in the early '60s and attempts in the last few years to phase out vinyl in favour of CDs. As with the 78, 7"s are being ditched for a format which is easier to store, harder to damage and altogether more modern and neat. Bearing in mind the comparative rarity of late '50s 78s, it may follow that in years to come, today's 7"s will become collector's items.

SOME RARE 78rpm SINGLES

ELVIS PRESLEY A MESS OF BLUES *(RCA 1194, 1960)* **£400**
(The King's rarest U.K. 78. Rumours that his next single, "It's Now Or Never", was issued as a 78 are unconfirmed.)

RONNIE SELF BOP-A-LENA *(Philips PB 810, 1958)* **£200**
(This rockabilly favourite has shot up in value in the last few years, principally because it wasn't issued on 45.)

JOHNNY BURNETTE DREAMIN' *(London HLG 9172, 1960)* **£200**
(Not the frenzied rock'n'roll of his mid-50s recordings, but a massive pop hit which sold peanuts on 78.)

ROY ORBISON ONLY THE LONELY *(London HLU 9149, 1960)* **£150**
(The Big O's first major hit, and his first single for U.S. label Monument. Once again, no-one bought the shellac.)

SID KING BOOGER RED *(Philips PB 589, 1956)* **£150**
(Another Philips rarity issued on Columbia in the U.S., this hillbilly number has also risen sharply in value.)

EDDIE COCHRAN THREE STEPS TO HEAVEN *(London HLG 9115, 1960)* **£150**
(Issued just after Eddie's death, this classic rock'n'roll ballad topped the singles charts, but the 78 sold zilch.)

CLIFF RICHARD FALL IN LOVE WITH YOU *(Columbia DB 4431, 1960)* **£125**
(The last-documented 78 by Britain's brightest pop singer, though later titles were possibly pressed for export use.)

SCREAMIN' JAY HAWKINS I PUT A SPELL ON YOU *(Fontana H 107, 1958)* **£125**
("I Put A Spell On You", an R&B classic, just missed out on a 45, because Fontana were slow to catch on to the 7".)

THE EVERLY BROTHERS LUCILLE *(Warner Bros WB 19, 1960)* **£125**
(A cover of the Little Richard rocker reinvented by Phil'n'Don. Issued in September '60, this is one of the last 78s.)

JOHNNY & THE HURRICANES ROCKING GOOSE *(London HLX 9190, 1960)* **£100**
(Another late entry from September '60 was this novelty instrumental from the top sax-led rock'n'roll combo.)

7" SINGLES

> ***"7" singles are cute, and feel nice in your hands."***
> *(David Gedge, the Wedding Present)*

Seven-inch 45rpm singles were introduced in the U.S. in 1949, and first appeared in Britain four years later. Compared with 78s, they were lighter, harder to break and, in most cases, also boasted better sound quality. By the late 1950s, they were outselling 78s, but they didn't replace them completely until 1961.

Throughout the '60s, '70s and '80s, 7"s dominated the singles market, so it isn't surprising that they're closely associated with the whole phenomenon of pop and rock. Indeed, some people regard them as something of a 'design classic', as much a part of the post-war teen experience as Levi jeans, Coca-Cola or Volkswagen Beetles.

During the 1990s, the 7" has lost considerable ground to CD, cassette and 12" singles, which together now outsell 7"s by more than three-to-one. The decline has been largely engineered by record companies and retailers, and has aroused a chorus of complaints from music lovers everywhere. In America, the 7" is all but dead, with few, if any, major labels producing any singles on this format. Only the small independents there are keeping it from extinction.

In Britain, though, we reckon the 7" will remain with us for some time to come, chiefly because of its appeal to collectors, whose buying-power has long been recognised by record companies. Although you're unlikely to find many chart-orientated dance singles on 7", indie and heavy metal bands still rely on the format to notch up early sales with limited pressings, like picture discs and special numbered or coloured vinyl editions. Labels such as Rough Trade and Sub Pop even have Singles Clubs, to which fans can subscribe.

The Clash's "Capital Radio" was given away by the 'NME' in a special 1977 offer. Copies now change hands for £30.

For collectors, the particular allure of the 7" is increased by its various quirks. These include everything from messages scratched into the run-out groove — check out the Smiths' and Morrissey's singles for a string of amusing epithets, including "Everyone is a flasher at heart"! — to colourful or unusual labels. In some cases, these peculiarities can affect the value of a record, as they may provide a key as to whether it's an original copy or not. The rare first pressing of David Bowie's 'Laughing Gnome' 7" can be identified by the inverted matrix number on its label, for instance — the '70s reissue has the number right way up.

Because of their 'classic' appeal, 7"s are by far the most popular format with collectors. The most valuable tend to be rare singles by rock and pop giants like the Beatles, Elvis, Queen, R.E.M., the Sex Pistols, David Bowie and U2, though obscure rock'n'roll, heavy metal and punk 45s can also sell for three-figure sums.

Another source of valuable 7"s are unsuccessful bands whose members later went on to find fame and fortune elsewhere. Before they were Status Quo, for example, Francis Rossi and Rick Parfitt were in a group called the Spectres. The three singles they recorded for the Piccadilly label in the mid-1960s were all total flops — but, because of the Quo connection, they currently change hands for around £150 each. It's a similar story with hundreds of other virtual unknowns, including R&B group Davie Jones & the King Bees (a teenage David Bowie and friends), whose 'Liza Jane' on Vocalion sells for £400, and Larry Lurex's £125-rated 'I Can Hear Music' (on EMI; actually Freddie Mercury doing a bit of moonlighting before Queen's first album appeared in 1973).

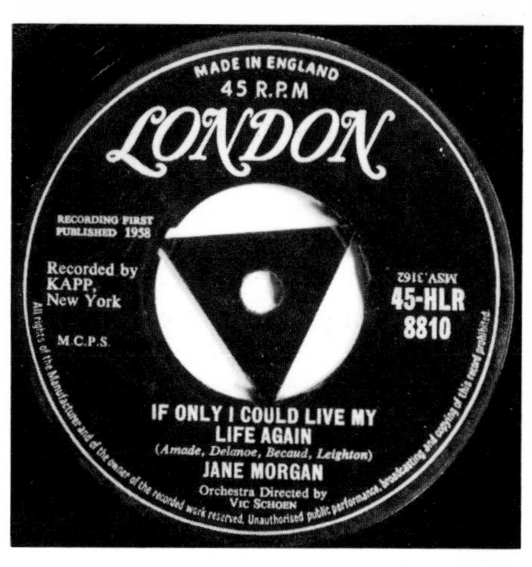

Many 7"s from the 1950s had 'tri-centres' like the one on this Jane Morgan single.

TRI-CENTRES

Up until the late '50s, most singles appeared with triangular — or 'tri' — centres, which were later replaced with round centres. Both tri and round centres could be punched (or 'dinked') out, allowing the records to be played on jukeboxes, which used a large adaptor instead of the more familiar thin spindle. If a tri-centre is missing, the record's value is reduced by about a third.

SOME RARE 7" SINGLES

BOBBY CHARLES SEE YOU LATER, ALLIGATOR *(London HLU 8247, 1956)* **£1,500**
(This rock'n'roll classic is generally regarded as Britain's most collectable 45. It once sold for over £2,000.)

WILLIE DIXON WALKING THE BLUES *(London HLU 8297, 1956)* **£1,500**
(The blues' greatest songwriter, if not performer. That hasn't stopped this 45 from selling for £3,000 on one occasion!)

RON HARGRAVE LATCH ON *(MGM 956, 1958)* **£1,500**
(Probably the rarest rock'n'roll record ever issued in the U.K. One copy recently sold for £2,000.)

JOHN'S CHILDREN MIDSUMMER NIGHT'S SCENE *(Track 604 005, 1967)* **£1,200**
(A legend in the record collecting world, this withdrawn psychedelic pop single featured Marc Bolan.)

THE PENGUINS EARTH ANGEL *(London HL 8114, 1955)* **£1,200**
(A doo-wop favourite from this L.A. vocal group. It topped the U.S. R&B charts, but flopped over here.)

THE CROWS GEE *(Columbia SCM 5119, 1954)* **£1,200**
(Another doo-wop vocal act, the Crows were from Harlem. Many of these 45s can be obtained more cheaply on 78.)

SEX PISTOLS GOD SAVE THE QUEEN *(A&M AMS 7284, 1977)* **£1,000**
(One of the most celebrated rarities of all time. Punk's prima donnas were naughty boys, so A&M refused to issue it.)

QUEEN BOHEMIAN RHAPSODY *(picture sleeve, blue vinyl, 1978)* **£1,000**
(This special 200-only edition was manufactured to commemorate EMI winning a Queen's Award for export in 1978.)

THE CHORDS SH'BOOM *(Columbia SCM 5133, 1954)* **£1,000**
(This Bronx-based doo-wop vocal group 45 was a massive U.S. hit on Cat, but made absolutely no impact over here.)

T. REX RIDE A WHITE SWAN *(Octopus OCTO 1, 1970)* **£1,000**
(The first pressing of Bolan's [nearly] chart-topping hit was abandoned when the label was rechristened as Fly.)

EPs (Extended Play)

Extended Plays had their heyday in the late 1950s and early '60s. They looked like 7" singles, and still played at 45rpm, but they contained roughly twice as much material as an ordinary single. Selling for about twice the price of a single, they were aimed at buyers who either couldn't afford albums or else wanted only a selection of an artist's hits. Usually, an EP came in a glossy, 'laminated' picture sleeve, looking like a miniature album cover.

EPs had their heyday in the '50s and '60s, but made an '80s comeback with 'indie' bands like Happy Mondays.

In the rock'n'roll era, the average music fan only bought LPs occasionally, so EPs provided a very welcome halfway house. Sometimes, artists used them to issue special collections of material, as with the Beatles' *Magical Mystery Tour* double EP, which contained unique tracks and was issued to coincide with the TV film of the same name. As a rule, though, EPs tended to contain material which was already available elsewhere, either on singles or albums.

Between 1960 and 1967, EPs had their own chart, though some of the Beatles' EPs sold enough copies to push them into the more important singles chart. By 1967, EPs were dying out, chiefly because albums had become more affordable. Also, in the wake of the Beatles' *Sgt. Pepper* and the Beach Boys' *Pet Sounds*, the LP was developing into an important art-form in its own right.

After 1967, EPs were reinvented as 'maxi-singles' — pretty much the same thing, only selling for the price of an ordinary single and not necessarily coming in a picture sleeve. In the early '70s, the Dawn label was particularly active in this field, issuing a whole series of four-track 7"s by artists like Mungo Jerry.

After punk started, EPs enjoyed a revival among indie fans, who liked the format's 1960s feel and the fact that they often sold at the same price as a normal single. Since then, they've remained popular with small labels, though, like the ordinary 7", they usually appear as limited editions.

Among the most collectable EPs are those by '60s beat acts like the Artwoods (who were led by Ronnie Wood's brother, Art) and the Kinks' Dave Davies. Also popular are vintage French EPs featuring British and American beat/psychedelic acts, many of which came in lavish picture sleeves. (Incidentally, standard two-track singles were rarely issued in that country until 1967.) But beware: EP vinyl records are easily damaged because the grooves are so close together, and pristine examples from 30 years ago are increasingly hard to find.

The Kinks' guitarist Dave Davies released the collectable "Hits" EP, worth £150, in 1968.

SOME RARE EPs

THE BO STREET RUNNERS BO STREET RUNNERS *(Oak RGJ 131, 1964)* **£750**
(Before this R&B beat band signed to EMI's Columbia label, they issued this extremely rare private EP.)

THE WILD OATS WILD OATS *(Oak RGJ 117, 1963)* **£500**
(Also recorded for the South London Oak label was the Wild Oats' EP, which is nearly as scarce as the above.)

THE PHARAOHS THE PHARAOHS *(Decca DFE 6522, 1958)* **£500**
(A doo-wop vocal group of American G.I.s taped this obscure EP for Decca while stationed over in Britain.)

THE ANIMALS I JUST WANNA MAKE LOVE TO YOU *(Graphic Sound ALO 10867, 1963)* **£300**
(Not the usual 7" EP but a one-sided four-track effort from Newcastle's "House Of The Rising Sun" hitmakers.)

THE BLUE MEN I HEAR A NEW WORLD *(Triumph RGXST 5000, 1960)* **£300**
(As ambitious as it is legendary, this sic-fi concept classic was the work of eccentric producer Joe Meek.)

GLENN ATHENS & TROJANS GLENN ATHENS & TROJANS *(Spot 7E 1018, 1965)* **£250**
(Spot was a tiny London label; Glenn Athens & Trojans were equally unknown but this EP boasts a killer R&B side.)

CAPTAIN BEEFHEART DIDDY WAH DIDDY *(A&M AME 600, 1971)* **£225**
(A promotional-only 'maxi-single'-styled EP consisting of the maverick U.S. blues genius's mid-60s A&M recordings.)

THE ARTWOODS JAZZ IN JEANS *(Decca DFE 8654, 1966)* **£225**
(The Artwoods are one of the biggest cult R&B acts of the 60s; and this EP consists of four exclusive tracks.)

AMOS MILBURN ROCK AND ROLL *(Vogue VE 170102, 1957)* **£200**
(Anything on Vogue is hard to find; but this top notch R&B collection of U.S. Aladdin recordings recently sold for £300!)

DOMINOES/SWALLOWS RHYTHM AND BLUES *(Vogue EPV 1113, 1956)* **£200**
(Another in-demand Vogue rarity couples tracks from two U.S. doo-wop vocal groups.)

12" SINGLES

Ironically, the 12" was launched in 1976, during a supposed world vinyl shortage caused by the Middle East oil crisis. Like the standard 7", 12"s played at 45rpm, but their extra size allowed for better sound quality — thanks to the wider grooves — and longer tracks. At first, these advantages were rarely exploited, and 12"s usually included the same material as the 7". But when dance-pop took off in the early '80s, the format came into its own, providing a vehicle for different remixes, extended versions and exclusive tracks.

12" singles came into their own in the 1980s. This is Paul McCartney's "Temporary Secretary", worth £20.

Towards the end of the '80s, the format became the centre of controversy when labels started issuing two or more 12"s of the same release — in addition to the standard 7", cassette and CD. This 'multiple formatting' meant that fans had to buy four or five different products if they wanted all the remixes or unique tracks available.

Not surprisingly, the 'remix' 12" got a bad name, and although fans of Madonna, Prince and Pet

SOME RARE 12"s

PAUL GARDINER STORMTROOPER IN DRAG *(Beggars Banquet BEG 61T, 1981)* **£250**
(An unreleased 12" from one of Gary Numan's backing musicians, this only reached the white label promo stage.)

LEVEL 42 SANDSTORM *(Elite DAZZ 4, 1979)* **£125**
(Prior to signing with Polydor, the jazz-funkers shared this single with Atmosfear, limited to a batch of white labels.)

QUEEN HAMMER TO FALL *(EMI 12 QUEEN 4, 1984)* **£125**
(This is the withdrawn 'live' sleeve, which was replaced by a plain red design before it reached the shops.)

PRINCE GOTTA STOP (MESSIN' ABOUT) *(Warner Bros LV 47, 1981)* **£120**
(The artist formerly known as's rarest single was released in two entirely different sleeves, both worth three figures.)

U2 U2: THREE *(EP, CBS 12-7951, 1979)* **£100**
(Bono & Co.'s first, Irish-only single, which came in a numbered, stickered CBS sleeve. Only 1,000 were made.)

ERASURE HEAVENLY ACTION (Yellow Brick Mix) *(Mute L12 MUTE 42, 1985)* **£75**
(This remix is the most expensive commercial release by Vince Clarke and Andy Bell. Has sold for over £100.)

ACT CHANCE *(ZTT BETT 1, 1988)* **£70**
("Chance" was withdrawn, making it one of the rarest ZTT singles. Act were Claudia Brücken and Thomas Leer.)

A-HA TAKE ON ME *(Warner Bros W 9146T, 1984)* **£70**
(First editions of "Take On Me", in a silver/blue sleeve with poster and stickers, are hard to find.)

JOY DIVISION AN IDEAL FOR LIVING *(Anonymous ANON 1, 1978)* **£65**
(A reissue of the Manchester band's debut EP on better quality vinyl, this is a classic indie post-punk rarity.)

THE ASSOCIATES COUNTRY BOY *(WEA YZ 329T, 1988)* **£60**
(They're best-known for "Party Fears Two", but this is their rarest single: it only reached the white label promo stage.)

Prince epitomised the glamour of '80s pop, and released a string of highly collectable 12"s.

Shop Boys treasured them, they were generally perceived as a rip-off. In the end, Gallup chart regulations put a stop to the practice, and these days the sales of only four versions of any single count towards the chart — though occasionally a second 12" or CD appears at the expense of a 7" or cassette single.

12"s are the standard format for club DJs, who are often sent special promotional-only releases to stir up interest in a new record or group. Several exclusive Paul Weller tracks have appeared as special 12" DJ pressings, including remixes of 'Kosmos' and 'Whirlpool's End', while the first Oasis record was a DJ-only 12" of 'Columbia'.

10"s

10"s were the standard format of the 1940s and '50s, and will always be identified with the classic eras of swing, jazz and rock'n'roll. Although at that time the industry standard for 10"s was 78rpm, some labels used other speeds — most notably 80rpm. Because a reliable Long Player (LP) had yet to be developed, long pieces of music were sold as stacks of 10" discs, which had to be changed every few minutes.

"It's A Shame About Ray" by the Lemonheads, one of many '90s groups to revive the 10" for limited edition singles.

10"s had their heyday with the birth of rock'n'roll, but by 1960, the format had been abandoned in favour of 45rpm 7"s. Since then, 10"s — playing at various speeds — have been resurrected as promotional gimmicks, as with Echo & the Bunnymen singer Ian McCulloch's 1984 solo single, 'September Song', which played at 78rpm and came in an old-fashioned brown paper sleeve.

Modern 10"s usually contain four tracks, as with Animals That Swim's "50 Dresses" EP, issued on the Ché label.

In the '90s, the 10" has undergone something of a revival, with indie-rock acts like the Lemonheads and the Levellers issuing collectable singles on this format. However, it's the rock'n'roll 78s from the end of the '50s (when they were being outsold by 45s) which command the highest prices.

In the '40s and '50s, most LPs appeared on 10", and several are extremely collectable. Top of pile are the debut album by Billy Ward & the Dominoes on Parlophone, which sells for around £500, and Johnny Burnette's *Rock'n'Roll Trio* on Coral, worth roughly the same.

LPs

> ***"When you get an LP back from the pressing plant you feel like you've achieved something. With a CD, well . . . "***
>
> *(Paul Weller)*

During the first quarter of this century, when record technology was in its infancy, engineers found it impossible to develop a commercially viable disc that could contain more than three or four minutes of music. To allow more playing time, the grooves on a record's surface had to be packed very closely together, but when this was tried, the music became quieter and the background hiss louder. What's more, the 'walls' between adjacent grooves would get thinner, making them even more brittle.

However, in 1926, the Edison Company in the U.S. claimed that they'd solved these problems and launched a Long Playing disc, or 'LP', which used fine 'microgrooves'. These records, made from a material called phenolic, rotated at 80rpm and had to be played by a special light-weight pick-up or stylus. However, they were very fragile, and the venture soon flopped.

Nearly 20 years later, in 1948, Columbia launched the 33⅓rpm vinyl LP (on both 10" and 12"), which immediately proved an enormous success. Within a year, sales had reached nearly 3.5 million units, and other companies started to produce their own vinyl LPs to cash in on the growing market. As technology progressed, the playing time of the 12" increased to over 20 minutes per side, and the modern LP was born.

However, pop and rock LPs continued to play second fiddle to singles until the arrival of the Beatles, the first artists to put as much care into their albums as their singles. By the late '60s, songs were getting longer and more sophisticated, and LPs like the Beatles' *Sgt. Pepper* suddenly seemed a better way to hear music than the three-minute pop single. In fact, groups like Led Zeppelin and Pink Floyd dispensed with singles entirely.

There are hundreds of collectable albums in every genre, but the big money tends to go for late '60s psychedelic, progressive rock and folk LPs. Most cherished are those on labels like Vertigo and Harvest, and obscure hard rock gems like Leaf Hound's *Growers Of Mushroom*. Another area of intense interest is 'private pressings' — records made by small labels in numbers sometimes fewer than 100, whose astronomical values often belie the fact that they're dreadful!

Original editions of the Small Faces' self-titled debut LP, issued in 1966 with red labels, now change hands for £30.

The Dominoes, whose 1958 album featuring Clyde McPhatter is currently worth £500.

It was never clear whether the Senseless Things' "Up And Coming" was an LP or a mini-LP.

As a rule, collectors prize the first pressing of an LP above any later editions or reissues, because they want the authentic 'period piece'. This is also true of singles; but while 45s are deleted fairly quickly, classic LPs are often repressed many times over the years, making it more difficult to tell when a particular copy was made.

In most cases, there are clues in the packaging, label design and vinyl thickness. '50s and '60s LPs were pressed on heavy vinyl and had 'laminated' (or glossy) front covers, while later pressings have no laminate and are far more flimsy. Anyone who wants details of the various editions of a particular record, and how they affect its price, is advised to invest in our *Rare Record Price Guide*.

Whether an LP is in mono or stereo can also affect its price (See MONO & STEREO).

SOME RARE LPs

(N.B.: These do not include private pressings, which are listed elsewhere)

JOHN LENNON & YOKO ONO UNFINISHED MUSIC NO. 1: TWO VIRGINS *(mono, Apple APCOR 2, '68)* **£750**
(The Beatles it wasn't: Rock's Bonnie & Clyde make weird noises in the name of art. Only a handful exist in mono.)

THE BEATLES PLEASE PLEASE ME *(gold/black label, stereo, Parl. PCS 3042, 1963)* **£700**
(This first pressing of the stereo edition with a gold/black label rose to over £1,000, but its value has now stabilised.)

LEAF HOUND GROWERS OF MUSHROOM *(Decca SKLR 5094, 1971)* **£700**
(Led Zeppelin-influenced hard rock was Leaf Hound's speciality, but no-one was interested at the time...)

DELANEY & BONNIE THE ORIGINAL DELANEY & BONNIE *(Apple SAPCOR 7, 1969)* **£600**
(The Bramletts' debut LP was meant to appear on the Beatles' Apple label but only reached the test pressing stage.)

JIMI HENDRIX ELECTRIC JIMI HENDRIX *(Track 2856 002, 1971)* **£600**
(A selection of tracks from Jimi's "Electric Ladyland" double LP made up this mail-order-only rarity.)

APPLE AN APPLE A DAY *(Page One POLS 016, 1969)* **£600**
(A psychedelic pop artefact which relied heavily on earlier singles, this LP originally came with an 'Apple' insert.)

THE ROLLING STONES THE ROLLING STONES PROMOTIONAL ALBUM *(Decca RSM 1, 1969)* **£600**
(Confusion still abounds as to whether the sleeve and/or record were pressed here or in the U.S. Either way, it's rare.)

JOHNNY BURNETTE TRIO ROCK AND ROLL TRIO *(10", Coral LVC 10041, 1956)* **£550**
(A legend not only in rock'n'roll but in rock music as a whole, this remains a jewel in the crown of any collection.)

BILLY WARD & DOMINOES FEATURING CLYDE McPHATTER *(10", Parlophone PMD 1061, 1958)* **£500**
(Rock'n'roll LP rarity No. 2 is this doo-wop set. The group were also responsible for one of the rarest-ever U.S. LPs.)

MELLOW CANDLE SWADDLING SONGS *(Deram SDL 7, 1972)* **£350**
(An Irish folk-rock group who'd issued a 45 four years earlier. A recent CD reissue reveals the LP's musical strengths.)

MINI-ALBUMS

During the late 1970s, record companies hit upon the idea of issuing mini-albums — LPs including five or six tracks, which sold for about half the price of a normal album.

These records were put out either to gauge the popularity of a new band, or because they provided a convenient resting place for a selection of songs that didn't warrant a full album release. In cases like the Senseless Things' *Up And Coming* debut, it's not immediately clear whether the record is supposed to be a long EP or mini-album — so it gets called both!

Scottish pop band Wet Wet Wet released this numbered 10" mini-LP in 1988.

CASSETTE ALBUMS

The cassette of the Stones' "Some Girls" LP.

By mid-1966, Philips' cassette tape had become standard, and other labels began to copy it. But the public was slow to respond. A 1971 survey showed that only 40% of tape machines sold that year were capable of playing cassettes.

Within a few years, though, cassettes were established as a rival to vinyl LPs and, later, CDs. They remain popular for use in personal hi-fis and car stereos.

Cassettes have rarely interested collectors, as they have little visual appeal and can suffer from relatively poor sound quality. The most sought-after cassette albums contain material unavailable elsewhere, though there are a few exceptions, such as David Bowie's *The Man Who Sold The World* tape with the rare 'dress' artwork, which changes hands for £20.

Cassettes are often given away free with music magazines, and some late '80s fanzine compilations contain rare versions of songs by groups like Carter U.S.M. and Manic Street Preachers. They're always worth more accompanied by the magazine.

Notable cassette rarities include the Cure's *Faith*, with their soundtrack to the film, *Carnage Visors*; and *I'm Sorry That I Beat You* by Mike Scott's pre-Waterboys group, Another Pretty Face. Also prized are early demos by Oasis, Supergrass and the Levellers.

SOME RARE CASSETTES

ANOTHER PRETTY FACE **I'M SORRY THAT I BEAT YOU** *(Chicken Jazz JAZZ 2, 1981)* **£45**
(From the Scottish band who evolved into the Waterboys, this came with a fanzine and a free badge.)

EURYTHMICS **RIGHT BY YOUR SIDE** *(RCA DA 4/EUC 001, 1983)* **£35**
(Not strictly a cassette in its own right but a promotional freebie shrinkwrapped with the single, and very hard to find.)

LEVEL 42 **TRUE COLOURS** *(double pack, Polydor POLHC 10, 1984)* **£35**
(As an incentive to buy the cassette edition, Polydor added a bonus tape featuring exclusive Level 42 remixes.)

THE BEATLES **THEIR GREATEST HITS** *(St Michael 1361/5701, 1984)* **£30**
(Only available in your local branch of Marks & Spencer, complete with a 64-page book in an album-sized box.)

THE DRONES **BONE IDLE** *(Valer VRS 1, 1977)* **£30**
(The 7" is easy enough to find, but few punk collectors own the far rarer cassette, housed in a 'cigarette box' sleeve.)

THE KLF **1987 (WHAT THE FUCK IS GOING ON?)** *(KLF Comm. JAMS LP 1, 1987)* **£30**
(Abba threatened to sue them, but more than a few copies of the LP and cassette slipped out before being withdrawn.)

GEORGE MICHAEL **WEMBLEY** *(Epic XPC 4060, 1991)* **£25**
(In the days before the ex-Wham! singer's legal dramas, this live tape was given away at the famous London venue.)

NEW ORDER **SUBSTANCE** *(box set, Factory FACT 200C, 1987)* **£25**
(Only 200 copies of the Manchester band's compilation came in a box set with an insert, hence the high asking price.)

MIKE OLDFIELD **IMPRESSIONS** *(Tellydisc TELLY 4, 1979)* **£25**
(A TV-advertised affair, both the LP and cassette were only available by mail-order and are now very elusive.)

RINGO STARR etc. **SCOUSE THE MOUSE** *(Polydor 3194 429, 1978)* **£25**
(The LP is worth around £80, but the cassette is also of value. A children's musical for a film that never happened.)

Continued on page 41

The Beatles, who are still easily the most collectable band in the world, 25 years after they split up.

The Clash's "White Riot" was inspired by disturbances at the Notting Hill Carnival.

"Something Else" by the Sex Pistols saw Sid Vicious reviving an Eddie Cochran song.

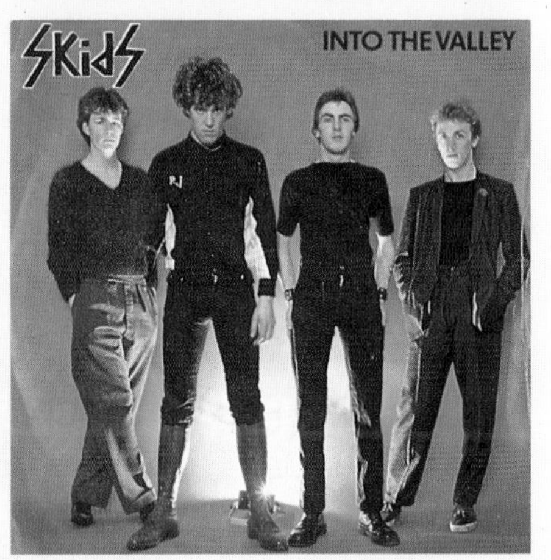

"Into The Valley" by the Skids, featuring future TV presenter, Richard Jobson.

"Playground Twist" was Siouxsie & the Banshees' third single for Polydor.

Scottish punk group the Rezillos scored a hit in 1978 with "Top Of The Pops".

Initial copies of the U.K. Subs' 1979 single, "Tomorrow's Girls", came on blue vinyl.

Debbie Harry found fame with Blondie, but she first recorded with psychedelic folk group Wind In The Willows in the late 60s.

THE CHANGING FACES OF THE SMITHS' SINGLES

Pools winner Viv Nicholson on the sleeve of "Heaven Knows I'm Miserable Now".

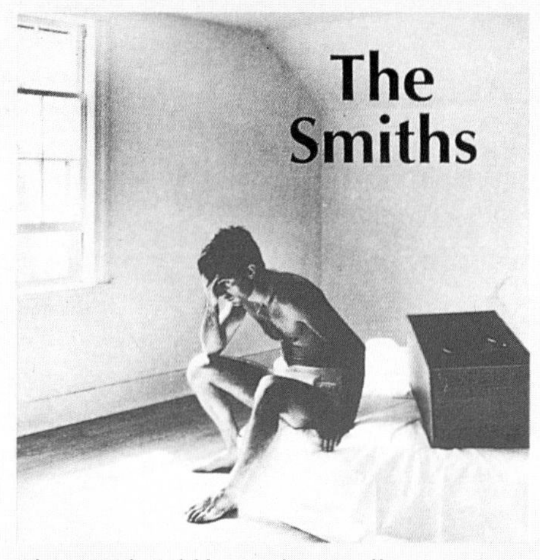

The Smiths' fifth single, "William, It Was Really Nothing", was a hit in 1984.

'Coronation Street's Pat Phoenix appeared on the cover of "Shakespeare's Sister".

"That Joke Isn't Funny Anymore" was lifted from the band's "Meat Is Murder" LP.

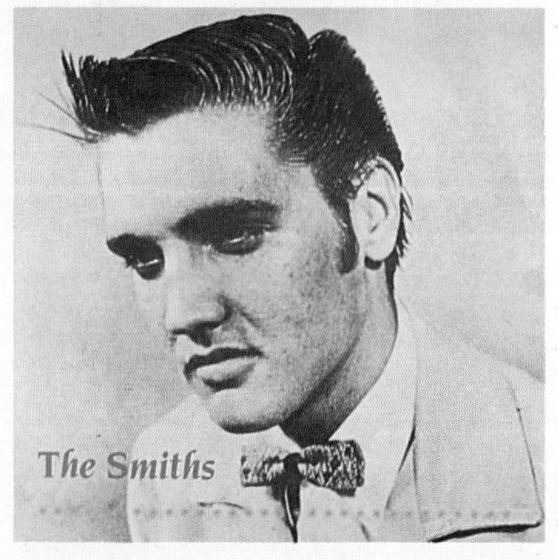

"Shoplifters Of The World Unite" pictured Elvis Presley looking faintly like Morrissey!

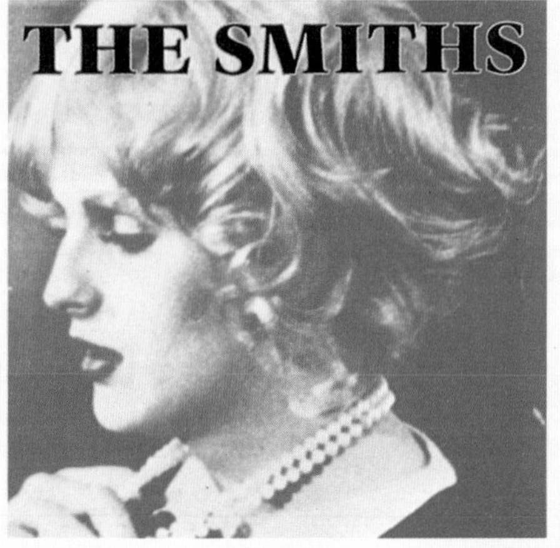

Andy Warhol protegé Candy Darling adorned the sleeve of "Sheila Take A Bow".

CASSETTE SINGLES

Although cassette EPs have been around since the mid-'60s, cassette singles — or 'cassingles', as they're sometimes known — didn't take off until the mid-'80s. In 1980, music biz entrepreneur Malcolm McLaren tried to market the cassette as *the* way to buy singles, issuing the first Bow Wow Wow's single solely on this format, but it wasn't until companies added exclusive material to cassette singles (as an incentive for fans) that people began to warm to them.

Occasionally cassettes are given away as freebies, like the live tape that accompanied Orange Juice's 'What Presence?!'.

Stourbridge rap-metal group Pop Will Eat Itself released the cassette single of "Sucker" in a 7"-square cardboard box.

8-TRACK CARTRIDGE

8-track cartridges first appeared in the early '60s, and were designed for in-car entertainment. They were much bigger than cassettes and contained a wide tape, on which were recorded four stereo tracks. As the stereo effect was achieved by having two signals running side-by-side, the tape actually contained eight tracks, hence the name.

Although they gave cassettes a run for their money in the late '60s and early '70s, they eventually disappeared, chiefly because they couldn't be fast-forwarded or re-wound on most machines, and because tracks were often edited carelessly to fit into four equal segments.

As 8-track music systems are obsolete, and tapes are generally uncollectable anyway, it's not surprising that this format is largely ignored by collectors. However, original Beatles and Stones 8-tracks do attract some interest, if only for their novelty value.

Now obsolete, 8-track cartridges were the last word in 1970s in-car entertainment.

Some reel-to-reel tapes by bands like the Beatles are collected for their novelty value.

REEL-TO-REEL TAPE

Before the introduction of tape cartridges and cassettes, pre-recorded music could be bought on 'open spools'. As their title suggests, these were single spools (or reels) which were played on small domestic reel-to-reel systems. These tapes — and the machines to play them — first went on sale to the British public in 1951, though a standard spool size wasn't agreed upon until a few years later. By this time, LPs had appeared on the scene, and though reel-to-reels remained popular with some hi-fi buffs well into the '70s, they eventually became obsolete. It's easy to see why: you had to fiddle about threading tapes onto the lead spool of the recorder every time you wanted to play them.

Despite this lack of enthusiasm, a few 'completists' will pay up to £30 for some Beatles and Rolling Stones reel-to-reels. In fact, two of the most valuable finds of recent years were on this format — a live recording by pre-Beatles group, the Quarry Men (which sold at auction for £78,000); and a bedroom rehearsal by Little Blue & the Blue Boys, an early version of the Rolling Stones (£50,000).

U2's "Achtung Baby" was one of the first LPs to appear on DCC — a new format yet to take off.

DCC

In October 1992, PolyGram introduced a new format called the Digital Compact Cassette — or DCC — which they hoped would eventually replace the ordinary cassette. Boasting CD sound quality, DCCs are the same size as existing cassettes, but work on an 'auto-reverse' system, and don't have to be turned over. As a result, they only have sprocket holes on one side, leaving the other free to carry a picture of the artist or album artwork.

Sales of DCCs have so far been slow, partly because they need to be played on a special system — which, incidentally, is designed to play ordinary cassettes as well. DCCs cannot be played on a standard cassette deck.

If they do become obsolete, pre-recorded DCCs will probably echo the fate of 8-tracks and reel-to-reel, and be collected by completists solely for their novelty value.

The Sugarcubes' "Life's Too Good" is one of a handful of albums that have already become collectable on the DAT format.

DAT

DAT — short for Digital Audio Tape — was launched as a commercial album format in 1991, but it has so far failed to catch on. Indeed, few, if any, albums now enjoy a DAT release. Considerably smaller than ordinary cassettes, DATs are capable of containing an hour or more of music, and boast sound quality comparable with that of CD. They need a special player, and the prohibitive price of these machines is one of the main reasons why this format has flopped commercially. Even so, DATs are still widely used in recording studios and by radio stations, who rely on its broadcast quality.

A handful of DATs have already become collectable, including the Sugarcubes' *Life's Too Good* and Erasure's *Supernature*.

Stiff Little Fingers singer Jake Burns was once a radio producer, and hence no stranger to DAT.

CD ALBUMS

> ***"I really hate the fact that vinyl's disappearing in favour of CDs. I like the size of the format, I like album sleeves. When they're on CDs, everybody's albums look the same."***
>
> *(Stuart Adamson, Big Country)*

Although working prototypes had been around since 1978, Compact Discs weren't officially launched until 1983, when Philips/Sony introduced them in Japan. The following year, they appeared in Britain, where the prohibitive price of CD players — about twice that of a quality record deck — initially slowed sales. However, by the end of the decade, the CD had become the most popular format on which to buy music.

Measuring 5" across, CDs contain digitally-encoded sound information under their surface, which a laser beam reads by scanning the disc. As there's no physical contact between the 'pick-up' and the CD, the discs do not wear out. To protect their surfaces, CDs are coated with a thin layer of protective plastic, which the laser beam ignores. Any build-up of dust or any small scratches on this transparent covering shouldn't impair the sound quality, though, as most of us know, CDs do 'jump' when faulty or greasy.

A great deal has been written about the question of whether CDs sound better than records. Although it's universally agreed that CDs give an exceptionally clear sound, they've been strongly criticised for their lifeless tone. However, as time passes, the number of dissenters seems to dwindle, though many people still rue the demise of the wonderful 12"x12" LP sleeve — and the fact that attempts to kill off vinyl have been largely industry- (and profit-) led. The fact that most record stores no longer stock vinyl has meant that fans have no choice but to buy a CD player.

SOME RARE CDs

ELTON JOHN THE FISHING TRIP *(4-CD, Happenstance HAPP 001, 1993)* .... **£200+**
(Ol' Reg knocked up this extravagant set especially for friends and acquaintances, though inevitably some slipped out.)

VARIOUS ARTISTS LONELY IS AN EYESORE
(in wooden box, 4AD CADX 703, 1987) **£200**
(Only 200 copies of this box set were made, which included a CD, video, cassette, etching and screen print.)

DAVID BOWIE ALL SAINTS *(own label, 1993)* **£100**
(Elton wasn't the only one: Bowie assembled this collection of instrumentals as an exclusive stocking filler in 1993.)

THE BEATLES YELLOW SUBMARINE *(box set, HMV BEACD 25/5, 1987)* **£75**
(The HMV retail chain created their own box sets for the Beatles CDs; "Yellow Submarine" is the rarest of the lot.)

MADONNA ROYAL BOX *(Sire 7599 264932, 1990)* **£60**
(Not strictly that rare but always expensive, "Royal Box" was a suitably grand collection from Ms Ciccone.)

TANGERINE DREAM FLASHPOINT *(Heavy Metal HMXCD 29, 1985)* **£50**
(This soundtrack from the German ambient veterans was issued when CD sales were still low, and was soon deleted.)

FREDDIE MERCURY MR. BAD GUY *(CBS CD 86312, 1985)* **£50**
(Ditto the comments for the Tangerine Dream title. Its value increased dramatically after Freddie's death.)

PROPAGANDA WISHFUL THINKING *(ZTT ZCD 20, 1985)* **£40**
(The rarity of this ZTT album is due to the fact that it was pressed up for export, so you couldn't buy it in the shops.)

THE KLF THE WHAT TIME IS LOVE STORY
(KLF Comms. JAMS CD 4, 1989) **£40**
(An early effort from Bill Drummond and Jimmy Cauty, sampling the song that was eventually a massive hit.)

GARY NUMAN STRANGE CHARM *(Numa CDNUMA 1005, 1986)* **£40**
(Along with Gary's earlier CD, "The Fury", this is presumably scarce because it was largely ignored at the time.)

"The Beatles — First" CD brought together some of the band's earliest recordings. CDs are becoming increasing collectable.

Among the most collectable CDs are titles issued in the mid-'80s when the format was relatively new. A notable example is Gary Numan's 1986 *Strange Charm*, now worth £40, and Elvis's 1984 *The Legend* 3-CD box set, which has changed hands for up to £180.

No doubt in years to come, CDs will be just as collectable as vinyl. There's one thought to bear in mind, though: as CDs are robust and are protected by their plastic 'jewel' case, which can be replaced if cracked, most will remain in Mint or Excellent condition with little effort from their owners. This means that most CDs will survive the years in very good shape, making examples with only the slightest damage — like a torn inlay book — virtually worthless.

Tangerine Dream, whose 1985 "Flashpoint" CD album currently changes hands for £50.

CD SINGLES

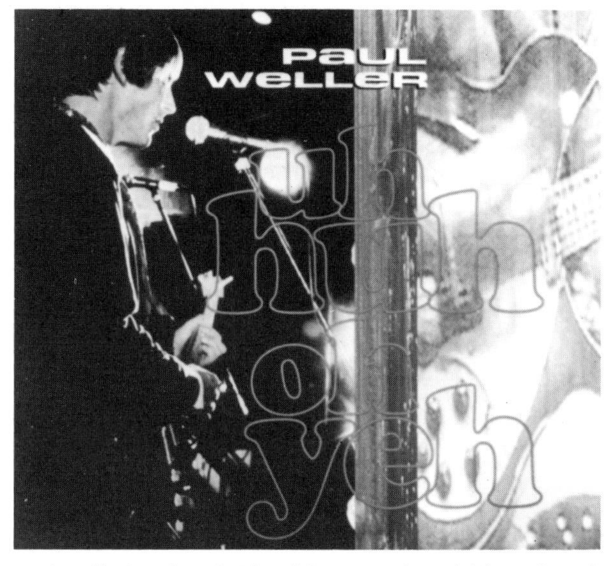

Paul Weller's "Uh Huh Oh Yeh" appeared as a fold-out digipak CD single. Digipaks are particular popular with collectors.

Not long after CD albums hit the shops, CD singles began to appear, and by the late '80s they were already outselling 7"s. To begin with, labels experimented with both 3" and 5" versions, but now 3"s have all but disappeared, primarily because people have found them awkward to handle.

In the 1990s, CD packaging has become more imaginative, with the advent of 'digipaks' — with fold-out cardboard covers — marking a considerable leap forward in design.

The first collectable CD single was a special promotional edition of Dire Straits' 'Brothers In Arms', now worth about £50. As with CD albums, many of the most valuable singles date from the mid-'80s, when the format had not yet taken off.

A special promo edition of Dire Straits' "Brothers In Arms" is one of the most collectable CDs.

SOME RARE CD SINGLES

U2 **I STILL HAVEN'T FOUND WHAT I'M LOOKING FOR** *(Island CID 328, '87)* **£75**
(An estimated price, as many dealers question its existence. Quite why it should be so rare is baffling.)

PAUL McCARTNEY **BIKER LIKE AN ICON**
(promo-only, Parlophone CDRDJ 6347, 1993) **£60**
(Never issued commercially — perhaps because of its lack of airplay — but a few DJ copies slipped out.)

GENESIS **TONIGHT TONIGHT TONIGHT** *(Virgin CD EP 1, 1987)* **£40**
(A special CD-only release, which many Genesis fans ignored back in 1987.)

DIRE STRAITS **BROTHERS IN ARMS** *(promo-only, Vertigo 884 285-2, 1985)* **£40**
(Once rated at a staggering £250, and hailed as the first-ever CD single, though it was only a promo.)

LED ZEPPELIN **STAIRWAY TO HEAVEN** *(promo-only, Atlantic CDLZ 1, 1990)* **£30**
(Another promotional-only single was this sampler, sent out to publicise the "Led Zeppelin" four-CD box set.)

METALLICA **ENTER SANDMAN** *(box set, Vertigo METCD 7, 1991)* **£30**
(A comparatively recent limited edition box set, with a value that reflects Metallica's dominance of 90s heavy metal.)

THE CHAMELEONS **TONY FLETCHER WALKED ON WATER**
(Glass Pyramid EMCD 1, 1990) **£30**
(Originally recorded for Geffen, this EP was withdrawn at the time, although copies have since slipped out.)

BRUCE SPRINGSTEEN **TUNNEL OF LOVE** *(CBS 651 295-2, 1987)* **£25**
(The Boss's most sought-after CD single — his first to be issued in the U.K., at a time when CD sales were low.)

QUEEN **THE INVISIBLE MAN** *(Parlophone CDQUEEN 12, 1989)* **£25**
(Many of Queen's early CD singles are now hard to find, but "The Invisible Man" is perhaps the rarest of all.)

ROLLING STONES **ROCK AND A HARD PLACE** *(CBS 655448-2 or 5, 1989)* .... **each £25**
(For £25, you can choose between a boxed set edition with a poster, or a tongue-shaped card sleeve design.)

RECORDABLE CDs

Recordable CDs (CDRs) are simply blank compact discs which, when inserted into a special CDR machine, can be encoded with music from a mastertape. Chiefly used in recording studios, they serve the same purpose as acetates once did, allowing the artist, producer, manager, etc., to have a copy of work in progress or an advanced copy of the finished music.

Most CDRs come in jewel cases with a plain insert providing a few basic details about the recording, and are of special interest to collectors if the material they contain is different from that released commercially.

These discs — which often have gold upper, and green-ish lower, surfaces — can only be recorded onto once, after which the music on the compact disc remains permanent, like a normal CD.

Recordable CDs are known as 'CDRs', and are used in recording studios to provide artists with a reference of their work.

MINI-DISCS

Mini-discs were introduced by Sony in 1992 as another future replacement for cassettes. Measuring roughly 2½" square, they resemble computer floppy discs, and again need to be played on a special machine. Their major selling point is that they are easy to use, and very hard to damage. However, as is the case with DCCs, it is still too early to determine whether they'll grow in popularity. Despite several expensive launch campaigns, the public still remains unconvinced.

If mini-discs flop, examples like Whitesnake's "Greatest Hits" will no doubt be collected in the future for their novelty value.

Singer Peter Gabriel has always been at the forefront of new technological developments.

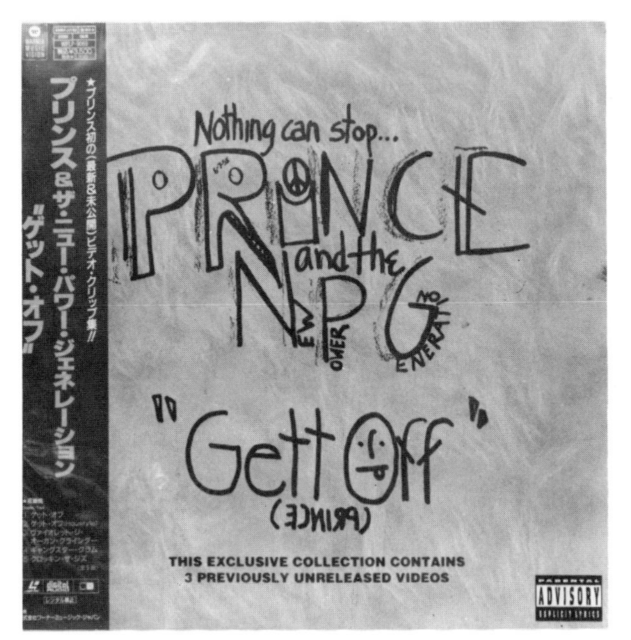

Laser discs are popular in the U.S. and Japan, but have yet to catch on in the U.K. This is Prince & the NPG's "Gett Off".

LASER DISCS

Popular in America but yet to catch on in Britain, laser discs are like CDs — only they measure 12" across and are encoded with both audio and visual information. They can contain anything from pop videos to movies, and are sometimes even used for karaoke, with the words and images coming up on a monitor while the music plays through a sound system. One drawback, though, is that each disc only contains about an hour of material, which can mean you need two or more for a whole film.

VIDEO

Since becoming popular in the early '80s, home-video has always been seen as an important companion to any record collection. At first, three different, non-compatible formats — VHS, Beta and Video 2000 — fought with one another to dominate the market. Video 2000 perished first, then Betamax, with VHS eventually emerging as the winner in the mid-'80s.

When they first went on sale, pre-recorded videos were comparatively expensive, retailing for around £25, but within a few years their price dropped dramatically, and an ordinary pop title tends to sell for roughly the same as a new CD.

Many early videos were later reissued, sometimes in different packaging and with different material. In a few cases, the originals can be very sought-after, as with Echo & the Bunnymen's in-concert film, *Shine So Hard*, which initially included a montage of rare on-the-road footage, called *Le Via Luonge*. These early copies now change hands for upwards of £25.

East 17's compilation video, "Pie & Mash". Some early videos can be very sought-after.

CD-ROM

CD-ROM is a computer disc which can only be played on a Personal Computer (PC) or Apple Macintosh with a special drive. Users can access music and visual images, and perform other activities like 'interviewing' the artist or playing games. But unlike CDi (see below), you can't store your own remixes, as these discs can only be 'read', not 'written to'.

Whether CD-ROMs will one day be an essential purchase for collectors remains to be seen, but the early signs are that there is a great deal of interest in this format.

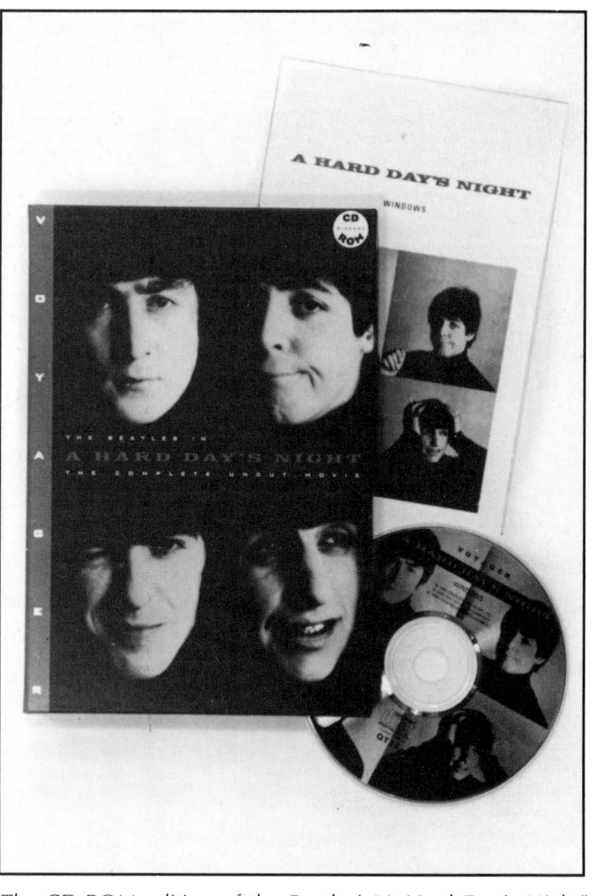

The CD-ROM edition of the Beatles' "A Hard Day's Night" features the famous 1964 movie in its uncut form.

CDi

This recent arrival is chiefly geared towards the computer games market, but is also used as a music format. Loaded into a special drive attached to a PC or Apple Macintosh, a CDi allows the user to 'interact' with the music and images the computer generates. This means you can, for example, remix tracks, create your own visuals, or devise games involving computer images of your favourite bands (!).

Some music CDi's are already becoming collectable, as with Rhythm King Records' *The Worlds Of...* various artists collection, which includes exclusive tracks by ex-Heaven 17 singer Glenn Gregory's dance project, Ugly.

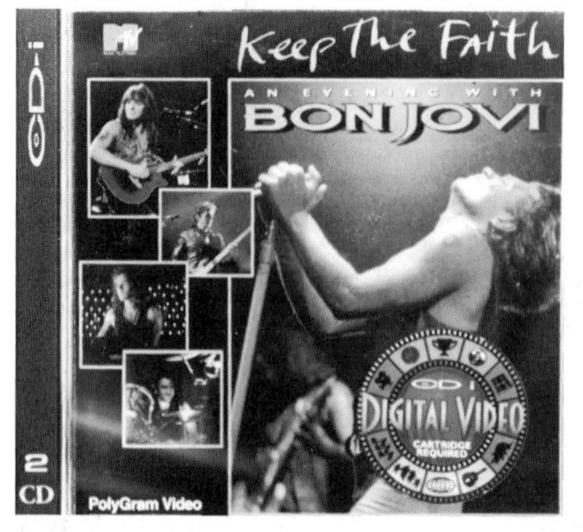

"Keep The Faith — An Evening With Bon Jovi" was issued in 1993 as a two-disc CDi.

CD PLUS

The latest 'multi-media' arrival, CD Plus has been jointly designed by Sony and Philips, and offers high quality sound with interactive graphics, unissued tracks and biographical information. Once again, the discs need to be played on a special computer drive.

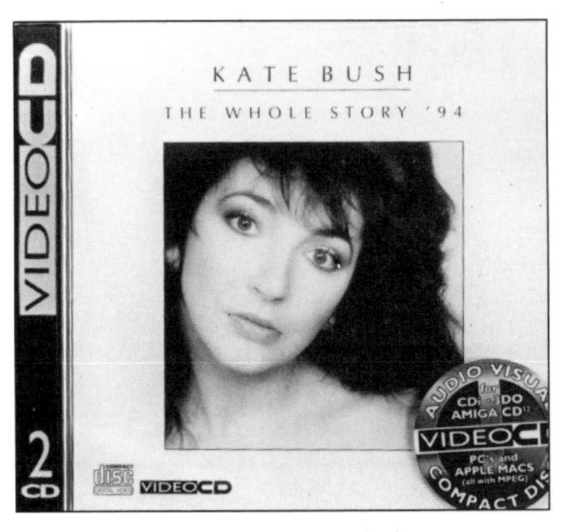

Singer Kate Bush's "The Whole Story '94" compilation was one of the first Video CDs.

CD Videos like David Bowie's "Sound & Vision Plus" include one audio-visual track.

VIDEO CD

Developed by Philips, who also pioneered the audio CD, this new format is used primarily for films and offers digital quality pictures and stereo sound. The discs can be played on CDi players fitted with a DV (Digital Video) cartridge. Early Video CDs include Pink Floyd's in-concert film, *Delicate Sound Of Thunder*, and David Bowie's *The Video Collection.*

CD VIDEO

CD Videos (CDVs) are 5" CDs with one audio-video track at the end. The audio-only material can be played on an ordinary CD player, but the last track must be played on a special machine. However, CDVs have already been superseded by Video CD.

Notable examples include several Freddie Mercury and Queen releases.

Queen in the late '80s: (L to R) Roger Taylor, John Deacon, Brian May and Freddie Mercury.

SPECIAL PRESSINGS

COMMERCIAL

LIMITED EDITIONS

The term 'limited edition' refers to any record produced in a relatively small quantity as a means of enticing fans to buy a new release. Some aren't really that limited at all, especially when a successful artist is concerned. This has led to the use of the term 'strictly limited edition' for items manufactured in numbers of less than 10,000 or so.

DOUBLEPACKS

As their name suggests, doublepacks are special releases which bring together two singles in a gatefold — or occasionally an ordinary — sleeve. Used as sales gimmicks, they normally comprise one disc which is identical to the standard single, plus another containing material unavailable elsewhere.

However, some doublepacks simply shrinkwrap together an ordinary single with an earlier release, though in such cases an explanatory sticker normally appears on the packaging.

Among the most collectable doublepacks are Kate Bush's *On Stage* EP, which sells for £35, and Pet Shop Boys' 'Suburbia', worth £12.

COLOURED VINYL

Records pressed on coloured vinyl have been around since the 1930s, but didn't become common in Britain until the late '70s, when many punk and new wave singles appeared in a variety of garish hues. At first, people couldn't wait to get their hands on the likes of the Dickies' 'Banana Splits' on yellow vinyl (naturally!) or clear vinyl copies of the Members' 'Sound Of The Suburbs'. But, by the early '80s, their novelty value had started to wear off.

"Feelin" by the La's came in this limited edition box set, containing a badge and three stickers.

The double pack edition of '80s band the Beat's "I Confess" included rare live recordings.

Even so, the idea has been revived every so often, most noticeably in recent years by punk-inspired groups like Hole, Therapy? and Carter USM, and independent labels like Detour and U.S. Sub Pop, whose grunge and rock releases often appeared on green, orange or white.

Usually, coloured vinyls are limited to only a few thousand copies, which means that they're often worth more than their black counterparts. However, there are some cases where the black copies are the rarer items — as with a couple of late '70s Stiff label LPs, Lene Lovich's *Stateless* and Wreckless Eric's *The Wonderful World Of....*

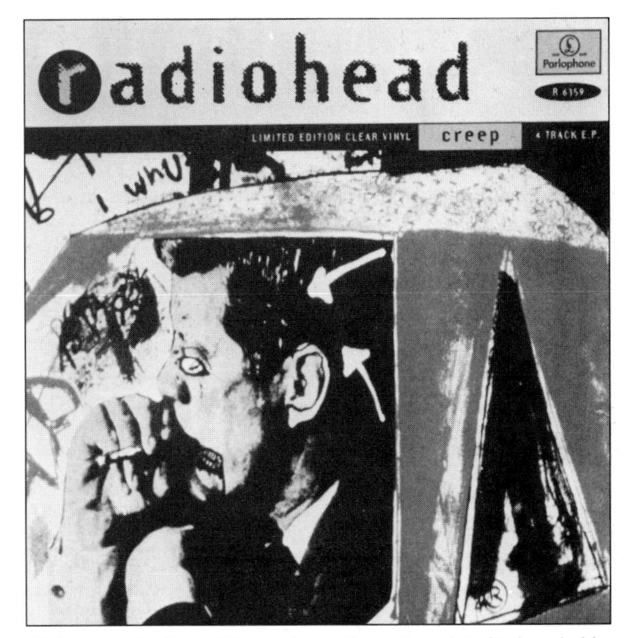

Coloured vinyl is still popular with rock and indie bands like Radiohead, who reissued their "Creep" 45 on clear vinyl.

The rarest coloured records include the royal blue 7" edition of Queen's 'Bohemian Rhapsody', distributed to 200 of EMI's in-house staff in 1978, and now worth a hefty £1,000, plus some early, semi-official Jimi Hendrix and David Bowie LPs. These were made by mischievous pressing plant engineers when the ordinary albums were being pressed, and are referred to as 'factory custom pressings'.

Carter USM, whose "Christmas Shoppers Paradise" gig freebie is now worth around £18.

PICTURE DISCS & SHAPED DISCS

After coloured vinyl had gone out of fashion in the early '80s, record companies began to rely heavily on picture discs to promote their records. As with coloured vinyls, these had been around since the 1930s, and were reputedly devised by David Sarnoff, the first person to pick-up the *Titanic*'s S.O.S. call in mainland America! Indeed, it was this claim to fame that landed him a job at RCA, where 20 years later he came up with the idea of making records a visual, as well as an aural, attraction.

The picture disc edition of Madonna's "True Blue" currently changes hands for £20. A similar "Erotica" disc is worth £350.

Picture discs soon caught on — in pre-war Germany, for example, there were several featuring portraits of Führer Adolf Hitler — but they were never much more than a novelty.

Modern picture discs are made by sandwiching a printed piece of paper between two sides of clear vinyl. Undoubtedly the rarest is Wings' *Back*

SOME RARE PICTURE DISCS

WINGS BACK TO THE EGG *(LP, Parlophone PCTCP 257)* **£1,000**
(It's hard to differentiate this in-house edition for McCartney's MPL staff from the hoards of counterfeits.)

MADONNA EROTICA *(12", Sire W 0138TP, 1992)* **£350**
(Withdrawn because of its infamous 'toe-sucking' image, only 100 or so copies exist, hence its astronomical value.)

ABBA VOULEZ VOUS *(LP, Epic EPC 11-86086, 1979)* **£60**
(One of the most in-demand picture disc albums which actually reached the shops at the time.)

QUEEN A KIND OF MAGIC *(12", EMI 12QUEENP7, 1986)* **£60**
(Not the first Queen picture disc but the most valuable, helped by an exclusive instrumental on the B-side.)

FREDDIE MERCURY BARCELONA *(12", Polydor POSPP 887, 1987)* **£60**
(The most expensive of several solo picture discs, which rocketed in value after his death. With Montserrat Caballe.)

THE CURE LOVESONG *(12", Fiction FICSX 30, 1989)* **£50**
(Test pressings were made for a proposed "Lovesong" picture disc, but the format never reached the shops.)

U2 WAR *(LP, Island PILPS 9733, 1983)* **£50**
(One that slipped through most U2 fans' net at the time. You could buy it over the counter — but not anymore!)

PRINCE PURPLE RAIN *(shape, Warner Bros W 9174P, 1984)* **£45**
(Cut into the shape of Prince on his outlandish motorbike, which he rode in the film of the same name.)

KATE BUSH THE KICK INSIDE *(LP, EMI EM CP 3223, 1979)* .... **£40-£45**
(There are two pressings of Kate's first album on picture disc, although they're worth roughly the same.)

MARILLION MARKET SQUARE HEROES *(12", EMI 12 EMIP 5351, 1982)* **£40**
(3,000 copies of Marillion's debut single were issued as a picture disc, which remains their top U.K. collectable.)

To The Egg LP, specially pressed for staff at Paul McCartney's offices, which fetches up to £1,000. Beware if you're offered one, though — there are many counterfeits on the market.

In the early '80s, shaped picture discs became popular. Often, the shape reflected a relevant theme, as with Police's 'Can't Stand Losing You', which took the form of a large police badge, and Irish band the Pogues' 'Sally MacLennane', which appeared like a shamrock. Among the most collectable shaped discs are Bruce Springsteen's 'Pink Cadillac' (no prizes for guessing its design) and Prince's 'Purple Rain', which pictures the singer sat astride a motorbike.

Shaped or picture discs are a popular gimmick with artists trying to get a high entry in the singles chart, and recent years have seen examples by everyone from R.E.M. and Nirvana to East 17 and Janet Jackson, most of them worth £4-£8 apiece.

Shaped discs are cut out by hand, and examples which have escaped the pressing plant uncut are usually worth more than their trimmed-down counterparts.

FLEXIDISCS

An obscure mid-'70s flexidisc, featuring an interview with pop group the Bay City Rollers. Flexidiscs are very easily scratched.

Flexidiscs are thin plastic records which are almost always given away free, usually with magazines or by fan clubs. Sometimes, they come with a new release — as with Elastica's self-titled debut album — though this is fairly unusual. As a rule, the sound quality of flexis is poor, so it's unusual for them to include any particularly important or historic recordings — though there are annoying exceptions! Normally, they contain interviews, spoken messages, studio out-takes or live tracks.

The most famous flexidiscs are probably the Christmas records issued to members of the Beatles Fan Club in the '60s, which now sell for between £45 and £75 apiece — if their cardboard picture sleeves are intact.

POSTCARD FLEXIS

Many postcards etched with grooves, and designed to be played like records, have surfaced over the years, with the most notable examples coming from Poland (though many are more likely to come from Putney!). They're also popular in the U.S.S.R., where they often form part of magazine-like gift packages.

In most cases, these flexis are unofficial, and they often won't play properly on an ordinary record player.

This interview disc came free with some copies of Julian Cope's 1987 album, "St. Julian".

Jukebox singles have large centre holes and are still common in countries like Italy.

INTERVIEW DISCS

Discs containing an interview are sometimes pressed up to promote a forthcoming release or event. Usually, they are limited editions, sent out to radio stations or the music press, though there is a label called Baktabak which specialises in releasing interview discs commercially.

It should be noted that recordings of spoken conversations are not governed by the same copyright laws that apply to music, and therefore virtually anyone can release an interview disc, if the conversation was originally taped with the artist's permission. Consequently, many such records are only 'semi-official'.

Among the rarest interview discs are American LPs from the early '60s, featuring the Beatles. These can change hands for up to £3,000. Despite the 'limited edition' tag given to the semi-official interview discs, however, these items rarely seem to raise much excitement from collectors — particularly as their sound quality is often dubious.

JUKEBOX SINGLES

In the '50s and early '60s, when pop music was rarely played on the radio, jukeboxes were one of the few ways record-buyers could check out the latest releases. In fact, there were so many jukeboxes around that record companies manufactured all their singles with push-out 'tri' or round centres, so they could be played on the machines.

Though jukeboxes were designed for 45s, some 78-only releases were pressed up in special 7" jukebox editions, as with Philips' very collectable 'JK' series. Jukebox discs coupling songs by two different artists were also common, as were singles containing two tracks lifted from a contemporary EP.

In the late 1960s, singles with 'tri' and round centres went out of fashion, and jukebox records with large centres were specially pressed by Polydor (for labels like Atlantic) and Philips/Fontana. These are not particularly collectable in their own right — partly because ex-jukebox singles are usually badly worn — though they can be valuable if they contain shortened versions of tracks, or feature unique couplings.

One of the most interesting jukebox singles is the Rolling Stones' 'Street Fighting Man', which included an extra track, 'Everybody Needs Somebody To Love', and played at 33⅓rpm. It currently changes hands for around £15.

Continued on page 61

Axl Rose, the controversial frontman of hard rockers Guns N' Roses.

SAME RECORD, DIFFERENT SLEEVE

Madness's 1981 single, "The Return Of The Los Palmas 7", came in this 'chefs' sleeve...

...And also in this scarcer 'cartoon' cover, which used artwork from a fan club comic.

"A Solid Bond In Your Heart" was the Style Council's stab at a Northern Soul song.

This edition is the more valuable of the two, and has a 'gatefold' sleeve that opens out.

The 'blue' version of the La's "There She Goes" is an EP with two bonus tracks.

The 'red' edition simply couples the title track with "Come In Come Out".

UNUSUAL SINGLES PACKAGES

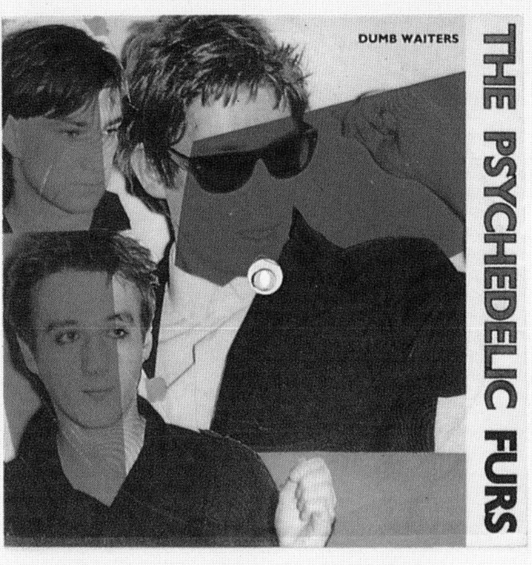

The Psychedelic Furs' "Dumb Waiters" came in a 'playable' sleeve etched with a groove.

Josef K's "Chance Meeting" was housed in this 'die-cut' Postcard Records sleeve.

"Uniform" by Inspiral Carpets was sewn into this cover made from camouflage material.

Nirvana producer Butch Vig's band, Garbage, issued "Vow" in a metal cover.

Menswear's debut single, "I'll Manage Somehow", came in a gatefold sleeve.

Orange Juice's "Lean Period" from 1984 was housed in a sealed brown paper bag.

Elton John, whose first recordings were with the mid-60s British R&B band, Bluesology.

OVERSEAS RELEASES

This box set of five Oasis CD singles was only available in France. The collection included four rare live recordings.

People don't always restrict themselves to collecting U.K. releases, as foreign issues often feature different packaging and tracks. In fact, records are sometimes put out abroad which never see the light of day here. An example is Nirvana's *Hormoaning* mini-LP, which was only issued in Japan and Australia, and includes the exclusive track, 'D-7'.

Some foreign territories are famous for high production values: Japanese releases, for example, often come in lavish packaging with lyric inserts and stunning artwork. Eastern European pressings, however, are notoriously basic, both in their packaging and their quality of vinyl.

SOME U.S. RARITIES

BOB DYLAN THE FREEWHEELIN'... *(LP, promo, Columbia CS 8786, 1963)* **£10,000**
(Unissued stereo version with "Talking John Birch Blues" and three other songs replaced on the commercial edition.)

THE BEATLES AND FRANK IFIELD ON STAGE
(U.S. LP, Vee Jay LPS 1085, 1964) **£5,000**
(To be worth the listed value, this has to come in the ultra-rare 'portrait' sleeve with a full-colour Fab Four painting.)

IKE & TINA TURNER RIVER DEEP, MOUNTAIN HIGH
(LP, Philles PHLPS 4011, 1966) **£4,000**
(Pressed in tiny quantities, without sleeves or producer Phil Spector's permission. Issued on A&M three years later.)

BILLY WARD & DOMINOES BILLY WARD & HIS DOMINOES
(10" LP, Federal 295-94, 1955) **£4,000**
(The first album to be issued by an R&B vocal group, this featured both Clyde McPhatter and Jackie Wilson.)

THE ROLLING STONES STREET FIGHTING MAN
(7" picture sleeve, London 909, 1968) **£3,000**
(One of the rarest sleeves in the world, withdrawn because of its image of police beating up demonstrators.)

THE FOUR TOPS BREAKING THROUGH *(LP, acetate, Workshop Jazz WSJ 217, '64)* **£2,500**
(The rarest Motown-related LP. Sleeve artwork definitely exists but it's thought it only reached the acetate stage.)

THE VELVET UNDERGROUND ALL TOMORROW'S PARTIES
(7" picture sleeve, Verve, 1967) **£2,500**
(Another hopelessly scarce picture cover, restricted to promotional use for just a handful of radio stations.)

PRINCE THE BLACK ALBUM *(LP, promo, Warner Bros 25677, 1987)* **£2,500**
(Only a few copies of this withdrawn album are known to exist, though it was bootlegged and later issued officially.)

JACK KEROUAC POETRY FOR THE BEAT GENERATION *(LP, Dot DLP 3154, 1959)* **£2,000**
(Incredibly rare collection by the famous American beat poet, which was withdrawn before release.)

JEFFERSON AIRPLANE TAKES OFF!
(LP, mono, different version to normal edition, RCA Victor LPM 3584, 1966) **£1,500**
(Contains the West Coast band's "Runnin' 'Round This World" and other alternate takes not on the final release.)

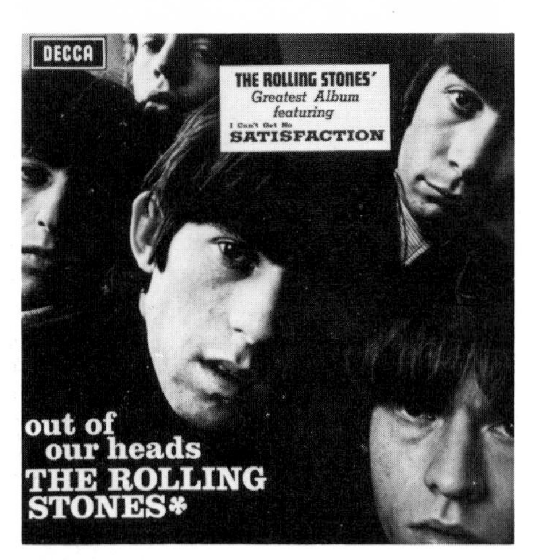

This export edition of the Rolling Stones' "Out Of Our Heads" LP was destined for Europe.

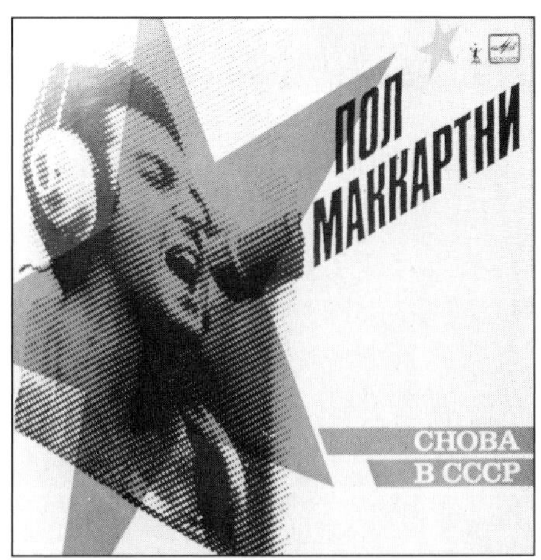

This Russian Paul McCartney LP was imported into the U.K. to meet demand from fans.

EXPORTS

In the 1950s and '60s, when overseas countries didn't have the facilities to press their own records, or couldn't manufacture enough copies of a British release to keep up with demand, it was common for the parent label in this country to help out. This involved pressing up the records here and shipping them out to the countries which needed them.

As foreign releases often featured different tracks and packaging, these 'exports' were often nothing like the copies available in this country. Indeed, sometimes they were completely unique. Not surprisingly, they're now of great interest, and though they were never sold in Britain, are usually regarded by collectors as U.K. issues.

The most famous exports are the Beatles singles and albums manufactured for sale in several European and South-East Asian countries, which are now worth between £70 and £800 each.

The term 'export' is now used much more generally for any record which is sent overseas to another country to be sold as an 'import'.

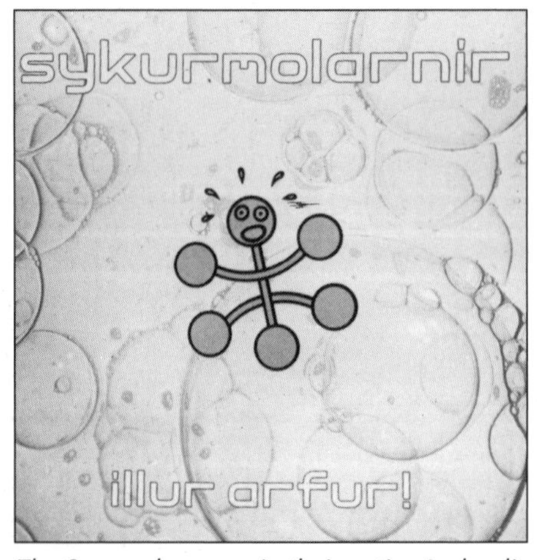

The Sugarcubes sang in their native Icelandic for this special foreign-language CD album.

An audiophile version of David Bowie's classic 1972 LP, "The Rise & Fall Of Ziggy Stardust".

IMPORTS

If a record is not released in a particular country — either because the record company can't find a label to distribute it there, or thinks that there will be no demand for it — then a shop or distributor might choose to 'import' some copies. This basically means that they buy up a batch from the foreign label, and pay for them to be shipped over themselves. As a result, imports are often expensive, but they allow fans to buy items that might otherwise be beyond their grasp.

Occasionally, so many copies of an imported record are sold in this country that it's pushed into the chart, which is what happened with the Clash's 'Bankrobber' single and the Jam's 'Just Who Is The Five O'Clock Hero?'. In fact, some imports, like the debut LP by '60s psychedelic band the Soft Machine, sold so widely in this country they're almost regarded as an ordinary U.K. release.

Other records imported in large numbers include U.S. and European dance/house/rap 12"s, sought after by DJs and fans keen to keep up with innovations outside the U.K.

SINGLES PACKS

In the early '80s, a group's hit singles were sometimes reissued together in a special pack. Notable examples include the *Madness Pack, Pistols Pack* and the blue vinyl *Police Pack,* all of which comprised six 45s. These items are worth £20-£25 each.

FOREIGN LANGUAGE DISCS

Throughout the history of pop, performers have been persuaded to re-record their hits in other languages, for release in foreign territories. Often the results are amusing results — just check out the French version of the Wedding Present's 'Why Are You Being So Reasonable Now?' ('Pourquoi Es Tu Devenue Si Raisonable?').

Among the best-known foreign-language discs are the Beatles' 'Sie Liebt Dich' ('She Loves You') — available in Germany and, strangely, America and Japan — and a string of Cliff Richard LPs with give-away titles like *When In Rome* and *When In Spain.*

AUDIOPHILE RECORDS

In the '70s, several record labels spotted a gap in the market for high-quality vinyl pressings of classic LPs, which would allow listeners to hear details of the original recordings that were often lost on the mass-produced discs of the day.

The "Police Pack" included six singles in a fold-out plastic wallet.

These 'audiophile' records were made of freshly-manufactured vinyl that was both hard and resilient, and could weigh upwards of 200 grams — making them almost twice as heavy as normal LPs. They were also mastered at half-speed, allowing the cutting stylus longer to etch the grooves accurately. They were also packed carefully in rice paper inner sleeves, which were supposed to be less abrasive than normal paper inners.

With such high production values, audiophile records were usually manufactured as exclusive limited editions, often by specialist American and Japanese record companies who licensed material from major labels (as with Mobile Fidelity's Stateside audiophile reissues of the Beatles' studio albums). Hardly any audiophile pressings originated from Britain.

Since the late 1980s, when CD albums began to dominate the market, audiophile vinyl records have become few and far between, although the more specialist market for vinyl has resulted in several series of high-quality pressings which have been aimed directly at the diehard record collector. In 1994, for example, Island Records reissued a handful of their classic albums — including Free's *Fire And Water* and Cat Stevens' *Tea For The Tillerman* — on 160-gram 'virgin' vinyl, and with their original gatefold sleeves and label artwork. However, these weren't strictly 'audiophile' pressings, as they simply replicated the original vinyl releases.

The latest craze is for 'gold audiophile' CDs, which are carefully remastered from the original tapes on digital equipment. Early examples like Paul McCartney & Wings' *Band On The Run* are already rising in value.

DEMOS, PROMOS, ACETATES, ETC.

DEMOS

(see also Promos)

Before the term 'promo' came into widespread use in the 1980s, records sent out free to the media to publicise a new release were known as 'demos' (short for 'demonstration' records).

Originally, they were meant for internal use only, so record company executives could hear new recordings before they appeared in the shops. But it was soon realised that demos could also be circulated among journalists and DJs to create a buzz.

As a rule, demos had different label designs to the ordinary copies sold to the public. For

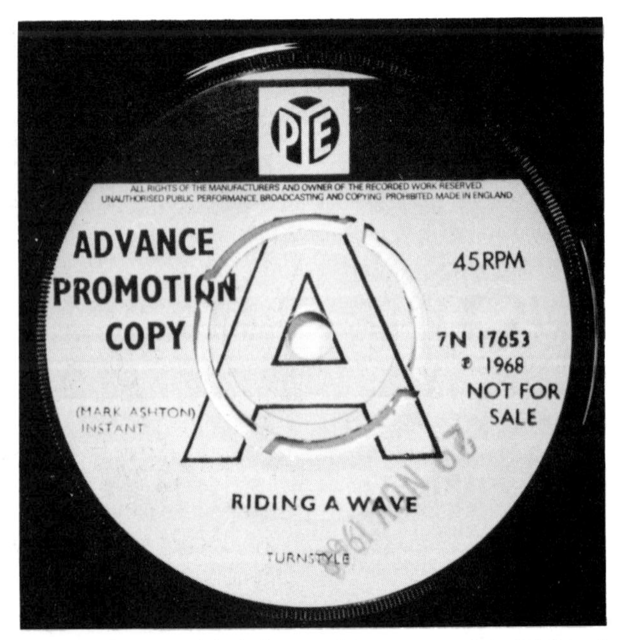

A typical '60s A-label demo. This is Turnstyle's "Riding A Wave", a psychedelic single from 1968, worth around £70.

instance, '60s demos on Parlophone, Columbia and HMV had distinctive white or green labels, superimposed on the A-side with a large red or white 'A'. This allowed a DJ to tell at a glance which side he or she was meant to play. For obvious reasons, these records are now referred to as 'A-labels'.

Attitudes towards demos vary: rock'n'roll collectors aren't too bothered about them, and often pay less for demos than normal commercial copies — particularly with obscure releases, which sometimes sold so poorly that the demos are easier to find. Fans of 'freakbeat' and British Psychedelia also seem indifferent, largely because the records are so rare they're happy to have them in any form.

Yet these are the exceptions rather than the rule. Most collectors prize A-labels for their exclusivity, and the majority of soul, pop and rock demos sell for far more than the corresponding 'stock' (commercial) issues. Examples by classic '60s groups like the Beatles, Rolling Stones, the Who and the Kinks are particularly collectable. For example, the demo of 'Love Me Do', the Beatles' first single, can sell for up to £1,000 — and not just because it spells Paul McCartney's name incorrectly!

In the '80s, the term 'demo' began to fall out of use, and was replaced by the word 'promo'.

PROMOS

(see also Demos, White Labels, Acetates & Test Pressings)

The term 'promo' is short for 'promotional', and is used to describe an advance copy of a new release sent out to the media, in the hope that it'll be reviewed or played on the radio. Until the late '70s, most promos were known as 'demos' (see above).

Promos fall into two distinct categories: those which are the same as the ordinary release, except for having a 'Not For Resale' sticker on the sleeve or a phrase like 'For Promotional Use Only' stamped on the label; and those which include different material or come in exclusive packaging. It's the latter that collectors particularly prize, of course, especially as U.K. promos are often manufactured in numbers of no more than 1,500 or so.

A 12" promo for Oasis's cover of "I Am The Walrus". The track was never released as an A-side, though it appeared on a flip.

In the 1950s and '60s, the free records distributed to DJs and journalists were more or less the same as the standard releases. But during the late 1960s and early '70s, it became increasingly common for different sleeves or packaging to be used, to make more of an impression.

An early example was the Rolling Stones' *Their Satanic Majesties Request*, a few promo copies of which came in a silk-padded sleeve. This item is so rare, in fact, that very few dealers have ever seen one, and if a copy came onto the market today it would probably fetch upwards of £750.

The early 1970s also saw the rise of exclusive 'promo-only' records. Again, the Stones were responsible for one of the first, *The Rolling Stones Promotional Album,* a special compilation featuring a unique combination of tracks. Other rare promo-only items include several singles by Led Zeppelin — the only British ones they ever made — and EMI's 'PSR' range of 45s by the likes of Cliff Richard and the solo Beatles.

By the late '70s, it was common for promo releases to come with anything from badges to flexidiscs and T-shirts — though most promos still took the form of stock copies with a 'For Promotional Use Only' sticker on their sleeve or label.

With the growing popularity of compact discs in the late '80s, record companies switched to CD as their main promo format and 'radio promos' were born. Often including a variety of special mixes or unique recordings, these are sometimes highly desirable artefacts, as indeed are 'samplers' — CDs (or LPs) featuring a selection of tracks from a particular artist or label.

The 1990s have seen promos turning into a huge area of collecting. They're especially popular with fans of Madonna, Prince, Pet Shop Boys, Belinda Carlisle, Erasure and Kate Bush, whose record companies tend to manufacture several different promos, each with unique combinations of tracks or exclusive material.

Dance collectors also put a premium on promos, as rare mixes — sometimes never released elsewhere — can appear on the 12" 'white labels' sent to club and radio DJs (often called, surprisingly enough, 'DJ copies').

Collectors are always keen to lay their hands on promos because of their air of

SOME RARE U.K. PROMOS

THE BEATLES, etc. **OUR FIRST FOUR** *(Apple, 4 x 7" [R 5722] incl. "Hey Jude" & three Apple-artist singles [APPLE 2, 3 & 4], with 4 inserts in box, 1968)* **£1,000**
(A presentation pack to launch their Apple label, hand-delivered to the likes of Harold Wilson and the Queen.)

THE ROLLING STONES **THEIR SATANIC MAJESTIES REQUEST**
(LP, padded silk sleeve, Decca TXL/TXS 103, 1967) **£750**
(Rumours abound that a few promo copies of the Stones' token stab at psychedelia came in a special fabric cover.)

THE ROLLING STONES **THE PROMOTIONAL ALBUM**
(LP, U.S. sleeve, Decca RSM 1, 1969) **£600**
(Designed for U.S. and U.K. radio stations to play old and new material prior to the release of their "Let It Bleed" LP.)

RINGO STARR **STEEL** *('Ringo Or Robin' Liberty's freebie, p/s, R.O.R. ROR 2001, 1972)* **£500**
(This one-sided 45 features the ex-Beatle drummer talking about his furniture design company over synth noises.)

LED ZEPPELIN **COMMUNICATION BREAKDOWN/GOOD TIMES, BAD TIMES**
(promo-only, Atlantic 584 269, 1969) **£350**
(Page, Plant & Co. never had an official U.K. single, though this powerful opener from their debut album came close.)

BLACK SABBATH **CHILDREN OF THE GRAVE/STATUS QUO** **ROADHOUSE BLUES**
(100 copies only, Phonogram DJ 005, 1972) **£300**
(Copies of this ultra-rare 45 were presumably pressed to promote the heavy rock output of Phonogram's Vertigo label.)

GEORGE HARRISON **SHANGHAI SURPRISE** *(1-sided 7", Ganga Publishing, & Vicki Brown matrix reads: SHANGHAI 1, 1986)* **£300**
("Shanghai Surprise" was Harrison's theme song to the Madonna movie of the same name. It remains unreleased.)

GENESIS **LOOKING FOR SOMEONE/VISIONS OF ANGELS** *(Charisma GS 1, 1970)* **£250**
(This 7" was sent out by the newly-formed Charisma label to promote their most promising signings, Genesis.)

PAUL McCARTNEY & WINGS **BACK TO THE EGG**
(promo-only, Parl. PCTC 257; some with T-shirt) .... **£250/£200**
(Not the legendary picture disc, but a black vinyl LP box set with badge, booklet, sticker, postcard & cigarette cards.)

DEEP PURPLE **HUSH!/ONE MORE RAINY DAY**
(in promo p/s, Parlophone R 5708, 1968) **£200**
(EMI occasionally promoted artists like Tyrannosaurus Rex, Pink Floyd and Deep Purple with promo picture covers.)

'exclusivity'. However, not all promos command sky-high prices — most are usually worth no more than double the value of the ordinary release, if that.

Incidentally, in the U.S., where there are many thousands of newspapers and radio stations, promos are manufactured in greater quantities than in the U.K., and are consequently easier to come by.

NB: Although promos have stickers saying they are 'not for resale' or are the 'property of the manufacturer', or else have a phrase like 'for demonstration purposes only' printed on their label — it *is* legal in Britain (through not in some European countries like Holland) to buy and sell them after the record has been released. The wording is designed so that any high-street record shops receiving them free don't sell them on to their customers.

ACETATES

In the 1950s and '60s, before cassettes were widely available, it was common for studio engineers to cut a few acetate discs at the end of each recording session, so the performer and producer could take them home to listen to.

Acetates aren't ordinary records, but aluminium discs covered in a layer of soft black vinyl called lacquer. Normally, they're one-sided and have a label printed with the name of a studio or the manufacturer (as with 'EMIdiscs'). Details about the tracks are usually hand-written or typed on the label.

Despite the fact that their sound quality deteriorates quickly — they're designed to be played just a few times — acetates are of great interest to collectors, especially when they contain unissued material or a different mix of a track. And, since only a handful of each are ever made, they're usually extremely rare.

Over the years, previously unknown recordings by the Beatles, Cliff Richard and Rolling Stones have all turned up on acetates, which have sold for hefty sums, despite their poor condition. Indeed, acetates containing rare material surface surprisingly often: in 1993, an acetate of an unreleased Jam single was auctioned by Sotheby's, causing much interest because of its unique version of 'Billy Hunt'.

Acetates by collectable groups are usually worth at least three or four times the value of their commercially released counterparts, and in cases where the version of the song is different, the acetate might easily fetch a three-figure sum.

Incidentally, when LP acetates come up for sale, they often consist of a set of two one-sided discs, with the other sides blank.

This acetate of a Shirley Bassey track was cut at the Beatles' Apple recording studio in Savile Row, Mayfair.

A one-sided promo for a Lynch Mob Beats remix of Paul Weller's "Whirlpool's End".

A test-pressing for the B-52's "Wild Planet" album. Note the primitive stamps on the label.

ONE-SIDED DISCS

The term 'one-sided' obviously describes any record with music on only one of its sides. Many flexis and freebies are one-sided, and since the mid-'80s there's also been a trend for one-sided discs with a laser-etched design on the flip (Sonic Youth's 'Halloween II' 12", for example). However, most one-sided discs are acetates or promos: a shortlived attempt to market commercial one-sided 45s failed.

TEST-PRESSINGS

Before any record is manufactured in large numbers, a few copies are run off to check that the final product sounds OK. These are called test-pressings, and are normally identical to the stock releases, except that they may have plain white labels and no proper sleeve. Some record companies — especially small indie labels — press up a few hundred extra 'test-pressings' to use as promos.

In most cases, test-pressings are worth no more than twice the value of their commercially-released counterparts. They are only more valuable if a projected release is halted at the test-pressing stage, making these the only copies in existence — as with T-Rex's 'Ride A White Swan' on the Octopus label, now worth about £1,000.

WHITE LABELS

This term refers to any promo, DJ copy or test-pressing with a white label, so there can sometimes be a certain amount of confusion about the specific nature of any particular record fitting this description.

White label promos usually have entirely blank labels or else labels with the track details printed on them, while test-pressings often have the information written on by hand.

During the '80s, 12" white label promos were common, though these days, most magazines and radio stations receive their promos on CD or cassette.

However, 12" white label promos are still popular with club DJs. If these records don't fill the floors, they may not see a commercial release — and hence they sometimes become collector's items.

A promo white label of the Bluetones' 1995 single, "Are You Blue Or Are You Blind?".

Sleeves, as well as records, can be mispressed. This Damned LP actually shows the Hot Rods!

MISPRESSINGS

At the manufacturing stage, the master plates which are being used to make a record occasionally get mixed up, with the result that a single or album ends up with the wrong material on its A- or B-side. If the mispressed track is a rare or unusual recording by the same artist, the record will be of special interest.

For example, some 12" copies of the Smiths' 'Shoplifters Of The World Unite' escaped from the pressing plant with 'You Just Haven't Earned It Yet Baby' on the A-side, a track that could otherwise only be found on their *The World Won't Listen* compilation.

Mispressings that result in the same track appearing on both sides are less interesting — though a copy of the Jam's 'When You're Young', which plays the flip, 'Smithers-Jones', on both sides, still fetches about £25.

Discs mispressed with a song by a different artist aren't usually collectable — unless they're by the Beatles, or someone of similar stature.

Several Smiths singles have been mispressed, including "Shoplifters Of The World Unite".

WITHDRAWN RECORDS

Withdrawn records are those which reach the shops for a short time, but are then recalled by the record company because of a legal dispute with the artist or a problem with the packaging. Sometimes, thousands of copies are sold before the shops are ordered to return the remaining stock — as with the Sex Pistols' 'Holidays In The Sun', which mischievously reproduced part of a Belgian Travel Service holiday brochure on its sleeve.

Occasionally, however, very few copies actually reach the public, instantly creating a rarity. For example, a 1978 solo recording by the Stranglers' Jean-Jacques Burnel was pressed up as a single in 1980, allegedly without his consent. When he learnt that 'Girl From The Snow Country' was about to go on sale, he threatened legal action and the record company recalled the single immediately.

The Soup Dragons' "The Sun Is In The Sky" was withdrawn from the shops, making it very rare.

In Britain, copies hadn't actually reached the shelves, but in Holland, the single went on sale for a day, and about 70 copies escaped, which are now worth about £125 each. Although the U.K. copies should have been melted down, a handful leaked out, and now change hands for upwards of £200.

The press kit for Thunder's "Behind Closed Doors" album included a CD, a publicity photo and a band biography.

PRESS KITS

To promote new releases or special events, record companies distribute a press kit to journalists, which is usually a folder containing information sheets, photographs and possibly a record, video, tape or CD. These can change hands for considerable sums —even the most unassuming Paul McCartney press kits sell for £25, for example, while the most lavish items can fetch up to £100.

"In The Studio", a 1988 U.S. radio show CD featuring Crosby, Stills & Nash.

RADIO SHOWS

Radio albums are special records containing complete broadcasts. They're made by only a handful of companies in the States, which then send them all over the country for use by local radio stations. These records and CDs usually concentrate on one artist, and often include rare live tracks and interviews unavailable elsewhere. The shows also include adverts, with pauses for the local stations to insert their own jingles.

The major manufacturers include Westwood One, whose 'King Biscuit Flower Hour' is a popular series. However, trade in these items is actively discouraged, as technically they remain the property of the radio station. Nevertheless they do occasionally appear on the collector's market, with a top example like U2's three-CD *Live From Dublin* selling for around £300.

BBC TRANSCRIPTION DISCS

The BBC sometimes transfers its programmes onto records, so they can be syndicated to other radio stations around the world. Recordings of 'in-concert' programmes are obviously very desirable, as they amount to an exclusive live album (as long as the BBC doesn't lease the material for commercial release, of course).

The BBC strongly objects to the sale of these discs, and they cannot be advertised for sale in Britain. And beware — most of those on the market are counterfeits.

The Sex Pistols, whose "God Save The Queen" on A&M is one of the most collectable 45s ever.

PACKAGING

Record companies know that people can sometimes be encouraged to make a spur-of-the-moment purchase on the strength of an eye-catching or unusual design. As a result, records and CDs have appeared in all kinds of packaging over the years, ranging from simple picture sleeves to lavish wooden boxes and metal cases. This chapter details all the different types that you're likely to come across.

PLAIN SLEEVE

A plain sleeve is simply a paper or cardboard sleeve without a design on it. Most are 'die-cut'.

DIE-CUT SLEEVE

Die-cut sleeves have a large circle punched out of their centre, through which the record's label can be seen. Sometimes, the design of the sleeve and label combine to create an artistic effect.

ART SLEEVE

The term 'art sleeve' is popular with European collectors, and refers to picture covers featuring a painting or design, rather than a photo of the artist. They were common in the 1950s and '60s, when each foreign territory would often devise their own artwork.

COMPANY SLEEVE

Up until the late-'70s, most U.K. singles were sold in company sleeves featuring the record label's name or logo. However, with the advent of punk, when picture sleeves became common, they began to disappear (though they are still used by some small independents). Famous examples include those produced by London and Decca in the '60s, and Postcard and Two Tone in the early '80s.

PICTURE SLEEVE

(also referred to as Picture Cover, Picture Bag)

Singles with sleeves featuring specially-commissioned artwork didn't become widespread in Britain until the late 1970s — though they were common in America and Europe since the '50s.

British labels originally felt that they were an unnecessary expense, especially as singles only have a short shelf-life. But when punk came along in 1976/1977, picture sleeves became a fashionable gimmick, and were so popular that most singles have had them ever since.

Not surprisingly, most of the rarest British picture-cover singles date from the '50s '60s and early '70s. Well-known examples including Bob Dylan's 'Leopard-Skin Pill-Box Hat' (£35) and George Harrison's 'Bangla Desh' (£75). Incidentally, unlike singles from the same period, nearly all EPs were issued in picture covers.

The term picture sleeve is often abbreviated to 'p/s', and picture cover to 'p/c'.

Different types of sleeve: 1. laminated (Bob Dylan) 2. die-cut (Elastica) 3 & 4. classic '60s picture covers (Traffic, Dusty Springfield) 5. art (Glide) 6. company (Postcard label).

LAMINATED SLEEVE

In the '50s and '60s, most album and EP sleeves were covered in a thin transparent layer of glossy material to protect the cardboard. Some early '50s albums had both sides of their sleeves 'laminated', but in the '60s, labels tended just to layer the front cover. As the laminate was folded over the back cover and glued down, these sleeves are referred to as 'flip-backs', 'flip-overs' or 'fold-overs'. Over the years, it's common for the covering to shrink slightly, leaving a thin, sticky tidemark around the edges of the flipped-back join.

POSTER SLEEVE

As their name suggests, these fold out into a poster. They've been common since the early '80s, and are sometimes called 'poster packs'.

GATEFOLD SLEEVE

Gatefold sleeves open out like the cover of a book, and are often used for double LPs or doublepack singles. Sometimes, as with the Rolling Stones' *Big Hits (High Tide & Green Grass),* they come with a booklet stapled inside.

INNER SLEEVE

This is the paper or plastic sleeve that protects a record from the cardboard outer sleeve. It often features photos, lyrics or information, and is considered an integral part of the packaging. Sometimes it's described as an 'inner bag'.

INSERTS

Usually a postcard or piece of paper, often containing song lyrics, artwork or written information. The absence of an original insert will decrease the value of a collectable record.

BOX SETS

Box sets fall into two categories: a) those including two or more records providing an overview of a group's work, and b) those which are simply a lavishly packaged edition of an ordinary release. In both cases, box sets often include extras, like booklets and lyric sheets or, in the case of some box set singles, badges, postcards or other freebies.

In recent years, record companies have anthologised the careers of many artists — including the Clash, the Stranglers, the Beach Boys and Abba — on multi-CD box sets. Often, these collections contain rare material.

NUMBERING

Many limited edition releases are numbered individually on their covers. The most famous example is the Beatles' 1968 'White Album', which Paul McCartney wanted numbered like the prints he'd seen in some art galleries. Obviously, there's competition among collectors for the low-numbered copies — in 1985, the cover of the '000 001' copy of the 'White Album', autographed by Ringo Starr, was sold at Sotheby's auction-house in New York for $715 (£550), and it would probably be worth at least twice that today.

SHRINKWRAPPING

Records are often sealed in a shrink-fitted polythene covering. Sometimes, this is done so that a free item such as a T-shirt, single or poster can be included within the packaging. Obviously, such 'shrinkwrapped' records are more desirable with the seal intact — even, ironically, if that means the record can't be played.

Packaging: 1. gatefold sleeve (Doors) 2. poster sleeve (Primal Scream) 3. inner sleeve (Jam) 4. box set (JAMC) 5. booklet (Buzzcocks) 6. numbered (The The) 7. shrinkwrapped (Prefab Sprout).

Different CD packaging: 1. long box (Mary Hopkin) 2. digipak (Dr. Robert) 3. jewel case (East 17) 4. slip case (Pearl Jam). A U.S. innovation, long boxes have now been abandoned.

LONG BOXES

In the late '80s and early '90s, some American CD albums were packaged in long, slim, cardboard boxes. However, these 'long boxes' were phased out due to pressure from ecological groups, who thought their lavish use of card was wasteful, and also because they were very easily damaged — for instance, when the CD was removed from the packaging.

SLIP CASES

Some CDs — usually CD singles — are sold in thin cardboard pockets, into which the disc 'slips'. Occasionally, these cases are lined with an anti-static material.

DIGIPAKS

Digipaks are one of the most lavish forms of CD packaging. They normally consist of a plastic tray (to hold the disc), which is attached to a cardboard sleeve which folds around the package. Often, one of the cardboard sections has a pocket containing a booklet or insert, though singles tend to have a simple 'gatefold' design.

It's highly likely that many digipaks will increase in value over the years, especially if they're limited editions. Like original cardboard LP sleeves, they damage easily, so it's important to handle them with care.

JEWEL CASES

A 'jewel case' is the term used for the plastic box in which most cassettes and CDs are housed. Most are of exactly the same design and therefore interchangeable and replaceable, though occasionally they're over-printed with a logo or image making them exclusive to that title.

Pulp's recording career stretches back to 1982, when they made their first appearance on a various artists compilation album.

COLOURED VINYL SINGLES

PICTURE DISCS

These Animal Men drew on heavenly inspiration for "The Sound Of The Youth".

Orange Juice's "Flesh Of My Flesh" pictured mutton chops — but not dressed as lamb!

1980's "New Amsterdam" by Elvis Costello showed the singer with a bunch of tulips.

Dodgy's "Making The Most Of" picture disc was numbered on its reverse side.

Brummie rap-metal outfit Pop Will Eat Itself scored a hit with "Ich Bin Ein Auslander".

One of many Levellers limited editions — the picture disc of 1993's "This Garden".

Jeff Beck, one of the three 70s guitar heroes who graduated from the Yardbirds in the 60s. The others were Eric Clapton and Jimmy Page.

ORIGINALS & REISSUES

REISSUES

In October 1973, when David Bowie was riding high on the success of *Ziggy Stardust* and *Aladdin Sane*, a skeleton sneaked out of his cupboard in the guise of 'The Laughing Gnome', a novelty single he'd cut for the Deram label back in 1967. Originally a flop, this record was back in the shops again, and selling like hot cakes to his somewhat bemused glam rock audience.

Although Bowie was annoyed that Deram was cashing in on his new-found stardom, the label was perfectly within its rights to re-release the record. They owned the master-tapes, and as long as they paid Bowie mechanical royalties, there was very little he could do to stop them.

'The Laughing Gnome' is a classic example of a reissued record — in other words, one that's been given a full release for the second time. The practice of reissuing happens all the time, and isn't necessarily a bad thing: reissues often make rare material widely available again. On the downside, though, they can make life difficult for collectors, particularly when a new pressing is virtually indistinguishable from an original copy — as we'll see later in this section.

In the 1930s and '40s, copyright laws were less precise and more difficult to enforce than they are today, and so reissues were often of dubious legal status. If a record was selling well in one country, another label might press up and sell its own copies, without ever paying royalties to the artist or person holding the rights to the the material.

The legality of such practices was made even more complicated by what was known as 'contemporaneous issuing', whereby record

A young David Bowie. All his LPs have been reissued but it's the originals which are still of most interest.

The original issue of George Harrison's 1970 hit, "My Sweet Lord", had a dark green cover.

When the single was reissued in the mid-70s, Apple used a totally different sleeve design.

labels — particularly in the States — would strike deals allowing other companies to put out their recordings, with the artists' names deliberately changed so they wouldn't have to pass on any royalities to the musicians! In this way, records by trad-jazzers like Irving Mills appeared under such unlikely pseudonyms as Jimmy Bracken's Toe Ticklers, the Kentucky Grasshoppers and the Whoopee Makers. As late as 1966, the Troggs' 'Wild Thing' appeared simultaneously on two separate labels in the States.

However, in the 1950s, the growing might of U.S. major labels like RCA, Columbia and Phillips resulted in the development of strict 'licensing' arrangements, which set out the terms under which another company could reissue material once it was given permission to do so. The number of unofficial reissues dropped sharply, though illegal copying or 'bootlegging' was never completely eradicated and, of course, it still continues to this day.

One of the most celebrated early reissues was Decca's 1966 edition of Johnny Burnette's *Rock And Roll Trio*, re-released because of the demand for the rare original. Interestingly, the reissue has become a collector's item in its own right, and now sells for around £18. (A 1956 original will cost you £500!)

It would be wrong to think that all of today's reissues are aimed at collectors, though. It's true that there's a huge market for CD reissues of classic or rare albums — but many re-releases are either second attempts to break a record into the charts, or else cash-ins after a track has been used on, say, a jeans or car advert.

TELLING AN ORIGINAL FROM A REISSUE

As a general rule, collectors prefer original records to reissues, and are willing to pay more for them. It's easy to understand why — reissues often skimp on extras like lyric inner sleeves, inserts or gatefold sleeves, and don't have the attraction of being the genuine, original artefacts from the time.

The difference in value between originals and reissues can sometimes be substantial, so it's important to know how to tell them apart. If a reissue appears on another label, or with a different catalogue number, then there won't be much difficulty. But problems can arise when a record is re-released by the same company, in a similar form to the original.

The Smiths' "How Soon Is Now" single was first issued on the Rough Trade label in 1984.

The cover of WEA's 1992 reissue used a photo of Vanessa Redgrave and David Hemmings.

However, close inspection invariably reveals minor differences. There might be a slight difference in label colour, or the song's title or writing credits may be printed in a distinctive typeface. The disc may even have a later or earlier copyright or publishing date, or a different record company address on the sleeve.

Take David Bowie's 'The Laughing Gnome', for instance. Although the 1973 reissue appears to have exactly the same Deram label as the original, there is, in fact, a small difference. On the 1973 disc, the matrix number (DR 39798) printed above the catalogue number is the right way up; on the original it's upside down. Because you can tell them apart, originals sell for £50, while reissues change hands for just £4.

Where an original and reissue can't be distinguished, the value of the former tends to drop. For example, the Charlatans' first EP, 1990's *Indian Rope*, was selling for around £20 until it was re-released in a virtually identical form. Today, both editions — and, unless you bought yours in 1990, who knows whether yours is an original! — sell for just £10.

In exceptional cases, a reissue may be the more valuable record. Freda Payne's 1973

Original copies of "Band Of Gypsys" by Jimi Hendrix were housed in a 'puppet' sleeve.

Later batches of the album sported a more typical image of the late guitar genius.

issue of 'Band Of Gold' on Invictus is actually worth more than the 1970 original on the same label, chiefly because far fewer copies of the reissue exist.

Castle reissued the Small Faces' "Ogden's Nut Gone Flake" album on CD in a metal tin.

CD REISSUES

Since the late 1980s, when the future of the Compact Disc was finally assured, most record companies have devoted considerable time and trouble to transfering the most popular records in their catalogues onto CD. Many of these CD transfers have been 'straight' reissues, simply including all the original material, but some have come with added extras, such as bonus tracks and sleevenotes.

Several small labels, including Demon, Sequel and Ace, have specialised in reissuing very rare vinyl albums on CD. Occasionally, the reissue reduces the value of the original LP, as with, say, progressive rock band High Tide's *Sea Shanties*. But records that are 'celebrated' rarities, such as the original release of Leaf Hound's *Growers Of Mushrooms LP,* rated at £700, tend to hold their price, even after they're reissued.

FIRST PRESSINGS

If a record is kept on catalogue for some time, it's quite likely that its packaging or label design might change slightly. Because it has never actually been deleted and then re-released, collectors refer to later copies as different pressings rather than reissues. Of course, the first pressing tends to be the most valuable.

Ol' blue eyes is back — legendary singer Frank Sinatra.

A classic illustration of this is the Beatles' first album, *Please Please Me*. When it was first released in April 1963, the labels had gold-coloured lettering on a black background. However, within a few weeks, after several thousand copies of the album had been sold, Parlophone decided to change the colour of the label lettering to bright yellow.

As a result, people are prepared to pay around £150 for a gold/black (mono) version of *Please Please Me,* compared with just £20 for a copy with the more common yellow/black design. In 1963, stereo editions of albums were pressed in relatively few numbers, so a gold/black *stereo* version of *Please Please Me* is worth around £700.

Of course, when different pressings can't be distinguished from one another, most fans are content with any record that appears to be of suitable vintage. Some experts do claim to be able to date records to the month or even week by looking at typefaces and label designs. But unless there's something obvious — like the inverted matrix number of 'The Laughing Gnome' — to convince the ordinary collector that a record isn't an original, values will not be greatly affected.

MONO & STEREO

At the end of the last century, people realised that a piece of recorded music sounds better when each of our ears is presented with a different aspect of the overall sound. In the same way, our eyes see slightly different parts of the whole scene, which our brains combine to make a full, three-dimensional picture.

At first, record companies found it very difficult to produce this 'stereophonic' effect. As a result, all commercially available recordings in the first half of this century were in 'mono', which meant that all the music was relayed as one solid plane of sound.

Behind the scenes, though, recording engineers were working hard to develop 'stereo', and in the mid-'30s the Gramophone Company in Britain patented a technique whereby two different signals were etched into just one groove, with the needle's up-and-down motion relaying one signal and the side-to-side motion the other.

Experiments continued for the next 20 years, but it was only after the introduction of vinyl, which was capable of carrying the finely-detailed stereo groove, that commercially available stereo records become viable.

The first public demonstration of a modern stereo record took place in Los Angeles in 1957, and within a year, the 45° stereo groove had been accepted in Britain and America as the industry standard. To begin with, only records by artists who appealed to an adult audience — like Frank Sinatra — were pressed in stereo, chiefly because you needed an expensive state-of-the-art 'hi-fi' with twin speakers to play them.

But by 1966, most LPs were being issued on stereo as well as mono, and with the introduction that year of cheap stylus cartridges that allowed stereo records to be played on mono equipment, the need for two different formats ended. By 1970, 'album

The first batch of the Stones' "Let It Bleed" had Decca's '60s logo. This is the mono edition.

A month or so later, Decca changed the label design to a boxed logo. This is a stereo copy.

Dr. Feelgood were leaders of the mid-70s R&B scene, a sharp contrast to the stadium-filling prog rock of the era. Interest in the band has increased since singer Lee Brilleaux's death.

monocide' was complete, though the mono format has occasionally been revived to recapture a vintage sound — as with Dr. Feelgood's *Down At The Jetty* in 1975.

With singles, mono remained the dominant format throughout most of the '60s, and stereo 45s only appeared regularly from 1969 onwards. Record companies knew that most pop singles were bought by teenagers, who often only had access to antiquated radiograms or portable players like the Dansette, that weren't fitted with stereo stylus cartridges.

Once stereo 45s were introduced, the market for mono singles quickly dwindled, and by the early '70s they were virtually obsolete.

FAKE STEREO

When it became clear in the mid-1960s that stereo was taking off, record companies began to issue stereo versions of many old albums — including those which were originally recorded in mono. By crudely remixing the master-tapes, and introducing a split-second delay between the two channels, engineers hoped to produce a stereo sound, but the results were often very poor. By the early 1970s, however, 'fake' or 'reproduced' stereo was discredited, and the practice stopped.

STEREO & MONO VALUES

Because they were initially produced in relatively small quantities, stereo albums from the late 1950s and early '60s are generally much harder to find than mono copies. Consequently, collectors tend to prize them more highly.

A good example is the Rolling Stones' 1965 *Out Of Our Heads,* which sells for around £35 in stereo and £25 in mono. With late '60s albums, the opposite is true: at £30, the mono edition of the Beatles' 1969 *Yellow Submarine* is worth about twice as much as the stereo.

However, many people prefer the mono version, because this was the mix that the group and producer put most work into. Will Sergeant, former guitarist with post-punk band Echo & the Bunnymen, relates the following tale about the Beatles' *Sgt. Pepper*, issued in June 1967:

"Geoff Emerick, who was the recording engineer on all the sessions, told me they spent three weeks doing the mono mix and then they all went off home. The producer, George Martin, then told Geoff to do the stereo mix on his own, because no one took it seriously. So he did it in three hours. It was no big deal — just stereo for the weirdos!"

In fact, the mono and stereo mixes of *Sgt. Pepper* are quite different — as, indeed, is the case with many other albums of the time, most notably Pink Floyd's *The Piper At The Gates Of Dawn*. For example, on the mono edition of *Sgt. Pepper* you can hear Paul McCartney shouting in the background on one track; on the stereo mix, you can't!

QUADROPHONIC

Quadrophonic sound took stereo a stage further, and split the music up into four different channels which were then relayed to four loudspeakers, arranged around the listener. 'Quad' enjoyed brief popularity in the mid-'70s, but quickly fell out of favour.

Mike Oldfield's legendary 1973 album, *Tubular Bells*, was originally issued in quadrophonic, and Mint copies today change hands for £20.

The Australian quadrophonic edition of Pink Floyd's "The Dark Side Of The Moon" album.

SOME RARE REISSUES

JOY DIVISION AN IDEAL FOR LIVING *(12" EP, Anonymous ANON 1, 1978)* **£65**
(A reissue of the Manchester band's rare indie 7" debut only months after it was deleted, on better quality 12" vinyl.)

JACKSON C. FRANK AGAIN *(LP, B&C BCLP 4, 1978)* **£50**
(Jackson C. Frank was an influential folk singer; this was an equally obscure reissue of his mid-60s Columbia LP.)

SLADE BEGINNINGS OF SLADE *(LP, withdrawn, Contour 6870 678, 1975)* **£50**
(A budget label reissue of "Beginnings", back in the days when Noddy Holder & Co. were called Ambrose Slade.)

CYRIL DAVIES THE LEGENDARY CYRIL DAVIES *(LP, Folklore F-LEAT 9, 1970)* **£50**
(The founder of British blues issued a hopelessly scarce LP in the late 50s. This reissue had four extra tracks.)

THE ARTWOODS ART GALLERY *(LP, Decca Eclipse ECS 2025, 1974)* **£45**
(Originally released in 1966, this London R&B band's sole album was later repackaged in a totally different sleeve.)

THE BEATLES THE BEATLES' FIRST *(LP, withdrawn, Polydor POLD 666, 1980s)* **£40**
(This second reissue of the Fab Four's Hamburg recordings pictured Ringo on the cover, who wasn't in the band then.)

EDDIE COCHRAN SINGIN' TO MY BABY *(LP, Liberty LBY 1158, 1963)* **£40**
(Originals on the London label sell for over £100; somewhat cheaper is this second edition, issued five years later.)

KILLING FLOOR ORIGINAL KILLING FLOOR *(LP, Spark Replay SRLM 2004, 1973)* **£40**
(A British blues rock outfit whose debut album from 1969 was reissued as part of Spark's retrospective Replay series.)

ALEXIS KORNER BLUES INCORPORATED *(LP, Polydor 236 206, 1967)* **£40**
(A reissue of the British blues legend's incredibly scarce 1965 album for the tiny Spot label, minus some of the tracks.)

JOHN TAVERNER THE WHALE *(LP, Ring O' 2320 104, 1977)* **£40**
(This contemporary classical LP was first issued on the Beatles' Apple label, and then on Ringo Starr's short-lived imprint.)

BOOTLEGS, PIRATES AND COUNTERFEITS

> ***"Why did you record all my phone calls? Are you planning a bootleg LP?"*** *(The Specials' 'Gangsters', 1979)*

Every year, thousands of CDs, cassettes and LPs are manufactured illegally. The vast majority are counterfeits of best-selling albums — the kind that are sold at street-markets. They are very poorly made, and most people regard them as a rip-off.

However, there's another kind of illicit release which is looked upon more kindly by some collectors. These are bootlegs, which are records featuring live recordings and studio out-takes that are unlikely to get an official release. Although they infringe copyright laws, it would be naive to pretend that they don't form an important part of collecting. In fact, they're often of immense archive value, providing rock historians with an invaluable reference of concerts and studio sessions.

The following section provides a guide to the different kinds you may come across.

BOOTLEGS

'Bootlegs' are illegal records containing material which isn't available on any official product, and can be bought on CD, vinyl or tape. Usually, they feature live performances or demos, though occasionally they include finished tracks which for some reason the label or artist didn't want released. Many people believe that bootlegs by some artists — including Bruce Springsteen, David Bowie and Bob Dylan — contain some of their best work.

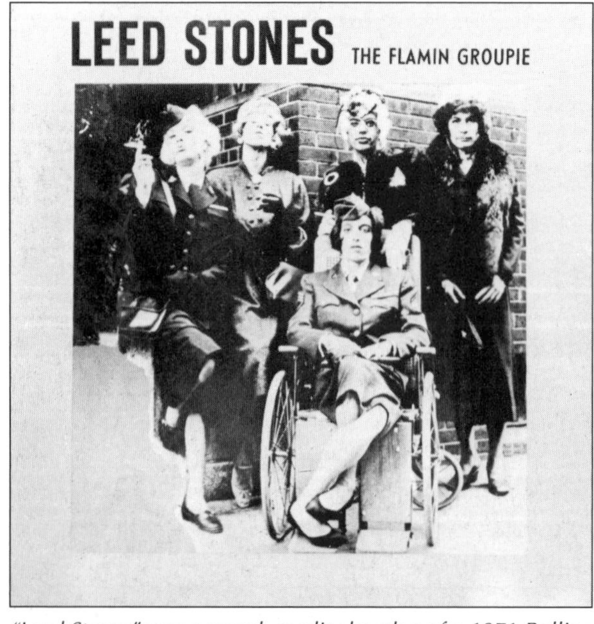

"Leed Stones" was a superb quality bootleg of a 1971 Rolling Stones live concert in — surprise, surprise — Leeds.

Bootlegging dates back to the pre-World War Two jazz era, when it was harder to prosecute record companies issuing material that didn't belong to them. However, rock bootlegs didn't start appearing until the late '60s, when LPs like Bob Dylan's *Great White Wonder* and the Rolling Stones' *Liver Than You'll Ever Be* surfaced in America. These records were initially sold quite openly and proved to be a roaring success — so much so, in fact, that the artists' official record companies were forced to release similar material to satisfy demand.

Within a few years, 'boots' had become part and parcel of collecting, though initially, many were pressed on inferior vinyl and had plain white sleeves and blank labels. However, many of today's CD bootlegs are made to the same high standards as their legal rivals, and albums like Nirvana's *Virgin Songs* and *Outcesticide* are welcome additions to any collection.

The problem is that the quality of unofficial recordings varies enormously. In the past, most live bootlegs were taped by audience-members with hand-held recorders, which not only picked up the group, but

"Tom And Jerry Meet Tico And The Triumphs", a bootleg of singer/songwriter duo Simon & Garfunkel's early recordings.

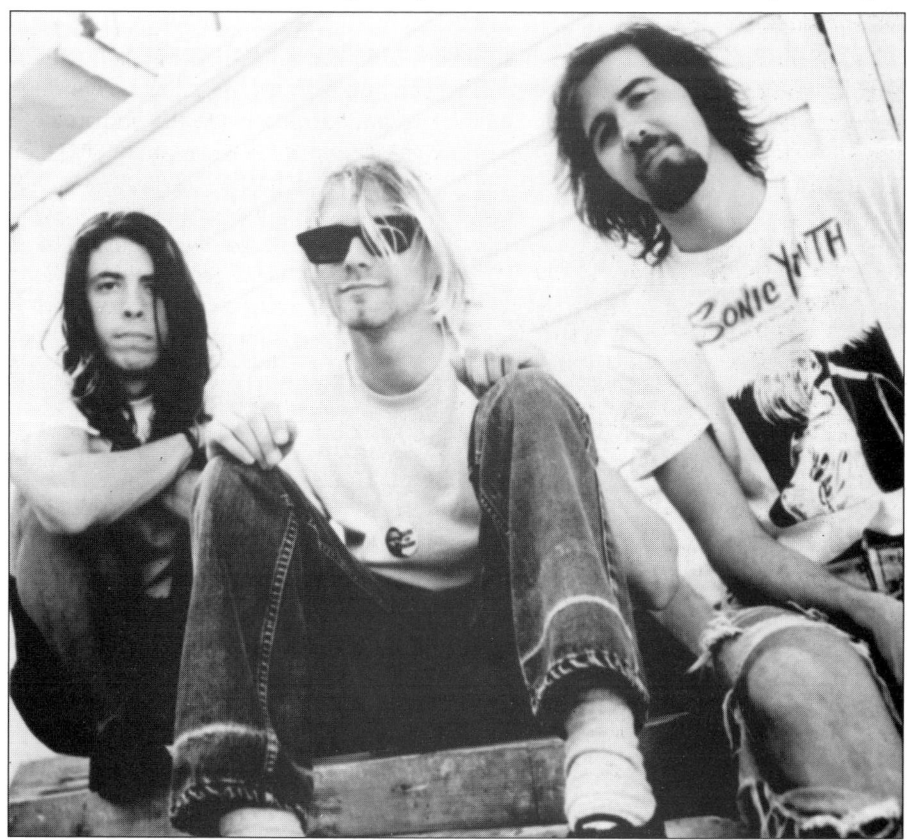

Million-selling U.S. punk band Nirvana are undoubtedly the most bootlegged band of the '90s.

also the conversations of people standing nearby. These days, however, it's common for recordings to made through the mixing desk, which obviously produces a much better result. Called 'soundboard tapes', they're made so the band can assess their performance, but it's usually not long before they're circulating among fans.

As you might expect, the quality of most studio bootlegs is usually good, though some originate from second or third-generation cassette copies, which results in muffled sound.

Ironically, many vintage bootlegs have became collectable themselves, with early, good-quality Dylan, Rolling Stones and Beatles items among the most valuable.

BUYING & SELLING BOOTLEGS

Although bootlegs provide a further dimension to collecting, buying them can have its practical drawbacks. There is, of course, absolutely no guarantee that any bootleg record, tape or CD will (a) play properly, (b) have reasonable sound quality, or (c) actually include the material listed on its cover.

But with fanzines and other underground publications often reviewing unofficial releases, it is possible to get an independent opinion before you actually part with your money. Naturally, that won't protect you from an unscrupulous dealer intent on selling you a *Guns N' Roses Live At Wembley* tape that is, in fact, totally blank, or a *Sex Pistols Out-Takes* LP containing Take That's first album. But usually, mishaps like this are the exception rather than the rule.

Official attitudes towards bootlegs differ considerably. Record companies despise them, arguing that unofficial releases rob them of millions of pounds in royalties each year — which isn't strictly true, as most fans who buy bootlegs are probably the first in the queue for the official products. Some labels have responded to the problem in a postive way, releasing their own 'Official Bootlegs' by major artists like Dylan and Frank Zappa.

Artists themselves seem to have mixed feelings, some regarding them as a back-handed compliment, while others express unease that fans are buying unpolished recordings or work-in-progress. John Lennon, though, used to make sure that he collected every new Beatles bootleg as it came out!

Some groups, like All About Eve and the Wedding Present tried to beat bootleggers at their own game, selling their own semi-official live tapes through their fan clubs. The Grateful Dead actively encourage gig taping — to dissuade fans from buying unofficial bootlegs.

Any band who attract a loyal following, like Stourbridge's finest, the Wonder Stuff, are an obvious target for the bootleggers.

Along with the Rolling Stones, Bob Dylan was one of the first artists to be heavily bootlegged.

PIRATES

Pirate records are simply cheap copies of official records in new, sub-standard packaging. Every year, millions are manufactured in the Middle and Far East, where copyright laws are hard to enforce. You'll find counterfeit tapes in markets selling for just a few pounds, but they usually suffer from very poor sound quality.

COUNTERFEITS

Unlike bootlegs, which usually contain unreleased material, counterfeits are exact (or almost exact) copies of official records. They are intended either as straight forgeries, or else as 'reproductions' — that is, cheap imitations for collectors unable to afford the originals. Among the most famous counterfeits are those of Paul McCartney & Wings' *Back To The Egg* picture disc, genuine copies of which sell for £1,000.

Sometimes, if it's difficult to tell a counterfeit from the original, the value of the real artefact will usually drop.

While bootlegging has a subversive charm, and results in the airing of material that might otherwise be left in the vaults, counterfeiting is universally perceived by artists, record companies and fans alike as out-and-out fraud.

EUROPEAN RELEASES — OFFICIAL PRODUCT OR BOOTLEG?

In recent years, there has been a flood of semi-official albums from the continent, which have invariably made their way into this country. These have included Bob Dylan and Beatles recordings from the '60s, Led Zeppelin rarities from the early '70s and Nirvana concert recordings from the '90s.

This situation arose due to discrepancies in the copyright laws which allowed some countries — particularly Italy — to exploit certain loopholes. While in Britain, a piece of music remained the property of the copyright owner for 50 years, in Italy, it was just 30 years.

Now, since July 1st 1995, when every country in the European Union agreed to adopt a new copyright law, this has been standardised. The period of copyright is now 70 years after a writer or composer's death, and this protection also applies to all works which were previously out of copyright.

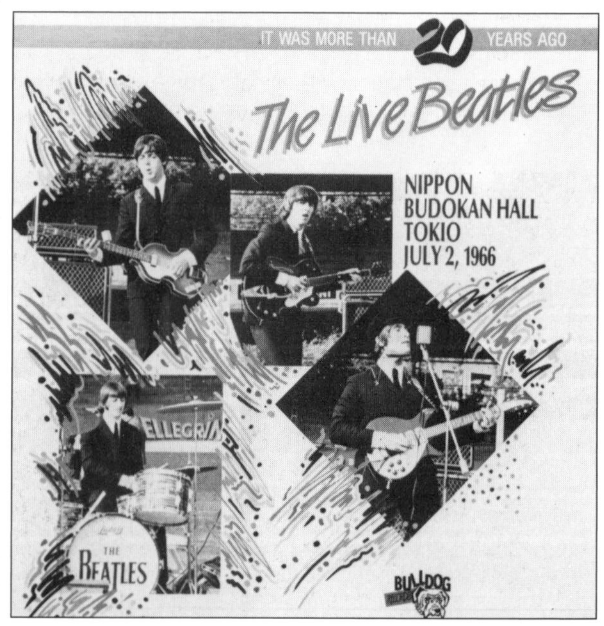

The Beatles are the world's most bootlegged band. Many CDs have surfaced in Europe which are illegal in the U.K.

WHAT'S IT WORTH?

A GUIDE TO VALUING RECORDS

Pricing rare records is one of the most contentious areas of collecting. People often argue about how much items are worth, and you'll frequently see dealers selling the same record at very different prices. But what is a record's true value? The basic answer is it's worth what anyone's prepared to pay for it at any given time. For example, an item that sells for £25 in a specialist shop may attract a bid of £35 in the heat of an auction sale, or be snapped up by a well-heeled foreign dealer for £40.

However, it is possible to come up with an accurate guide to the values. *Record Collector* magazine pioneered the pricing of records in the U.K., and every monthly issue of the magazine features complete discographies with up-to-date values.

ESTABLISHED RARITIES

With established rarities, like many '60s soul, progressive rock and punk releases, pricing isn't really a problem, because specialists know from experience how often the items appear for sale, and what the demand is like.

They're aware, for example, that the Who's *Ready Steady Who* EP on Reaction is scarce enough for people to pay £30 for it and that the Sex Pistols' 'Rock'n'Roll Swindle' with the withdrawn American Express picture sleeve is actually very common, and is barely worth a fiver.

NEW AREAS

The real difficulties arise when new areas of collecting open up. Sometimes a genre will emerge — like Exotica (basically anything strange or kitsch from the '50s and '60s) — in which albums that were previously worth a nominal £5 suddenly start selling for

The Who's "Ready Steady Who" EP featured tracks played on a mid-'60s TV special.

The Sex Pistols' "Great Rock'n'Roll Swindle" single initially came in this picture sleeve.

Supergrass became instantly collectable when "Caught By The Fuzz" gave them a minor hit.

many times that amount. This is true of LPs by Martin Denny & His Orchestra, whose lilting Hawaiian sounds have recently won new converts on the club scene.

New groups can also present a problem, particularly when their fan base is expanding rapidly, which pushes up the values of their early limited editions. For instance, in April 1995, indie band Supergrass's rare debut single on Backbeat, 'Caught By The Fuzz', was selling for £12-£15. A month later, when the band's debut album sailed into the Top 10, its value rocketed to £25 — but it later stabilised at £20. During these turbulent periods, dealers often don't know whether they're over- or under-pricing the records, and sometimes they'll simply invite offers.

BOOK PRICE

In recent years, the publication of our *Rare Record Price Guide* — compiled with the help of scores of specialised dealers — has helped standardise values, and many collectors now sell items at 'book price'. Even so, prices can still vary considerably, especially when there's interest from foreign buyers, who'll often pay over the odds for items they know they're unlikely ever to see for sale in their own country. (This is particularly true of progressive rock, punk and Beatles records.)

In such cases, dealers with a large number of overseas clients will invariably raise their prices. Of course, some shops offering a specialist service may also charge more, while others make a name by selling items at knock-down prices.

The bottom line is that it's always worth shopping around — and never forget that rarities sometimes turn up at car boot and jumble sales for next to nothing.

LPs by middle-of-the-road artists like Mrs. Mills can usually be picked up for under £1.

A GUIDE TO FACTORS AFFECTING PRICE

Here's a summary of the key points affecting values, which are always taken into account whenever we price an item in one of our complete *Record Collector* discographies:

A) SUPPLY & DEMAND

Competition for scarce items pushes up values — which is why the one-off pre-Beatles acetate, 'In Spite Of All The Danger', is worth tens of thousands of pounds, while the huge-selling 'Agadoo' by Black Lace can't be given away.

B) CONDITION

If a record is worn or damaged, it will always sell for less than the Mint 'book price' (see Condition section). 1950s and '60s discs are particularly hard to find in perfect condition.

Interest in 'exotica' has increased the price of LPs by Martin Denny & His Orchestra.

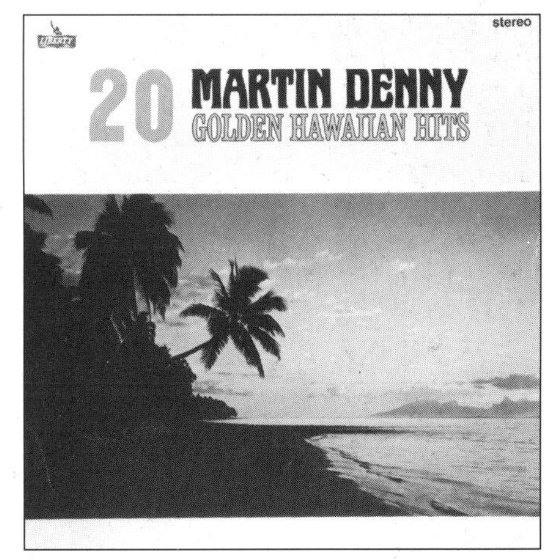

Martin Denny's "20 Golden Hawaiian Hits" first appeared on Liberty in 1965.

"Back To Front Vol. 4" brings together many obscure European punk rock rarities.

Progressive rock band Stone Angel's self-titled 1975 LP sells abroad for up to £600.

C) CHANGING TASTES

As artists go in and out of vogue, so their records fluctuate in price. 'Thru The Flowers', the 1987 debut single by indie band the Primitives, was given the thumbs up by Morrissey, who was then hugely popular. As a result, copies quickly began changing hands for upwards of £40. But after the ex-Smith went off them, and the band fizzled out, the value tailed off. The single now sells for about £15.

D) FOREIGN DEMAND

Well-heeled foreign collectors — particularly from Japan and Germany — are often prepared to pay top prices. Some genres are affected more than others, like progressive rock, punk and the Beatles.

E) REISSUES

If a rare single or album is re-released, the price of original copies may fall. However, experience shows that rarities which have achieved a certain celebrity — such as John's Children's 'Midsummer Night's Scene' or the Sex Pistols' 'God Save The Queen' on A&M — can rise in price every year, even though you can often buy exactly the same music on CD in your local record shop.

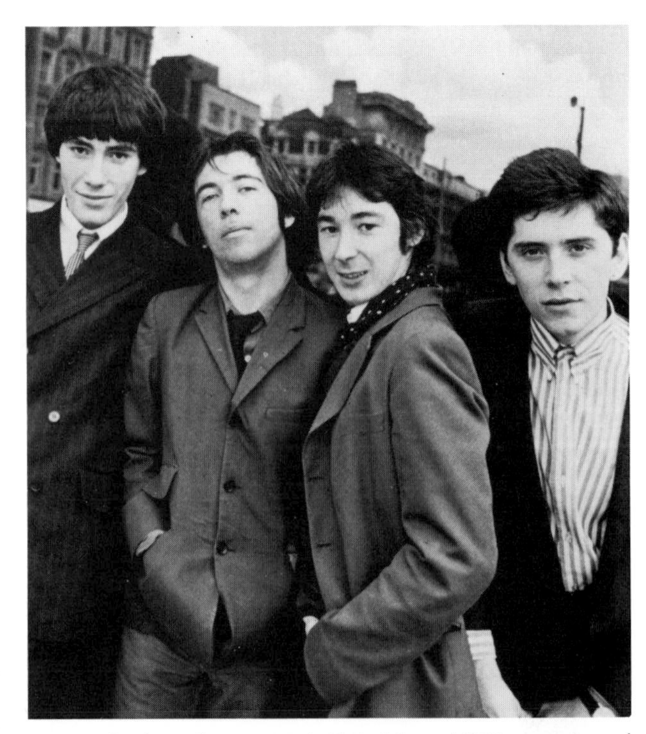

Buzzcocks' first release, 1977's "Spiral Scratch" EP, was reissued in 1979. The original is worth £15 and the reissue £5.

Marc Bolan, who started recording as a solo artist in the mid-60s, and went on to lead John's Children and then T Rex.

The Everly Brothers returned to their rock roots with the 1965 LP, "Rock'N Soul".

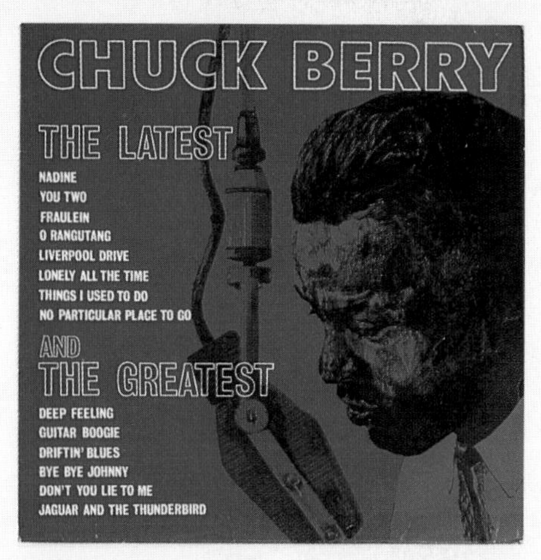

Chuck Berry's "The Latest And The Greatest" was released by Pye in 1964.

One of the best-selling rock'n'roll albums ever in Britain was Buddy Holly's hits LP.

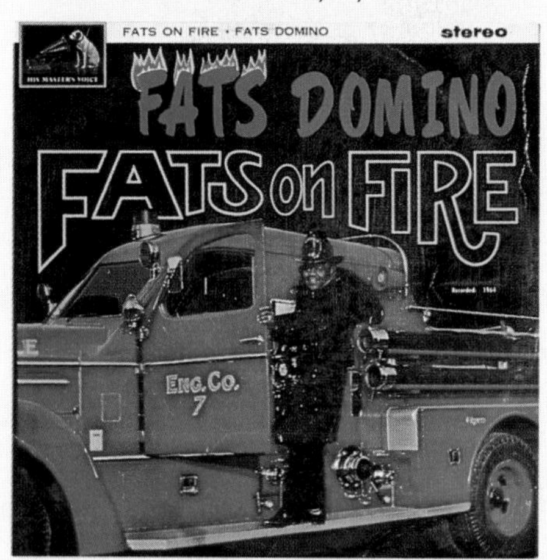

Fats Domino was one of the 50s rockers whose careers were revived in 1964.

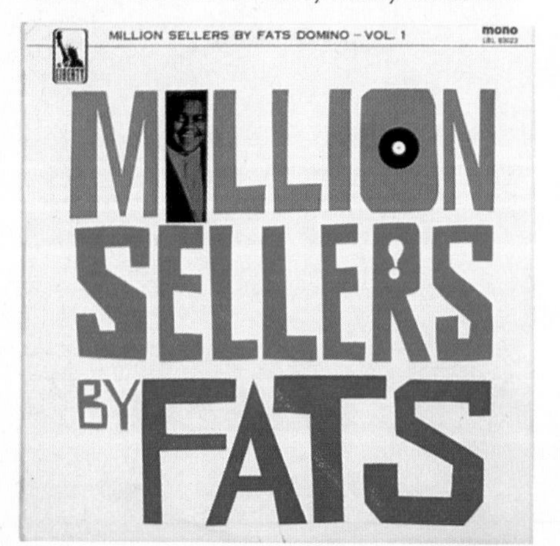

Many of Fats Domino's classic hits from the 50s were included on this Liberty LP.

Gene Vincent made an ill-fated comeback in 1969 with this LP on John Peel's label.

Elvis Presley at the height of his fame as a rocker in the 50s. His early Sun recordings revolutionised pop music.

The U.K. edition of the Beach Boys' first LP, which was released in 1962.

This soundtrack LP for Sonny and Cher's first movie was only issued in America.

Paul Revere and the Raiders scored lots of U.S. hits, but never broke through in Britain.

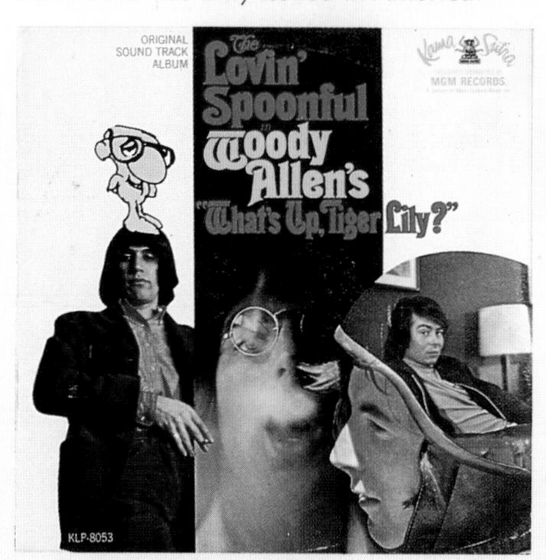

This soundtrack LP for an early Woody Allen movie was never released in the U.K.

"All Strung Out", a 1967 folk-rock LP by the popular duo Nino Tempo & April Stevens.

"Half & Half" was split between Frankie Valli solo tracks and Four Seasons songs.

BUYING AND SELLING

WHERE TO LOOK

Some collectors like to spend their money in high-street record stores, buying new releases and limited editions that may become collectable in the future. However,those who want to get hold of old records will need to look further afield.

The first port of call for collectors are local second-hand **specialist shops**, which can stock everything from recent CDs to vintage items from the 1950s onwards.

Occasionally, you can pick up a real bargain, especially if the shops adopt the practice used by London's famous Music & Video Exchanges, which drop the price of each item with every week it remains unsold. For the most part, though, professional dealers price their goods according to *Record Collector's Rare Record Price Guide*, and as a result, customers tend to have to pay the going rate.

The same is true of **record fairs** — indoor events for which dealers hire a stall. Regional fairs take place in most towns every few weeks, while big cities like London and Birmingham regularly host large weekend events, billed as 'international fairs'.

But there are bargains to be had. Collector Daren Butler picked up a rare acetate of the Cure's 'Lament' flexidisc at a 1993 Wembley fair. Only five acetate copies of this item are thought to exist, so Daren was more than a little surprised to find one in an anonymous-looking box. "It was just sitting there among some other stuff," he remembers. "I got it for £30, but it's actually worth nearer £200."

Generally, though, music fans who want to pick up an old record at a knock-down price have to take a more imaginative approach to buying, and this means scouring **junkshops**, **jumble sales**, **charity shops**, **car-boot sales**, and **house clearances** for items priced at just a few pounds or pence. In fact, these places have yielded some very lucrative finds over the years — as illustrated by some of the letters that arrive at *Record Collector*.

A rare hard vinyl test pressing of the Cure's "Lament" flexidisc.

"I have just had the biggest shock of my collecting career," wrote an Oxford-based music fan two years ago. "Yesterday I went to a car-boot sale in search of some LPs, but nothing much was forthcoming. I was browsing through various boxes of junk, when I spotted an old single on the London label among four or five old 45s. It only cost me 10p and I didn't buy anything else.

"When I got home, I looked up its value in your *Rare Record Price Guide*, and I had to ask my wife to verify what it said! I had bought a pristine copy of the Penguins' 'Earth Angel' on London (HL 8114, 1955), which had a black label with gold lettering. Is it *really* worth £1,200?"

The answer is yes, which proves that even the most celebrated rarities sometimes turn up for 10p!

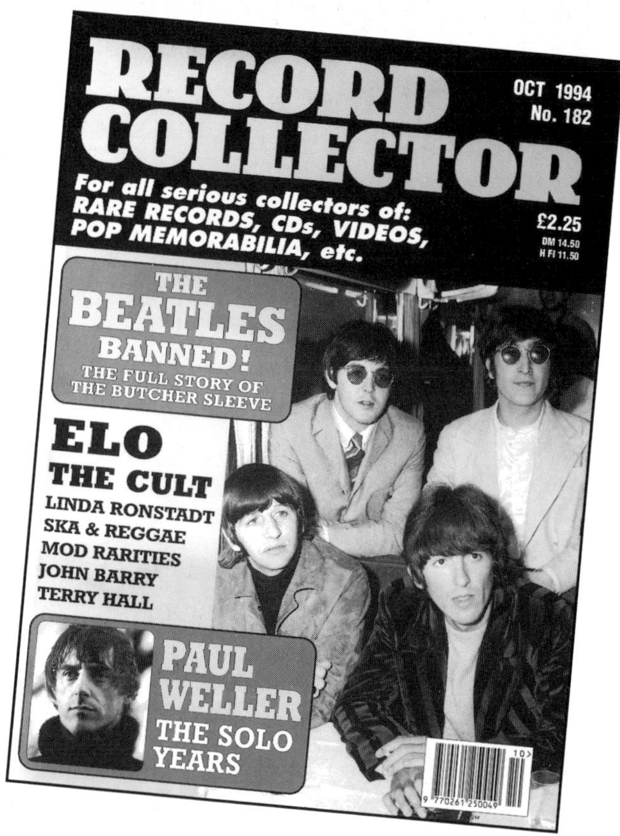

With around 200 issues under its belt, 'Record Collector' is still the best place to find records and CDs on sale by mail order.

Another fruitful place to find bargains is **auction houses**. Although sales of individual records are few and far between, whole collections are often sold off as part of a larger sale. Normally, you'd be expected to bid for the whole collection, and may end up competing with dealers who have hundreds of pounds to spend.

However, sometimes collections are offered as a number of different lots, and it's here that you may get lucky. Dealers tend to decide in advance what they're going to bid for and the maximum price they'll pay. Consequently, some lots don't attract any bids at all, leaving the field clear for you to jump in and pick up a bargain for the lowest possible price.

It's also worth remembering that it's the auctioneers' job to sell as much as possible, so they may accept a bid of just a pound or two for an unpopular lot. Sometimes, they sell anything left over at the end to anyone offering them a reasonable sum.

Auctions are usually good fun and can yield some great finds. However, if you've only got £30, make sure you don't scratch your head when the bidding for that rare Beatles acetate tops the £15,000 mark — you might have a lot of explaining to do when you get home.

BUYING RECORDS BY MAIL-ORDER

Another convenient way of buying records is by mail-order. Most of the trade centres around *Record Collector* magazine, which includes adverts for around 50,000 records and CDs each month. These range from old 78s to contemporary pop records, and are offered for sale by both large companies and individuals. You'll also see adverts for posters, tour passes, autographed photos and a wealth of other memorabilia.

SET SALE & AUCTION

There are two basic types of advert in *Record Collector*: listings and display. Most individuals take out a listings ad, which, as its name suggests, is basically a list of the records they're selling, together with details of their address and how much extra to add for postage and packaging.

Usually, the vendor states the price of each item, and this is called a **Set Sale**. However, with a very rare item, people may be asked to write in with offers. The person tendering the highest bid will, of course, receive the item. This is referred to as an **Auction** sale.

Here is an example of the kind of advert placed in *Record Collector* by a private trader:

SET SALE

Write to: JOHN SMITH, 57 ANYSTREET, ANYTOWN AN3 TN1, ENGLAND. Tel: (0103) 890987. P&P £1.75 + 50p.

Format	Item	Condition	Price
CD	ABBA Classic Abba (dbl. play orchestral CD)	EX/M	9.99
LP	ALICE COOPER Ladies Man (rare live THBM005)	VG/EX	9.99
CD	ALL ABOUT EVE, Every Angel (EVENCD7 UK)	EX	6.99
LP	BRIAN AUGER & TRINITY, Befour (RCA Victor 1970)	M/M	10.99
LP	B-52s Mesopotamia (Island 1982)	EX/M	6.99
LP	JOHN BARRY, Thunderball (UAS5132 US)	VG	19.99
LP	SHIRLEY BASSEY With Nelson Riddle (Columbia, ST '62)	VG/EX	7.99
CD	BLACK SABBATH, Trashed (PRO-A-Z102 US promo 12")	EX	9.99
LP	DAVID BOWIE Profile (German Teldec Red Decca 1979)	EX/EX	12.99
CD	BJORK, Venus As A Boy (Holland 2trk)	EX	5.99
CD	BJORK, Human Behaviour (4trkAustralia)	EX	7.99
12"	BELINDA CARLISLE, Vision Of You (UK pic, sealed)	M	7.99
7"	PHIL COLLINS, Thru These Walls (US 524 dj UK promo ps)	EX	7.99
LP	BING CROSBY, The Early Thirties (AH88 mono)	VG	9.99
7"	DEVO Come Back Jones (PC b/w Social Fools, grey)	EX/VG	2.49
12"	DR FEELGOOD She's A Wind Up (ltd. edn. UA 1977)	VG/EX	5.99
7"	DURAN DURAN, Various Japanese Singles	ea M/M	8.00
7"	FALL Rowche Rumble (PC, SF11 1979)	EX/M	8.99
7"	GENESIS Spot The Pigeon EP (PC Charisma 1977 PC)	VG/VG	7.99
LP	JIMI HENDRIX Birth Of Success (MFP 1970)	M/EX	6.99
7"	BUDDY HOLLY, Learning The Game (45Q72411 UK)	VG	7.99
LP	BUDDY HOLLY, Greatest Hits	EX	11.99
LP	JOHN LEE HOOKER, Driftin Thru The Blues (Holland)	EX	14.99
7"	KING KURT, Ring Dang Do (KurtG2 dble pack UK)	EX	5.99
CD	LENNY KRAVITZ, Let Love Rule (VUSCD10 UK 3")	EX	7.99
12"	KRAFTWERK, Neon Lights (signed Hutter/Hilpert)	M/EX	20.00
7"	FREDDIE MERCURY, I Was Born To Love You (double pack)		26.00
12"	FREDDIE MERCURY, Barcelona (pic disc, songs on wrong sides)		50.00
LP	MOVE, Flyback (rare Fly 1971)	EX/M	11.99
7"	PEARL JAM, Alive (UK white vinyl ps)	EX	7.99
CD	PEARL JAM, Spin The Black Circle (SAMP2467 promo)	EX	9.99
LP	GENE PITNEY 24 Sycamore (SHM 1977)	VG/EX	6.99
7"	PRINCE, Mountains (Japan promo)	EX	39.99
7"	PUBLIC IMAGE LTD. Death Disco (Virgin 1979)	M/M	6.99
LP	DIANA ROSS Greatest Hits (Tamla Motown g/f 1973)	VG/VG	8.99
LP	SMALL FACES Small Faces Big Hits (Virgin V2166)	M/M	10.99
12"	TELEVISION Marquee Moon (Elektra 1977)	EX/EX	7.99
LP	T. REX, Slider/Tanx (CBS Israeli copies)	ea M/M	10.00
LP	JOE WALSH So Far So Good (US ABC1540)	VG/EX	5.99
LP	WHO Live At Leeds (Track 1970 + all insert)	M/M	13.99
7"	XTC Life Begins At The Hop (PC, Virgin 1979 PC)	EX/M	4.99
7"	NEIL YOUNG, Needle & Damage Done (Spain promo ps)	EX	14.99

HOW TO REPLY TO A SET SALE OR AUCTION

The procedure for responding to a **Set Sale** advert is as follows:

a) Telephone or write to the advertiser stating which records you are interested in buying. If you're writing, it may be worth sending a stamped addressed envelope (SAE) to ensure a quick reply. DO NOT SEND ANY MONEY AT THIS STAGE.

b) If the record is still available, the advertiser should reply promptly to your letter or call, telling you how much the total cost will be, including postage and packing.

If the record has already been sold, the advertiser won't normally contact you — unless, of course, you included a stamped addressed envelope with your letter.

c) If a sale is agreed, send the vendor a Postal Order or cheque for the required amount. Vendors living abroad usually prefer to receive payment by International Money Orders (available from your local post office).

The procedure for replying to an **Auction** sale is slightly different:

a) Send the advertiser a list of items you want, stating how much you're prepared to pay for each one. Auction lists often have a closing date, so make sure your bids are posted early. If you want to know whether or not you've lodged the highest bid, enclose an SAE. However, some advertisers specify 'winners only notified'.

b) If you do offer the highest amount, the advertiser will advise you of the total price (inc. P&P), just as he or she would if it was a Set Sale.

Record Collector is often asked how much people should bid in a postal auction. All we can suggest is that you set yourself a cash limit, just as you would at any other auction, and that you don't offer more than the record is worth to you. Obviously, there is no point in wasting a stamp on a ridiculously low bid or offering well over the odds for an item which you could buy elsewhere for less.

Remember that the advertiser may only receive a handful of bids for many items, so there is always a good chance that a sensible, fair bid will be successful.

DISPLAY ADVERTS

Large mail-order companies often take out 'display' ads in *Record Collector*, like the ones below:

EXTRA RECORDS

102 High Street, Slattington, Anywhereshire AN1 3NE
Tel: (01890) 123456, Fax: (01890) 567890
Open 9.00am – 6.00pm Monday to Saturday

ALMA COGAN A To Z 1950-1966 (3-CD set, 88 tracks) £20.99
THE CHANTAYS Pipeline (CD) £13.99
EVERLY BROTHERS UK Singles (22 track Ace CD) £7.99
HANK MARVIN & THE SHADOWS Best Of (CD) £12.99
CRICKETS Something Old, Something New (CD) £9.99
SAPPHIRES Best Of (CD) £7.99
ADAM FAITH Best Of EMI Years (dbl CD) £12.99
LONNIE MACK Home At Last (CD) £10.49
TEX OWENS Cattle Call (Bear Family CD) £12.99
VENTURES Another Smash/Colourful (2-on-1 CD) £11.99
PATSY CLINE Discovery (CD) £10.99
CLARENCE CARTER Best Of: Snatchin' It Back (CD) £8.49
PETULA CLARK The Nixa Years Vol. 1 (CD) £9.99
BILLY FURY Play it Cool (video) £10.99
GENE VINCENT Ain't That Too Much (import CD) £12.49
THE SURFARIS Wipe Out (US CD) £13.99
CONWAY TWITTY Number 1s Vol. 1 (US CD) £10.99
TORNADOS Telstar Original Sixties Hits Of... (CD) £5.99
WILLIE MITCHELL Walkin' With (Rollercoaster CD) £8.99
HEINZ Tribute To Eddie (Rollercoaster CD) £8.99
DICK DALE Unknown Territory (CD) £12.99
RUTH BROWN Miss Rhythm (dbl CD) £11.99
ROCKIN' DOO WOP 1954-64 various (CD) £7.99

Postage rates: UK & EC: £1.25 per item
REST OF THE WORLD: £3.50 per item

Methods of payment: 1. Postal orders/cash by Recorded Post only.
2. Cheques made payable to Extra Records.
3. International Money Order.

As you can see, it's normally made clear how to respond to the advert.

LEGAL SAFEGUARDS

All *Record Collector* advertisers must comply with the laws laid down in the Trade Descriptions Act. This means that vendors giving misleading or false information are liable for prosecution.

In practice, few problems arise, and those that do are almost always settled by the advertiser refunding the buyer's money. If you are dissatisfied with the condition of any record you buy, then write to the advertiser, stating the problem.

If you don't receive a satisfactory reply, then let *Record Collector* know, and we will do our best to investigate the matter. It's our policy to ban any fraudulent advertisers from the magazine — though we very rarely have to take such a drastic step.

Formed in the late 1970s, the Cure remain one of the most collectable bands in the world.

BEWARE!

Very occasionally, collectors have the misfortune to come into contact with an unscrupulous dealer, who has no qualms about ripping off his, or her, customers. Such people are a rarity in this business, but you still need to be wary.

One dodgy practice is 'skimming', which entails removing the surface scratches on a record by polishing it on a machine. To the eye, the record looks Mint, but when played it sounds like chips frying! Other underhand procedures include counterfeiting and passing off reissues as originals.

SELLING

Collectors often fund their own purchases by selling the records they've picked up for next to nothing at car boot sales and junkshops, but don't want to keep.

Selling items through *Record Collector* is simple. First you place an advert — a section in the magazine explains the procedure in detail — and then you await the replies from other collectors interested in what you have to offer. You then contact the buyer telling him, or her, the total amount they need to send you, including expenses for postage and packing. If you are auctioning a record, you obviously contact the highest bidder as quickly as possible after the closing date.

Unsuccessful bidders need only be notified if they've enclosed an SAE.

SELLING TO A DEALER

Dealers make their living from buying and selling records, so it's important for them to make a profit on every item. As a result, they will only pay you a proportion of the going rate for any record you offer them. Sometimes this will be as little as 30 or 40 per cent, though 50 per cent is more normal. Even so, it's always worth haggling.

In fact, you'll probably get a much better deal if you're prepared to trade your records for other discs from the dealer's stock. This way, you should get a more favourable rate of exchange.

SENDING RECORDS THROUGH THE POST

PACKING A RECORD PROPERLY

Records sent through the post should always be properly packed in special 7" or 12" postal envelopes or 'mailers', available from specialist shops and mail-order firms. Before placing the record in the envelope, it should be sandwiched between two pieces of stiff card, to ensure it doesn't get bent. CDs are more robust than records, but again, it's sensible to pad out the envelope prior to posting, or to send them in a special 'Jiffy' bag lined with polythene air pockets. Plastic CD cases are particularly prone to damage if they're not packed carefully.

POST OFFICE SERVICES

The Post Office offers several special services for sending important or valuable items:

a) RECORDED DELIVERY provides proof of posting and requires a signature on delivery. However, compensation for loss, damage or delay is limited to a maximum of 100 times the basic first class rate (which currently works out at £25). Packages are handled along with ordinary post, and there are no special security procedures.

b) SPECIAL DELIVERY provides proof of posting and requires a signature on delivery. It also guarantees the package reaches its destination before 12.30pm the next working day — if it doesn't, the Post Office will refund twice the Special Delivery fee. Again, at the time of writing, the maximum compensation in event of loss or damage is £25.

c) REGISTERED provides proof of posting and requires a signature on delivery. It also guarantees the package reaches its destination by 12.30pm the next working day, *and* insures it for up to £500.

d) REGISTERED PLUS is similar to registered but the insurance is up to £2,200.

The Post Office recommends that valuable items — including rare records — should be sent by **registered** mail. Registered and Registered Plus provide evidence of posting and delivery, plus special security arrangements during transit.

For an additional charge, you can insure your package against 'consequential loss' — that is, extra expense incurred over and above the actual cost of the items, due to loss or delay. You can also combine **Special Delivery** with **Registered Post** to ensure the package arrives before 12.30pm the next working day.

These services only apply to the U.K — ask at any Post Office for details about sending records overseas.

N.B: DO NOT send cash through the post unless it's in a registered envelope. Despite the fact that this warning is printed in *Record Collector* every month, people are still doing it, and *still* losing their money.

1960s Psychedelic LPs

The Turtles' "Happy Together" album took its name from their big 1967 hit single.

The second part of Jimi Hendrix's legendary "Electric Ladyland" album, issued in 1968.

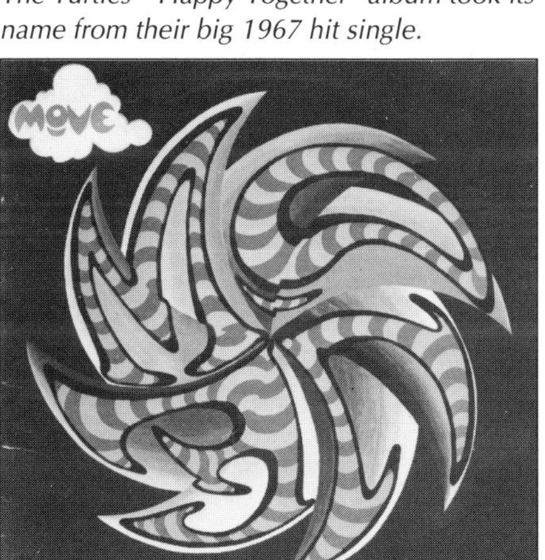

The Move's self-titled 1968 LP was housed in this colourful, psychedelic sleeve.

Wynder K. Frog lent his Hammond organ wizardry to the "Sunshine Super Frog" LP.

The superb "Introspection" album by the End was produced by Rolling Stone Bill Wyman.

Issued in 1967, Pink Floyd's first album was titled "The Piper At The Gates Of Dawn".

CONDITION & GRADING

The values quoted for records in this book and in our *Rare Record Price Guide* refer to copies in perfect — or 'Mint' — condition. Items that are damaged in any way, or show signs of wear, will always be worth significantly less. Many households may have old and battered Rolling Stones and Beatles LPs tucked away in a cupboard somewhere, but these aren't really what collectors are looking for. Usually, fans buying a second-hand record will expect it to play well, look OK, and include any original extras like inner sleeves or inserts.

In cases where a Mint copy isn't available, most people are happy to settle for records in Excellent or Very Good condition (see grading system below). Indeed, some fans prefer buying items with a small amount of wear, because they're cheaper and sound perfectly adequate. Collectors of '50s and '60s labels like London, Parlophone or Phillips often don't have the choice, as truly 'Mint' examples of some releases rarely come onto the market.

Of course, not all non-Mint discs are impaired to the same degree, so *Record Collector* has developed a standard grading system to enable people to work out what their records are worth.

Primal Scream are one of many contemporary rock bands whose early releases are in demand.

78s are made out of brittle shellac and break very easily — ask Rosemary Clooney!

It's still possible for thirty-year-old records, like this Cliff Bennett LP, to survive in good nick.

GRADING SYSTEM FOR CONDITION

N.B. Although the definitions primarily refer to records, they also can be used for CDs and cassettes. In such cases, the CD or tape itself will usually be 'Mint', as they are hard to damage, but inserts and cardboard covers may only be 'Good' or 'Fair'.

The definitions of the grades are as follows:

MINT:
The record itself is in brand new condition, with no deterioration in sound quality. The cover and extra items such as the lyric sheet, booklet or poster are also in a perfect state of repair. Where appropriate, collectors sometimes refer to 'Unplayed' copies.

EXCELLENT:
The record shows slight signs of having been played, but there is no substantial reduction in sound quality, and the cover and the packaging have been well cared for, but may be slightly creased or worn.

VERY GOOD:
The record has obviously been played a few times, but without any major deterioration in sound quality. Some wear and tear on the cover or extra items is acceptable.

GOOD:
The record still produces a reasonable sound but is noticeably crackly and/or distorted. Although showing wear and tear, neither the record, the cover or the contents display any major defects.

FAIR:
It's noticeable that the record has been played so much that the sound quality has deteriorated badly. The cover and contents may be folded, scuffed, etc.

POOR:
The record is still just about playable but has not been cared for properly and displays considerable surface noise and other deterioration in sound quality. The packaging may be torn, stained, defaced or even missing.

BAD:
The record will not play properly due to scratches, bad surface noise, etc. The cover and contents may be badly damaged or even missing.

Once you have determined which of these definitions applies to your record, you can then work out its value on our 'Ready Reckoner', printed on the next page. Assuming that you know the 'Mint' value of the disc — which can be found in *Record Collector*'s *Rare Record Price Guide* — this chart will tell you how much an 'Excellent', 'Very Good', 'Good', 'Fair', 'Poor' or 'Bad' copy is worth in comparison.

OTHER DEFECTS

When an item is offered for sale by mail-order, it's normal practice for the vendor to state its condition. Sometimes, the grade is accompanied by short-hand details about any defects the item has, so that people know exactly what they're getting.

The most common defects — all of which will affect the price of an item — are as follows:

WRITING ON LABEL or COVER (WOL/WOC): This refers to any writing or scribbling on the label or cover, or to the presence of an ink stamp saying, for instance, 'Property Of The Radio Station'.

TEAR ON LABEL/COVER: Covers and labels are sometimes torn when price or reference stickers are removed, though the term can also describe any other rip in the packaging. Covers that have split along one or more edges will also affect the value, even if they've been stuck back together with tape.

SLIGHT EDGE WARP: This is probably the most common kind of warp in a vinyl record, caused by a pressing fault or exposure to heat. Even in cases where the record can still be played, and sounds perfectly OK, it's important to alert buyers to this defect. When the record can't be played, it's always graded as 'Bad'.

Warping is one of the collector's biggest worries, as buckled discs are irreparable.

NO COVER (NC): This term usually refers to EPs and LPs only. With singles, the absence of a picture sleeve where one was originally issued is denotated by 'no p/s'.

NO CENTRE: This refers to singles which have had their centres punched out so they can be played on jukeboxes. However, many foreign records — including all U.S. singles — are manufactured without centres, as indeed were some late '60s and early '70s U.K. singles on labels like Atlantic and Fontana.

READY RECKONER

Mint	EX	VG	Good	Fair	Poor	Bad
500	400	275	200	150	75	25
300	240	170	120	90	45	15
250	200	140	100	75	35	12
200	160	110	80	60	30	10
150	120	85	60	45	25	8
125	100	70	50	40	20	7
100	80	55	40	30	15	5
75	60	45	30	22	10	4
50	40	28	20	15	8	3
40	32	22	16	12	6	2.50
30	25	17	12	9	4.50	2
25	20	14	10	8	4	1.75
20	16	11	8	6	3	1.50
15	12	8.50	6	4.50	2	1
12	10	7	5	3.50	1	—
10	8	5.50	4	3	—	—
9	7	5	3.50	2.50	—	—
8	6	4.50	3.25	2	—	—
7	5	4	2.75	1.75	—	—
6	4.50	3.50	2.50	1.50	—	—
5	4	2.75	2	1.25	—	—
4	3.25	2.25	1.50	1	—	—
3	2.50	1.75	1	—	—	—
2	1.75	1	—	—	—	—

This chart will help you work out the value of a record in any condition. If you find a record which is worth £10 in Mint condition, but your copy is only in Very Good condition, then you can read across the appropriate line and discover its value — in this case, £5.50. As few collectors are interested in records in Poor or Bad condition, we consider that any disc worth less than £10 in Mint condition is virtually worthless in Poor or Bad condition.

1960s Jamaican Ska & Reggae Rarities

'Independant Jamaica Calypso" by Lord Creator was the first 45 on Island Records.

"Madness", Prince Buster's classic ska single which inspired the band of the same name.

Ska/reggae label Pama kicked off with Carlton Alphonso's "Where In This World".

Hugh Godfrey's "A Dey Pon Dem" was the first single to appear on the Coxsone label.

"You Don't Care" by the Techniques put the Treasure Isle label on the reggae map.

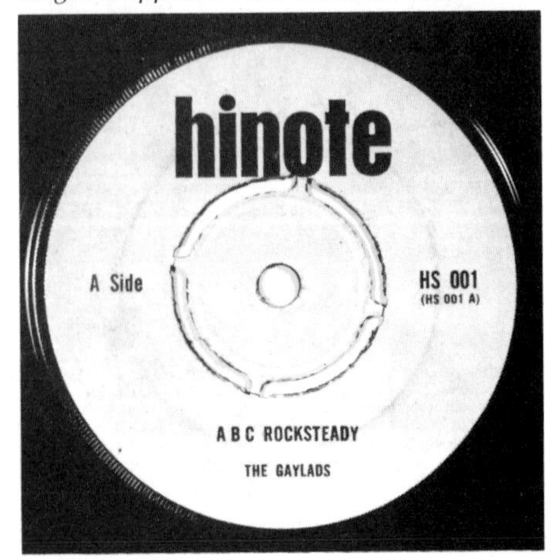

The Hi-Note label began in the late '60s with the Gaylads' "ABC Rocksteady" single.

RECORD CARE

As the condition of your record is so important, it's vital that they're looked after properly. Items suffering from scratches, blemishes or warping are always worth far less than those in perfect condition (see item on 'Condition' on page 108).

For the most part, looking after your collection is simply a matter of common sense: most people realise that playing records with a badly-worn stylus isn't going to do them any good, or that packing items together too tightly in a storage space will result in scuffed sleeves.

Even so, there are several key points about record care that everyone should be aware of:

HANDLING

If a vinyl record is not handled carefully, it will quickly start to suffer from small surface scratches and other faults. You can obviously reduce the wear by storing it in its proper sleeve and keeping your fingers away from the grooves. Never return an album to its cardboard cover without first putting it back into its inner sleeve.

Despite manufacturers' claims that CDs will play perfectly well with dirt on the surface, it's still advisable to handle them by their edges and centre.

STORING

Records should always be stored upright — preferably on purpose-built wooden shelves — and kept away from dampness, direct sunlight and heat (especially radiators). Lying records on top of each other eventually leads to warping as well as damage to their sleeves. Where possible, discs should be kept in protective PVC outer covers, which can be bought at most record fairs, collector's shops and through ads in *Record Collector* magazine.

A record can be cleaned safely using lukewarm water and a mild detergent like liquid soap.

EQUIPMENT

Playing a vinyl record with a worn stylus can damage it irreparably. If your stylus is showing signs of wear, change it immediately. Normally, when you buy a replacement it will state how many hours' worth of playing time the stylus will give you. If it doesn't, then ask the retailer.

Never play modern vinyl discs on vintage record players which don't have suitable styluses, or have an old-fashioned mono 'needle'.

STATIC & DUST

When you play a record on the turntable, a small charge of static electricity builds up on its surface, attracting dust. Before you play a disc, wipe it with the type of anti-static cloth or brush available from most specialist record shops and hi-fi centres.

Renowned rock'n'roll and TV personality Doc Cox cleaning a treasured Howlin' Wolf 78 on the legendary Chess label!

CLEANING

Collectors have always argued about the best way to clean a record. The traditional method is to wash the disc in a bowl of lukewarm water, containing just a touch of liquid soap, and to wipe the dirt off afterwards with a soft cloth. As long as the record isn't submerged for more than a few seconds at a time, no harm will come to the vinyl or label.

Or at least that's the theory. Many people consider this method to be crude, arguing that detergents and tap water contain impurities that may damage the vinyl. Their alternative suggestion is to use a specially-prepared cleaning solution, or to remove the dirt with a 'cleaning machine'.

The recommended solution is made up of one part isopropyl alcohol (IPA) to four parts distilled water (both liquids are available from high-street chemists). To this, you can also add a 'wetting agent', which reduces the surface tension of the solution, allowing it to penetrate deeper.

Cleaning machines, like the Moth and Nitty Gritty, can be ordered from specialist record shops, but are generally very expensive. Once the dirt has been loosened with a cleaning solution, these devices carefully scoop or suck it out. Any remaining dirt can be removed by playing the record, and then wiping the stylus clean with a suitable soft brush.

Alcohol-based cleaning solutions should **not** be used on 78s, because they attack the shellac material from which the discs are made. These should be cleaned with distilled water.

CDs can be cleaned by wiping them with a soft cloth. This method is particularly helpful in stopping CDs from jumping.

INSURING YOUR MUSIC COLLECTION

Although your record collection may have taken years to build up, and be worth hundreds or thousands of pounds, you'll find that it is very difficult to insure against loss or damage. The majority of brokers just aren't interested in offering you a policy.

One of the major problems is the lack of 'recognised consultants' in this field. Record collecting is a relatively new pastime, and most brokers have yet to acknowledge that, say, the Sex Pistols' 'God Save The Queen' on A&M is worth £1,000 or Madonna's 'Erotica' 12" picture disc sells for £350.

What's more, little — if any — research has ever been done into the likelihood of a stack of old rock'n'roll 78s smashing during transit to a record fair, or of an entire collection of Oasis rarities warping in a summer heatwave. With no statistics to go on, insurers are unwilling to risk their money.

A spokesman for one of Britain's leading firms admits: "We wouldn't insure your records on their own, but they would be covered under a general household policy for fire, flood and theft. I suppose if you did have individual records worth many hundreds of pounds each, then we'd recommend you make special arrangements with us."

Under a standard household policy, each record doesn't have to be itemised, but in the event of a claim, the onus is on the owner to prove that the item in question is worth the amount being claimed for, and also that they owned it in the first place. Insurers aren't necessarily going to believe that a smouldering lump of plastic you retrieved from a fire is the remnants of a £500 Delaney & Bonnie album.

Once a record has been washed, make sure that it's dried quickly using a non-abrasive cloth.

There are various ways of keeping records clean, from cloths to carbon fibre brushes.

It's more likely that your policy insures your whole collection for a nominal sum, usually around £1,500, which would be payable if it was stolen or badly damaged.

Another U.K. insurance heavyweight had the same attitude, saying: "If it's an actual collection of specific records which are valuable then we wouldn't insure them. But if an existing customer wanted to insure his records, then we'd look at it a bit more favourably, but the most we'd cover it for would be £1,500." As this sum is barely enough to replace 150 standard-priced vinyl albums, the message seems to be if you need insurance, see a specialist.

Needless to say, these are few and far between. In fact, a recent edition of the brokers' standard reference book, *Insurance Buyers Guide To Schemes, Packages & Unusual Risks,* lists only one — Blake Marston Priest Ltd. operating the eight-year-old Magpie Collector's Policy, catering for specialist collections.

Their policy covers accidental loss or damage (including fire and theft), and features a number of benefits over and above those found in standard household policies. However, they do insist on the installation of security devices for collections insured for £20,000 or over.

There is one other insurance company which deals in records, Stamp Insurance Services, but they are predominantly concerned with classical records. They don't rule out jazz or 'specialised collections', but offer a resounding "No thanks!" to punk, indie and heavy rock records.

Record insurance is still obviously in its infancy. Statistics just aren't available for the number of copies of Queen's 'Bohemian Rhapsody' on blue vinyl getting lost in the post, or boxes of indie singles being pinched in the Coventry area. Such facts and figures would obviously give insurance companies a better idea of the risks involved, and would allow them to design specific packages attractive to ordinary collectors. Until that happens, the Magpie Collector's Policy seems to offer the most comprehensive service.

Magpie Collector's Policy, Blake Marston Priest Ltd, 52 Station Road, Egham, Surrey TW20 9LB.

Stamp Insurance Services, 2 Bakery Meadow, Puddington, Tiverton, Devon EX16 8LW.

P.J. Proby's "Enigma" LP, one of a series of wild and wonderful 60s LPs by the singer.

Tom Jones is now being acknowledged as one of Britain's finest soul singers.

David McWilliams' first LP included his hit single, "The Days Of Pearly Spencer".

"The Adventures Of Keith" was issued after the singer scored a major hit with "98.6".

Robin Gibb issued this album during his split from the Bee Gees in the late 60s.

Nilsson's "Pandemonium Shadow Show" established him as a late 60s cult favourite.

Wynder K. Frog's "Sunshine Super Frog" was one of the strangest LPs of 1967.

The Animals' 1964 debut LP showcased their vibrant brand of British R&B.

"Emotions" was one of the Pretty Things' classic 'freakbeat' LPs from the mid-60s.

Georgie Fame covered some fine U.S. soul records on "Sweet Things" from 1966.

The second LP by Them, the group which included Van Morrison from 1963 to 1966.

The self-explanatory "Autumn '66" by the Spencer Davis Group, with Steve Winwood.

The Rolling Stones billed themselves as the greatest rock'n'roll band in the world during the 60s, and they're still just about the biggest concert draw in rock.

Neil Young, who began his recording career in 1963 as a member of the Canadian instrumental group, the Squires.

Ex-Manfred Mann singer Paul Jones starred in the controversial 1967 film "Privilege".

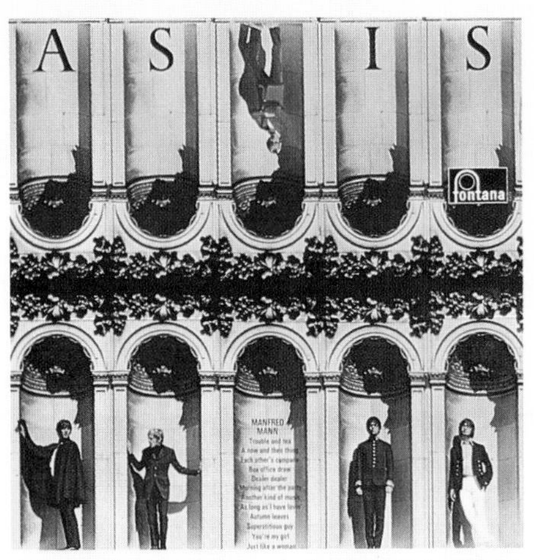

Manfred Mann recorded "As Is" in 1966, with Mike D'Abo taking Paul Jones' place.

"In Memoriam" was released by Immediate when the Small Faces split in 1969.

P.P. Arnold joined the Small Faces on the Immediate label for her "Kafunta" LP.

The rare original version of Neil Young's first LP, without his name on the cover.

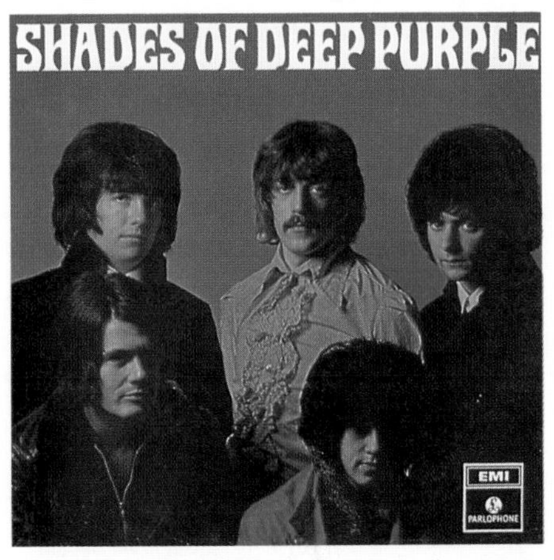

"Shades Of Deep Purple" appeared in 1968, and included their U.S. hit single, "Hush".

PSYCHEDELIC LPs

Jimi Hendrix's "Rainbow Bridge" — not a soundtrack LP, despite what the cover claims.

The Blues Magoos' collectable debut LP, featuring the hit "We Ain't Got Nothin' Yet".

"Four Sail" by Arthur Lee and Love, one of the top California bands of the late 60s.

The suitably psychedelic cover for the Savage Resurrection's 1968 debut album.

"Projections" by the Blues Project, led by sessionman/producer Al Kooper.

"Outside Inside" by Blue Cheer, reckoned by some to be the first heavy metal band.

The Jimi Hendrix Experience pictured in typically flamboyant dress at the start of 1968.

Besides his own enormous back catalogue, Prince has also been responsible for writing and producing records by dozens of artists.

TYPES OF MUSIC PEOPLE COLLECT

Most people first become collectors because they're fans of a particular artist, and they want to track down as many of their releases as possible. Many never lose that early infatuation with their favourite star. These are the fans who devote their lives to buying every possible permutation of Madonna's records from around the world, or who won't be satisfied until they've managed to find every original magazine article about the Beatles from the 60s.

Other collectors take a wider view of the subject. Rather than concentrating on a single artist, they put all their energy and enthusiasm into one genre — which can be anything from punk to reggae or country to blues.

In the same way that the mainstream music business has become more and more fragmented in recent years, supporting all kinds of specialist areas, so the record collecting market has become the home for dozens of small, tightly-defined genres — each one with its own musical heroes and heroines, and its own mega-rarities.

The next section of the book is devoted to the 24 most popular genres, which straddle an incredible range of musical styles. But they all have one thing in common — a well-organised collecting scene, dominated by diehard dealers and enthusiasts who can show off a dazzling amount of expert knowledge.

Our introductions to these major genres explain why people are so fascinated by these areas, what and who they collect, and how to spot a potential bargain, or a legendary rarity. Top U.K. rarities are listed for each of the genres, and its major artists.

ROCK'N'ROLL

Golden age: **1954-1959**
Top U.K. rarity: **BOBBY CHARLES' 'See You Later Alligator'**
(7", London HLU 8247, 1956) **£1,500**

There's a book entitled *What Was The First Rock'n'Roll Record?*, and the fact that fans and historians are still arguing about the answer proves that rock'n'roll is the most slippery of all the genres. In its widest sense, rock'n'roll — or sometimes rock and roll — is used to refer to everything and anything that is part of 'rock culture' since the mid-'50s. The Rolling Stones billed themselves as "the greatest rock'n'roll band in the world", and that title has been claimed by everyone from the Clash to Guns N' Roses since then.

Everyone agrees that original rock'n'roll grew out of an unholy marriage between R&B, pop and country music, and that Bill Haley & the Comets were the first act to take the new style onto the world stage with 'Rock Around The Clock' in 1954 (7" copies on Brunswick with gold label lettering are now worth £60; the 10" 78rpm edition sells for just £8).

Bill Haley was quickly followed by Elvis Presley and Jerry Lee Lewis, both of whom initially recorded for producer Sam Phillips' legendary Sun label, based in Memphis, Tennessee. In Britain, Elvis's early singles were picked up for distribution by HMV, while Lewis's appeared on London. As with most of the first rock'n'roll records, copies are rarer on 45, with the 7"s of 'Heartbreak Hotel' (with gold label lettering) and 'Whole Lotta Shakin' Goin' On' selling for £150 and £30, respectively.

A variety of stylistic ingredients made up this new music — the 12-bar blues structure, souped-up country guitar licks, R&B saxophones, and the kind of overt sexuality that up until then had only been seen and heard in black American R&B clubs.

Hence the confusion about rock'n'roll's origins: there are plenty of uptempo country and R&B songs from the late '40s and early '50s which sound just like rock'n'roll to enthusiastic ears. But the acknowledged giants of the genre all crossed over into the pop market, even when — like Chuck Berry and Bo Diddley — they were operating in strict R&B territory.

1960's "A Lot Of Dominos" contained the hit single, "Walking To New Orleans", and was Fats' eighth British LP.

Ultimately, rock'n'roll isn't so much a musical style as a way of life. There's precious little in the grooves to link Chuck Berry's 12-bar street poetry (check out 'No Money Down'; £200 with a tri-centre) with Buddy Holly's delicate ballads ('Blue Days, Black Nights'; £350 on Brunswick), or Elvis Presley's rockabilly raunch with the vocal group R&B of the Coasters ('Searchin'; £30).

What links them is the effect they had on teenage listeners in the 50s. All these artists, and plenty more — notably Jerry Lee Lewis, Little Richard, Fats Domino, Eddie Cochran and Gene Vincent — sparked a revolution in the minds of everyone who heard them. In the era of Doris Day and Bing Crosby, they sounded like an incitement to riot, which is exactly what the first Teddy Boys did when they heard Bill Haley's music in their local cinemas or dance-halls.

Rock'n'roll is the music of 1950s teen life — the first musical genre aimed specifically at kids, rather than adults. That's why Elvis Presley is still regarded as the king of rock'n'roll, even though he hardly cut a rockin' tune after 1958; why Jerry Lee Lewis's fans stayed loyal through more than a decade when he abandoned rock for country; and why Chuck Berry can still fill venues around the world, 30 years after his last major new song. Rock'n'roll changed the lives of an entire generation, and the barriers it demolished could never be rebuilt.

Collecting notes: As you'd expect from a genre that crosses so many musical and racial boundaries, rock'n'roll divides into many different categories. As the separate section on Rockabilly shows, many people concentrate solely on that particular brand of uptempo hillbilly country, tinged with rhythm and blues. Other diehards are obsessed with the R&B/pop crossover that is epitomised by Bill Haley, who took 'jump blues' standards from the '40s and '50s and turned them into pop records.

Some people only collect doo-wop singles that were sufficiently upbeat to qualify as rock'n'roll; others are only interested in white pop singers who added a backbeat and a faint air of menace to their '50s pop songs, like Bobby Darin and Pat Boone. (Look

Bill Haley & His Comets' first U.K. hit in 1954 opened the door for rock'n'roll in Britain.

out for their U.K. debuts 7"s: respectively, 'Rock Island Line' [Brunswick 45, £70] and 'Ain't That A Shame' [London, £25].)

Original releases by all of the '50s giants, however, from Elvis to Buddy Holly, are avidly collected, and first pressings of LPs with a brief shelf-life, like Elvis Presley's 1957 *Christmas Album*, can be worth upwards of £70. Indeed, Presley's first two LPs, *Rock'n'Roll* and *Rock'n'Roll No. 2*, sell for £200 apiece.

There's often a huge chasm between the value of U.S. and U.K. editions of the same record — for instance, the American 7" of the Penguins' doo-wop classic 'Earth Angel' is worth just a few dollars, while the British edition on London is worth nearer £1,200. (It was a million-seller in the States but flopped over here.)

In fact, London issued records by a large proportion of the classic American rockers, while others emerged on Parlophone, Columbia, Brunswick and Vogue-Coral. With all these labels, factors like the presence of the original 'tri-centres' come into play, which can often help to distinguish first editions of many '50s singles from later repressings. Period EPs and LPs are invariably very valuable, particularly if they pre-date 1960.

Although rock'n'roll is universally accepted as an American style of music, Britain produced many pretenders to the throne. Billy Fury and Cliff Richard are held in highest regard (Fury's four 1959 singles on Decca are worth between £18-£90; Cliff's recordings from 1958/59 are just as pricey), while the likes of Vince Eager, Cuddley Dudley and Tommy Steele are remembered fondly enough to push their early singles into the £8-£20 bracket.

ROCKABILLY

Golden era: **1950-1959**
Top U.K. rarity: **JACKIE LEE COCHRAN's 'Mama Don't You Think I Know'** *(7", Brunswick 05669, 1957)* **£800**

Although it's commonly used as another term for rock'n'roll, rockabilly actually refers to a very specific style of music — as its aficionados would be the first to point out.

1950s American rock'n'roll was a blend of influences from country and R&B, but it was always aimed at the national — or even international — audience. Rockabilly was a uniquely Southern style, rooted firmly in country music, and played almost exclusively by singers who had their roots on the country circuit. As early as 1950, singers like Ernest Tubb ('Thirty Days', Brunswick, £40), Hank Williams ('Lovesick Blues', MGM, 78, £15) and Hank Snow ('My Two Timin' Woman', HMV, 78, £7) were starting to combine uptempo country songs with a strong backbeat. 1954 saw guitarist Scotty Moore playing what was effectively the first rockabilly guitar solo, on a Sun Records single by the otherwise unknown Doug Poindexter. And later that year, Moore was in the studio when Elvis Presley recorded his first single, combining an R&B song, 'That's All Right Mama', with the country hit, 'Blue Moon Of Kentucky'. With its sparse instrumentation, ferocious vocal and musical swagger, and unashamedly Southern sound, Presley's single defined rockabilly.

All across the South, singers heard his early Sun sides and were inspired to add some fire to their country music. While that country influence was quickly lost on most of the mainstream rock'n'roll hits, it was instantly recognisable on rockabilly performances by other Sun artists like Jerry Lee Lewis, Carl Perkins and Johnny Cash, and pioneers on other labels like Charlie Feathers, Mac Curtis and Jackie Lee Cochran.

This 1970s Carl Perkins compilation included rock'n'roll classics such as "Blue Suede Shoes" and "Honey Don't".

Like the vampire that refused to die, rockabilly managed to survive the gradual watering-down of rock'n'roll in the late 1950s, and a decade later, at the height of psychedelia, many of the original pioneers were still turning out raucous singles on tiny local labels. By the early 1970s, a genuine rockabilly revival began in Britain, and since then there has been a regular series of reissues and compilations issued on both sides of the Atlantic.

Collecting notes: Many U.S. and U.K. singles from the '50s now change hands among enthusiasts for

The wild music and lifestyle of Jerry Lee Lewis helped to define rock'n'roll and rockabilly.

hundreds of pounds. Apart from material by major artists like Elvis Presley ('Heartbreak Hotel', HMV, £150 with gold lettering) and Jerry Lee Lewis ('Whole Lotta Shakin' Goin' On', London, £30) only a minute number of rockabilly 45s were issued in Britain at the time — but those that were, like Mac Curtis's 'You Ain't Treatin' Me Right' on Parlophone (£700) and Jackie Lee Cochran's 'Mama Don't You Think I Know' (£800), now rank among the rarest U.K. releases of all time.

There is also a steady market in '70s rockabilly compilations on labels like MCA and Epic, which introduced British fans to some of the American '50s classics for the first time. The continued popularity of the genre has been reflected by the success of younger artists working in the style — from the pop hits of Shakin' Stevens to the underground cult that grew up around the Cramps.

COUNTRY

Golden era: **1950-1955, late '60s, mid-'70s, early '90s.**
Top U.K. rarity: **JIM REEVES' 'Bimbo'**
(7", London HL 8014, 1954) **£150**

Country music is often referred to as 'the white man's blues'. Up to a point, the comparison holds water, because one definite strand of country was working-class music, expressing the trials and tribulations of struggling to survive in a harsh and unfriendly world.

But there has always been more to country than sentimental bar-room laments and rhinestone-clad stars. The roots of the music go back to the late 19th century, when the folk songs which were being sung in the fields, hills and mountains of America's Southern States started to reach the towns. By 1900, rural performers were consciously making commercial careers out of their singing — mixing these folk strands with gospel, blues and Tin Pan Alley novelty songs.

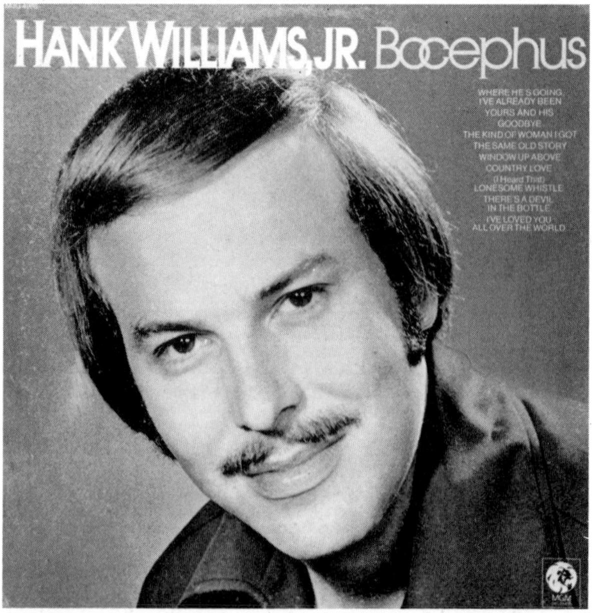

The first country record was issued in 1922, though the style was known as hillbilly until the late 1940s. The most important early sessions took place in 1927, when Victor Records recorded the Singing Brakeman, Jimmie Rodgers, and the gospel-flavoured trio, the Carter Family.

Within a few years, the Grand Ol' Opry was broadcasting weekly concerts across the Southern states, and related styles began to be incorporated into the country mainstream — the

"Bocephus" was the nickname country's greatest star gave to his son, Hank Williams Jnr., and the title of Jnr.'s 1975 album.

Hank Williams, America's greatest ambassador of country, formed his first band back in 1936.

crystal-clear harmonies of mountain music, which grew into what we know as bluegrass; the cowboy songs popularised in movies; and Western swing, a mixture of traditional fiddle music and '30s jazz which evolved in Texas.

After the Second World War, Nashville established itself as the centre of the country industry. Hank Williams (*Hank Williams Sings*, MGM, 10" LP, £35) became the music's first real superstar, and his cracked vocals, swinging rhythms and unashamed sex appeal set the mould for much of what has happened since. Many young country singers helped create rockabilly in the mid-'50s, while those who spurned this youth-orientated craze opted for a more sedate style.

Since then, the history of country has been a pendulum swing to and from the dreaded influence of pop. The creation of the Nashville Sound in the '60s, led by singers like Patsy Cline (*Showcase*, Brunswick, £18) and Jim Reeves ('Bimbo', London, £150), was followed by the more rootsy Bakersfield country of Merle Haggard (*I'm A Lonesome Fugitive*, Capitol, £12) and Buck Owens ('Everlasting Love', Capitol, £6) — which in turn inspired country-rock pioneers like Gram Parsons and the Byrds. Pop took control in the 70s, before Ricky Skaggs and Emmylou Harris pulled the music back to its roots. And the recent explosion of country on the U.S. pop market has led to further accusations that the music is sacrificing its soul to Hollywood.

Collecting notes: Despite its massive place in American musical history, country has only occasionally enjoyed any kind of street-credibility in Britain, and it's still possible to build up a large collection of seminal country records for a relatively small price. Among U.K. releases, 1950s LPs by artists like Slim Whitman, Jim Reeves and Johnny Cash fetch good money, while early 45s on the London label by Reeves and the country artists who cut rockabilly records for Sun in Memphis are eagerly sought-after.

From the '60s, there's demand for albums by major artists like George Jones, Patsy Cline and Merle Haggard — particularly those which weren't issued in Britain. In the States, collectors are willing to pay $100 or more for scarce LPs by Waylon Jennings or George Jones, but the market in Britain is much more specialised.

Certain sub-genres command cult followings in Britain, such as the Texas singer-songwriters like Guy Clark and Townes Van Zandt, the bluegrass of Bill Monroe & the Country Gentlemen, and even early rarities by modern stars like k.d. lang and Ricky Skaggs. And country-related releases by rockabilly and rock performers — everyone from Jerry Lee Lewis to the Flying Burrito Brothers — remain very popular among mainstream collectors.

BLUES, R&B & DOO-WOP

Golden ages: **1935-1939, 1948-1965**
Top U.K. rarity: **WILLIE DIXON's 'Walkin' The Blues'**
(7", London HLU 8297, 1956) **£1,000**

Blues and jazz are almost impossible to separate before the early 1930s, when many jazz songs followed the familiar 12-bar blues structure, and often featured the word 'blues' in the title. While the jazz combos were filling the clubs of America, however, out in the fields and the small towns, individual singers and guitarists were perfecting the acoustic styles known as country blues or delta blues (after the Mississippi Delta).

Performers like Robert Johnson and Son House drew on worksongs and laments that had been passed down through the black community since the days of slavery. The blues was the language of oppression, and from the very beginning it was used to convey pain — romantic, physical or financial.

Few of the '30s acoustic bluesmen were ever recorded, but pioneering producers and archivists like John Hammond Snr. and John Lomax did succeed in either persuading the likes of Johnson to record in a professional studio, or else captured their music on tape where they lived. Nearly sixty years after he died in obscurity and poverty, Robert Johnson (*Robert Johnson*, Philips, £50) is now regarded as one of the musical giants of the 20th century — on the basis of a few dozen recordings he made during his brief adult life.

As blacks migrated from the American South to the Northern cities in search of steady work, the blues travelled with them. In Chicago, the delta acoustic sound was transferred into the clubs and dance-halls, and onto electric instruments, by guitarists like Muddy Waters (*With Little Walter* EP, Vogue, £120) and Howlin' Wolf (*Rhythm And Blues* EP, London, £75), while Mississippi-born B.B. King (*Take a Swing With Me*, Blue Horizon, £45) continued to ply his trade in the Northern states.

Their ferocious Chicago blues recordings inspired the Rolling Stones, the Yardbirds, the Pretty Things and many other white mid-'60s U.K. blues bands, and contributed several standards to the rock'n'roll repertoire, like 'Mannish Boy' (alias 'I'm A Man'), 'Little Red Rooster' and 'Got My Mojo Working'. Most of the major Chicago figures ended up on the city's Chess Records label, including Little Walter, Buddy Guy and Sonny Boy Williamson.

Meanwhile, the Californian jazz bands of the '20s and '30s had been succeeded by rhythm-and-blues combos playing what blues scholars came to know as urban blues or 'jump blues'. Apart from the 12-bar format, they had little in common with the Chicago school, as they lent heavily on brass instruments and adopted a much smoother, less

B.B. King's blend of R&B and Delta Blues inspired the likes of guitar legend Eric Clapton.

confrontational style. Pianists like Louis Jordan (*Louis Jordan* EP, Melodisc, £40) also graduated from this tradition, which was a direct influence on the mid-'50s rock'n'roll of Bill Haley & the Comets.

Also in California, and on the East Coast in Philadelphia and New York, some R&B singers formed vocal groups who were inspired partly by the cool harmonies of '40s combos like the Inkspots ('Here In My Lonely Room', Parlophone, £15), and partly by the rhythm of 'jump blues'. The result was doo-wop, which showcased four or five-part harmonies, often over the most rudimentary of instrumental backing.

Doo-wop groups like the Penguins, whose legendary 'Earth Angel' on London is worth around £1,200, crossed over into the white pop market, and by the mid-'50s there were hundreds of white doo-wop groups — some of them blatantly covering the latest black hits, and others (like Dion & the Belmonts) developing their own material. Purists regard the white 'imitators' as virtually sacrilegious, but often there's little difference in sound between the white combos and their black predecessors.

If the '30s was the classic era of acoustic blues, there was a revival in the 60s, based around the folk and protest movement. Many long-forgotten bluesmen were rescued from retirement and sent out on the college circuit, and the '60s saw a deluge of new recordings from musicians who either hadn't seen a microphone for 30 years, or had never been taped before.

For different reasons, the electric blues giants of the '50s also underwent a commercial revival in the '60s, as the British and American blues booms led by the Stones, Alexis Korner, Paul Butterfield and John Mayall encouraged rock fans to listen to the originals. Before the end of the decade, the white musicians were repaying their debts by working with their heroes in the studio, though again the purists regarded these blues/rock crossovers as essentially flawed.

Since the '60s, many of the century's most important blues performers have died, and the tradition has relied increasingly on younger musicians repeating the style of their heroes — or, like Robert Cray, moving the blues close to soul. But one man remains as a link through 50 years of American blues: the eternal John Lee Hooker, who first growled his idiosyncratic, erratic and unsettling blues into a studio mike in 1948, and is still recording in the mid-90s.

John Lee Hooker's "Don't Turn Me Away From Your Door" was a popular album with '60s U.K. blues revivalists.

Collecting notes: Original 78s by Robert Johnson and his contemporaries from the '30s and '40s are worth a small fortune, as they sold in comparatively small quantities and in restricted areas of the U.S.

John Lee Hooker, that most laid-back of bluesmen, is one of the world's most influential artists.

A handful of blues 78s also appeared in Britain in the '40s and '50s, aimed mostly at American servicemen, and titles like John Lee Hooker's 'Need Somebody' (London, £40) and Muddy Waters' 'Walkin' Blues' (Vogue, £30) would be high on most collectors' wants lists.

During the '50s, London Records in Britain issued a shortlived 'Rhythm And Blues' series, exposing the U.K. to EPs by artists like Muddy Waters and Howlin' Wolf. The blues boom of the early '60s persuaded Pye International, who then controlled the Chess Records catalogue, to unleash a blitz of R&B releases over a period of four years — after which Chess launched its own logo in this country, just too late to capitalise on the blues revival. These Pye and Chess releases are much more common than the '50s releases on London, but can prove more difficult to find than their U.S. equivalents.

Original U.S. blues albums from the '50s, however, are always sought-after. By contrast, many singles by the top blues performers sold in enormous quantities without ever reaching the U.S. pop charts, and though all Chess releases are collectable, they're not necessarily as valuable as you might think, tending to sell in the £5-£10 range.

A number of blues performers, like Little Milton, Rufus Thomas and Joe Hill Louis, recorded for Sam Phillips' Sun label in Memphis, and very few of these 78s and 45s sold particularly well. The cachet of the famous yellow Sun label has transformed many of these obscure releases into legendary collectables.

Golden era: **1963-66**
Top rarity: **BO STREET RUNNERS' *Bo Street Runners* EP**
(7", Oak RGJ 131, 1964) **£750**

In the '50s and early '60s, British pop blatantly followed what was happening in America. The U.K. scene was overwhelmed with unimaginative cover versions of U.S. pop hits, and producers shied away from anything that sounded too raucous or wild.

Meanwhile, teenage musicians all over the country were listening to imported R&B and soul records from the States. When these influences were combined with the sound of American rock'n'roll, the result was what came to be known as beat music — which began as a straight imitation of American records, and turned into a style that swept the world between 1963 and 1965.

Although it was the Beatles and the other Liverpool 'Merseybeat' groups like Gerry & the Pacemakers and the Searchers who made the initial breakthrough, similar beat scenes were evolving in Birmingham (the Moody Blues, Spencer Davis Group), Manchester (the Hollies) and other major cities in England and Scotland.

Howie Casey and the Seniors were the first Liverpool beat band to make a record ('Double Twist', on Fontana, £15), but the success of the Beatles in 1963 transformed

Manchester's Hollies were signed to EMI in the wake of the Beatles' huge success in 1963.

the history of British pop. Hundreds of beat groups made records in the early-to-mid '60s. Aside from the rarities connected with the Beatles, who soon outgrew the 'beat' fashion, collectors tend to focus on the less successful artists from the era — like the Remo Four ('I Wish I Could Shimmy Like My Sister', Piccadilly, £12) — and those with the strongest leanings towards R&B, like the Animals (*I Just Wanna Make Love To You,* 12" EP, 99 only, £250) and the Pretty Things (*On Film* EP, Fontana, £70).

1966's "Animalisms" was the Animals' last album in the U.K. and is now considered their rarest and most valuable.

Indeed, the latter pair were an integral part of Britain's very own R&B scene, which ran in parallel to the beat explosion. Led by the Rolling Stones, it provided a springboard for everyone from the Kinks and Them (fronted by Van Morrison) to Manfred Mann and jazzer Georgie Fame. Between 1965 and 1967, the scene took on board elements of rock, psychedelia and folk, turning bands like the Who, the Small Faces and the Creation from straight R&B Mod bands into magnificent, three-dimensional pop-rock giants.

However, the Rolling Stones remained the champions of British R&B, with guitarists Brian Jones and Keith Richards paving the way for future stars like Eric Clapton, Jeff Beck and Jimmy Page — all of whom served in another top R&B act, the Yardbirds.

Gerry & the Pacemakers were Liverpool's second most popular group after the Beatles. This is their third EP.

Collecting notes: It's still possible to pick up original singles by the 60s' popular beat groups for just a few pounds apiece. But LPs and EPs from this era can be very collectable, even by major chart acts like the Hollies (*Stay With The Hollies,* Parlophone stereo LP, £45), Gerry and the Pacemakers (*I'm The One,* Columbia EP, £12)

Gerry & the Pacemakers were the first act to take their first three singles to No. 1 in Britain.

and the Fourmost (*First And Fourmost*, Parlophone, £70).

The rarest beat singles, however, are either mini-classics of British R&B, or else have connections with later superstars, like David Bowie's debut single as Davie Jones & the King Bees ('Liza Jane', Vocalion Pop, £400); the Warriors, featuring future Yes vocalist Jon Anderson ('You Came Along', Decca, £35); and the first 1964 single by Joe Cocker ('I'll Cry Instead', Decca, £30).

In the States, where the beat groups formed part of a much-hyped 'British Invasion' in 1964, it was quite common for U.S. companies to release albums that included songs not issued in Britain. Almost all U.S. releases had different artwork, and often track listings, to their U.K. equivalents, enhancing their appeal to collectors — particularly as it's the U.K. versions that tend to have been reissued on CD.

With most original '60s LPs by the Who, the Kinks and the Small Faces selling in the £20-£35 range, the biggest challenge is provided by rare export EPs and picture sleeve singles. Look out for the export editions of *The Kinks* EP (Pye NEP 5039), worth £300 in its picture cover, and the Who's 'My Generation' (Decca AD 1001), which changes hands for £100 in its original sleeve.

The Artwoods' 1966 *Jazz In Jeans* EP also deserves a mention. Group leader Arthur Wood was the older brother of Rolling Stone Ronnie Wood, and this tenuous Stones link, plus the fact that the Artwoods played a brand of blistering R&B, has pushed the record's price up to £225.

After the initial beat boom cooled down in 1965, many of the groups disbanded. Others hardened their R&B sound and began recording in a style known today as Freakbeat (see 'Psychedelia').

Golden eras: **1926-1935, 1944-1958**
Top U.K. rarity: **TUBBY HAYES' *Down In The Village***
(Fontana 680998 TL, 1963) **£200**

Jazz is almost impossible to define. What can you say about a brand of music which includes Bessie Smith moaning blues ballads, and Ornette Coleman destroying conventional ideas about rhythm, melody and harmony? What links the carefully constructed big band arrangements of Duke Ellington with the jazz-rock crossovers of Miles Davis and John McLaughlin?

Like rock'n'roll, jazz is as much an attitude — and a sense of tradition — as a distinct musical genre. But its history begins in the early years of the 20th century, with elements of ragtime, blues and pop blending into a form of black music that allowed room for improvisation, and encouraged syncopation (a shift of rhythm away from a strong central beat).

After that, you're on your own — following the vocal links between Bessie Smith (check out 1934's 'Do Your Duty' 78, Parlophone, £25) Billie Holiday (*Billie Holiday*, 10", Columbia, £15) and Ella Fitzgerald (*Souvenir Album*, 10", Brunswick, £15) perhaps, or the big band sound through Count Basie (*Basie's Best*, 10", Brunswick, £15) and beyond. Two figures dominate pre-1950 jazz, however: Louis Armstrong, who established the importance of an individual voice — vocal and instrumental — at the heart of a small jazz group; and Duke Ellington, who grew out of the small Dixieland combos to pioneer the art of scoring complex, often thrilling arrangements for a jazz orchestra. (Look out for the rare picture sleeve version of Armstrong's 'We Have All The Time In The World' on United Artists, worth £30, and the 10" *Ellington's Greatest* LP on HMV.)

The arrival in the mid-'40s of Charlie Parker — whose LPs first appeared in this country a decade later on labels like Vogue, Melodisc and Columbia (all £15-£18) — shattered all the normal rules about harmonies and key signatures, and divided the jazz world in half. The experimenters followed and then built on his example, mixing melody and astonishing improvisation, and developing the cult of individual virtuosos and composers like Miles Davis (*Quintet*, 10", Esquire, £25) John Coltrane (*Blue Train*, Blue Note, £20) and Thelonious Monk (*Quintet*, 10", Esquire, £18). In turn, these geniuses inspired

Ella Fitzgerald's "George & Ira Gershwin Songbook" album was issued in 1964, with a cover painting by Bernard Buffet.

Controversial, trail-blazing trumpeter Miles Davis took jazz into new realms in the 1950s.

many psychedelic rockers in the late '60s, and the circle was completed when rock fans were inspired to listen to the jazzmen who had influenced their own heroes. Meanwhile, another strand of jazz musicians rejected these avant-garde tendencies, and concentrated on more conventional melodies, rhythms and harmonies. In Britain, this return to the ragtime sounds of the '20s and '30s led to a trad jazz boom, which produced household names like Acker Bilk, Kenny Ball and Chris Barber.

Elsewhere, particularly in the stable of artists built up by Blue Note Records in New York, jazz veered closer and closer to R&B, broadening further in the '70s to create fusions of rock, funk and Latin music. The '80s saw the British club scene take jazz-dance to its heart, and the rise of a new style of slick jazz-funk called acid jazz, after the label of the same name. And, with hip-hop acts sampling and name-checking legends like Donald Byrd, Herbie Hancock, Freddie Hubbard and Hammond organ groover Jimmy Smith, demand for the original records rocketed.

Today, it's increasingly difficult to distinguish jazz from blues from soul, and one fan's jazz genius is another fan's soul giant. Jazz now ranges from free-form experimentation to note-perfect imitations of every style since Dixieland at the start of the century.

Collecting notes: Original 1950s and '60s LPs by the leading names are always collectable, particularly if they haven't been transferred onto CD. However, very few albums fall outside the £12-£35 price range — though look out for LPs by British artists like Tubby Hayes (*Down In The Village*, Fontana, £200), Joe Harriott (*Free Form*, Jazzland, £50) and Don Rendle (*Roarin'*, Jazzland, £75).

There are tens of thousands of jazz 78s kicking around, but the vast majority are only worth a few pounds. The most valuable tend to be 1920s and '30s recordings by the likes of Bessie Smith, or by legends like Louis Armstrong.

Finally, a note about the most collectable jazz label of them all, Blue Note, which has been issuing records in American and Britain since the '50s. Any Blue Note originals are of interest to completists, though some of the highest prices are reserved for the soul-tinged '60s and '70s classics which are current club favourites.

Continued on page 145

LATE 60s & EARLY 70s LPs

Marc Bolan pictured in typically flamboyant mood on the T. Rex "Great Hits" album.

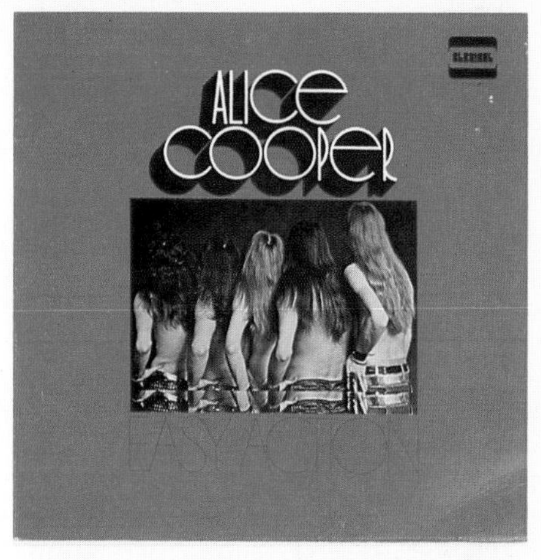

Alice Cooper's 1970 album "Easy Action", released on Frank Zappa's Straight label.

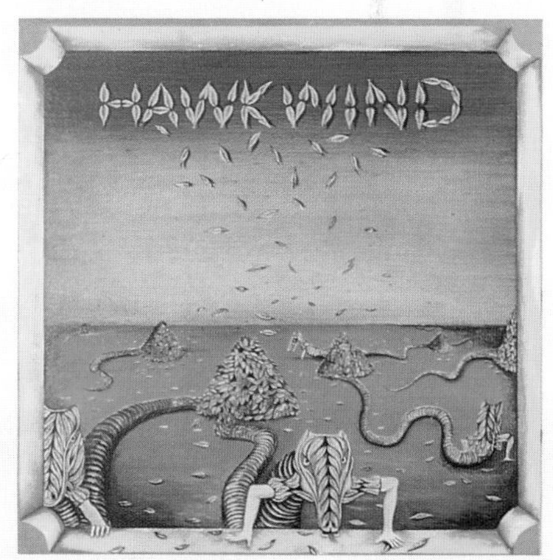

Hawkwind's 1970 debut LP, featuring their rarest single, "Hurry On Sundown".

The Soft Machine's second LP, issued by EMI's newly-formed Probe label in 1969.

Legend featured Mickey Jupp, who turned up years later as a solo artist on Stiff.

Graham Bond's "Solid Bond" compilation featured tracks recorded in 1963 and 1966.

60s SOUL LPs

Black artists often didn't appear on album covers in the 60s, as this 1964 LP shows.

"Take A Look", a set of early Aretha Franklin songs issued to cash in on her later success.

"Away We A Go Go", a classic Motown LP by Smokey Robinson and the Miracles.

The Supremes' "A Go Go" featured some wonderful Holland/Dozier/Holland songs.

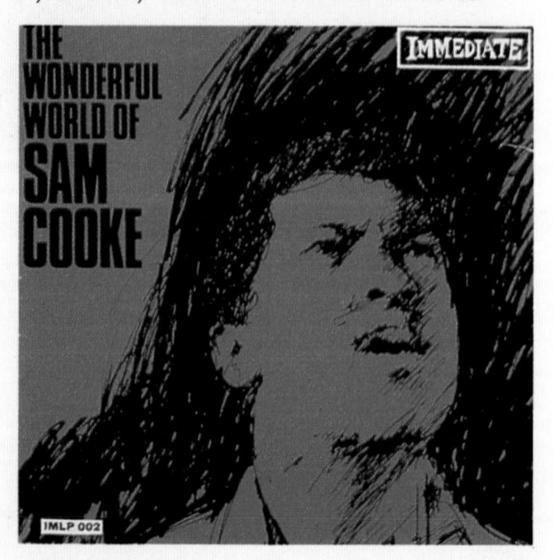

Immediate issued "The Wonderful World Of Sam Cooke" two years after his death.

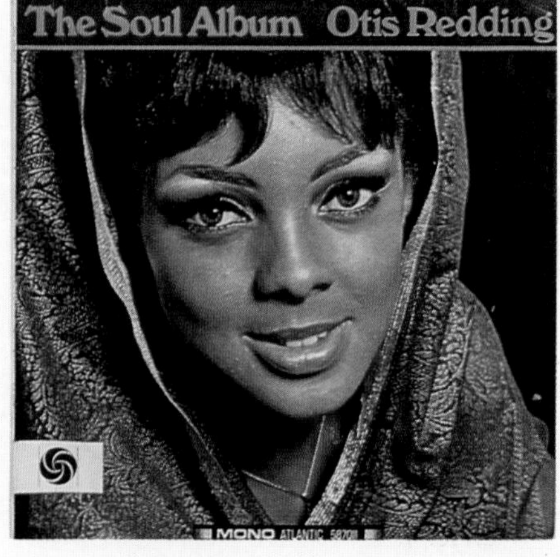

Otis Redding became the standard-bearer for the Southern soul sound in the mid-60s.

Michael Jackson at the height of his early teenybopper success with the Jackson 5.

Lenny Kravitz broke through at the end of the 80s with a sound that owed much to 70s soul and psychedelic 60s rock.

60s GIRL GROUPS & U.S. POP

Golden era: **1961-1966**
Top U.K. rarity: **THE CRYSTALS' 'There's No Other Like My Baby'** **£90**
(7", Parlophone R 4867, 1962)

It might seem strange to classify '60s pop as a specialist genre, when everything from Engelbert Humperdinck to Frank Zappa was regarded at the time as 'pop'. But during the steady march of progress from Elvis Presley's return from the army in 1960 to the birth of the Woodstock generation in 1969, a series of short-lived pop crazes sparked cult followings which have survived to this day.

The girl group phenomenon was actually a hangover from the doo-wop era of the late '50s, when the predominantly male domination of the U.S. vocal group scene was challenged by female pioneers like the Chantels, whose U.K. debut 7" on London, 'Maybe', is now worth around £300. But during the first half of the '60s, girl groups became a major force in American pop.

1963's "Then He Kissed Me" was the Crystals' biggest hit.

The Shirelles made the initial breakthrough, capturing the feelings and fears of teenage female America with a series of upbeat songs like 'I Met Him On A Sunday' (Brunswick 7", £40) and 'Tonight's The Night' (London, £12), though they didn't chart in the U.K. until 1961's wonderful 'Will You Still Love Me Tomorrow?'. Many of their hits were co-written by Carole King — who became an unofficial cheerleader for the entire movement. But it took the entrepreneurial and musical talents of producer Phil Spector to transform the Shirelles' aims into a movement that would sweep around the world.

Spector had been schooled in Los Angeles teen pop in the '50s, before he migrated to New York to join the legendary writing and production team of Jerry Leiber and Mike Stoller. The experience he gained there proved invaluable when he launched his own Philles label in 1961. His first signings were the Crystals, and over the next two years he added Darlene Love, Bob B. Soxx & the Blue Jeans and the Ronettes to his roster.

Spector regarded his artists as interchangeable nonentities, and reckoned that it was the sound of 'his' records that sold, not the faces behind them. He invented a cacophonous, overpowering production technique called the 'Wall Of Sound', which involved dozens of musicians playing simple parts simultaneously in the studio. Together with the plaintive teenage romance songs written by Carole King, Jeff Barry and Ellie Greenwich (among others), this technique defined the girl group sound, and sparked hundreds of imitations around the world. Diehards have an endless appetite for anything which bears even a hint of the Spector influence.

While Spector was conquering America from the East Coast in the early '60s, the West Coast was spawning its own pop genres. Surf music reflected the lazy teenage lifestyle of middle-class white kids around L.A. It divided neatly into two camps — the instrumentalists, led by guitarist Dick Dale (whose 'Miserlou' was revived for the soundtrack to the hit movie, *Pulp Fiction*), who attempted to capture the sound of the waves and the liberation of the surfing experience in music, and the vocal groups, like the Beach Boys and Jan & Dean, who captured the beach scene in words. Early U.K. rarities from these groups include, respectively, the £50-rated 'Ten Little Indians' on Capitol and the 'Baby Talk' 78, worth £45.

A handful of producers, writers and performers cornered the market, and released dozens of cash-in singles between 1961 and 1965 under a variety of pseudonyms. When the Beach Boys inaugurated a fad for records about hot rod car racing with the B-side, '409', the surf pioneers followed suit — adding engine noises to their guitar instrumentals, or reworking their lyrics. As with the girl groups, the rest of the world quickly picked up on this trend and surf records emerged from places that were hundreds of miles away from the nearest beach.

This compilation of early Phil Spector recordings includes obscurities by the Paris Sisters, Gene Pitney and Curtis Lee.

The girl groups and surfers were both swept away by the 1964 British Invasion led by the Beatles. But America quickly rallied with its own beat group sound. Like the Beatles, America's young rockers were inspired by the lyrical depth of Bob Dylan and the folk protest movement, and when groups like the Byrds and the Turtles allied Dylan's words to the smooth harmonies and interlocking electric guitars of the Beatles and the Searchers, folk-rock was born.

The new genre depended heavily on 12-string guitars (as played by the Byrds' Jim McGuinn),

An early line-up of the Beach Boys from 1963, with singer/guitarist David Marks (far right).

Spectoresque percussion, and two- or more normally three-part vocal harmonies. The Byrds were the undoubted masters of folk-rock, but the style rapidly became the standard sound of American pop, touching everyone from ex-crooners like Bobby Darin to former folk singers like Phil Ochs.

Ironically, Bob Dylan — who had influenced the entire folk-rock genre — never really slotted into its radio-friendly approach. Instead, he continued to experiment with ever more outrageous lyrical metaphors, and when others began to imitate his drug-fuelled fantasies, the stage was set for an entire generation of garage and folk-rock bands to drift seamlessly into psychedelia — or acid-rock, as it was known at the time.

Collecting notes: As the girl groups, surfers and folk-rockers were almost exclusively American, most of the prime rarities — and indeed most of the available material — were only released in the States. Even so, very early U.K. singles by the Chantels and Shirelles can be pricey, as too can those by the Beach Boys and pre-surf era Jan & Dan, which generally fall in the £18-£50 range.

Everything produced by Phil Spector is of interest to specialists, and minute label variations on the singles issued by his Philles Records company can make an enormous difference to their value. Hit singles by artists like the Ronettes and the Crystals can be found for only a few pounds, so the big money is reserved for Philles records that weren't given full commercial release, or for obscure Spector soundalikes, often only available in one of the 50 U.S. states.

All the major girl group hits were released in Britain, where they are usually worth more than their American equivalents. Particularly sought-after here are the EPs and LPs by Spector groups, the Shirelles (*The Shirelles Sing To Trumpet & Strings* EP, Top Rank, £80), the Chiffons (*The Chiffons* LP, Stateside, £40) and their contemporaries, which are much harder to find than the singles.

It's a similar picture with the surf, hot rod and folk-rock fields. In each case, the classic records of the genre are the ones which were the biggest hits — like the Beach Boys' 'Surfin' U.S.A.' and 'Little Deuce Coupe', and the Byrds' 'Mr Tambourine Man'. But there are scores of soundalike releases by obscure artists which can fetch large sums, like the Duals' 'Stick Shift' (on Star Revue, £500) and Carol & Sheryl's 'Go Go G.T.O.' (Colpix, £150). In Britain, the same rules apply: the singles are collectable, but usually fairly easy to find, while the albums — beyond the Top 10 hits by the Beach Boys and the Byrds — are more of a challenge.

INSTRUMENTALS

Golden age: **1957-1963**
Top U.K. rarity: **BLUE MEN's *I Hear A New World***
(7" EP, Triumph RGXST 5000, 1960) **£300**

Forget Elvis Presley and the Beatles — there's a whole sub-sect of collectors out there who want the vocalists to get out of the way so they can hear the band. 1950s rock'n'roll was dominated by charismatic wild men, like Little Richard and Jerry Lee Lewis. But for instrumental collectors, the hooklines of their favourite records were provided by guitars, saxes or pianos, not singers.

The late '50s and early '60s were the golden age of instrumental rock'n'roll, when artists like Duane Eddy, the Shadows, Johnny & the Hurricanes and the Tornados notched up dozens of hits. But instrumentals had always been part of popular music — not just in jazz, which has always been at least 50% vocal-free, but also in blues and country (thanks to hot-pickers like Chet Atkins and Merle Travis). In Britain, guitarist Bert Weedon's instruction books taught a generation of rockers how to play.

The loud, brash and thrilling blues bands that filled American clubs in the '40s and '50s regularly kicked off their shows with swinging instrumentals, as a way of warming up the musicians and the crowd before the arrival of the singer. The wailing tenor

The Shadows' "Jigsaw", recorded in 1967, was the instrumental outfit's eighth U.K. LP, and reached No. 8.

In Britain, the tremolo effect was the trademark of the Shadows' guitarist, Hank Marvin.

saxophone became a vital part of the R&B band, and musicians like King Curtis (whose *Have Tenor Sax, Will Blow* on London sells for £25) and Lee Allen ('Walking With Mr. Lee', HMV, £25) easily stepped over the line from blues to pop in the '50s. In particular, Curtis lent his instantly recognisable 'yakety sax' to many of the hits by the Coasters.

The white rock group Johnny & the Hurricanes borrowed his sound wholesale for a string of hits, while Duane Eddy pioneered a thunderously deep, heavily echoed guitar style for a lengthy career as an instrumental king. Dozens of other combos scored instrumental hits, like the Champs ('Beatnik', London, £20), B. Bumble & the Stingers (*The Piano Stylings Of B. Bumble* EP, Stateside, £20), Sandy Nelson (*Teen Beat*, London, £25 in stereo) and Bill Doggett (*Dame Dreaming* 10" LP, Parlophone, £25).

But the most influential style of rock instrumentals — RIs, as they're known to fans — came from the guitar groups. Using the classic rock line-up of two guitars, bass and drums, the Ventures in America and the Shadows in Britain inspired literally thousands of imitators.

Even now, Neil Young admits that the Shads' Hank B. Marvin was his prime inspiration as a teenager. Using Fender Stratocasters or Telecasters, the instrumental quartets concentrated on tight, ultra-slick arrangements, letting the slightly reverbed or echoed lead guitar take all the strain. The accent was on melodies rather than noise — the exact opposite, in fact, of the proto-grunge guitar noise produced by the anti-hero of the '50s RI scene, Link Wray.

British producer Joe Meek was a keen aficionado of all kinds of instrumental music, and his RGM production company issued dozens of RI tracks — notably the Tornados' eerie 'Telstar'. Instrumentals were perfect for conjuring up other-worldly or exotic sounds, as was discovered by everyone from surfers like Dick Dale to the Easy Listening orchestras of Martin Denny and Ralph Marterie.

The surf/hot rod fads were the final flourish of the RI scene, which perished under the onslaught of the beat boom and the British Invasion in 1964. The next time that instrumentals played a major part in the rock scene was in the late '60s, when the Grateful Dead and Cream used extended, improvised solos as a vehicle for psychedelic experimentation.

Collecting notes: Almost every instrumental from the late '50s and early '60s has a collector in hot pursuit, whether it's a raucous saxophone-driven rocker or a lazy orchestral melody. But the highest prices are paid for the rarest rockers, particularly original albums by the likes of the Champs (*Go Champs Go!*, London, £30), Duane Eddy (*Have Twangy Guitar, Will Travel*, London, £25) and the Shadows. Ironically, among the Shadows' scarcest, most collectable singles are those on which they sing, such as 'Feelin' Fine', credited to 'The Drifters' (Columbia, £50).

U.S. star Duane Eddy gave the world the 'twangy' sound.

Joe Meek collectors are keen to complete the full set of Meek productions, or related records with a 'RGM Sound' credit on the label, regardless of whether they're instrumentals or vocals. Watch out for early releases on the Triumph label, which Meek himself briefly ran in 1960, and names like the Honeycombs, John Leyton, Cliff Bennett and the Rebel Rousers, Heinz, Tornadoes, Screaming Lord Sutch, and Mike Berry & the Outlaws.

Multi-racial instrumental soul outfit, Booker T. & the M.G.'s, famous for their "Green Onions".

SOUL

Golden era: **1962-1970**
Top rarity: **FRANK WILSON's 'Do I Love You (Indeed I Do)'**
(7", U.S., test pressing only, Soul 35019, 1965)
£8,000

When Ben E. King scored a hit single with 'What Is Soul?', he was asking a more difficult question than he might have imagined. Recognising a soul record when you hear one is easy enough — after all, what are Marvin Gaye's 'Heard It Through The Grapevine' or Jackie Wilson's 'I Get The Sweetest Feeling' if they aren't soul? But describing it is something else.

Just as urban American R&B built on the foundations of pre-war blues, so soul was a natural progression from the gospel-tinged R&B of the 1950s. While R&B tended to keep to certain standard chord changes and song structures, soul was looser and more expressive — taking its title, obviously enough, from the 'soul' that singers put into their performance. Drawing on the musical accompaniment of the blues, the passion of gospel, and sometimes the delicate vocal control of doo-wop, soul music quickly became the voice of early '60s black America.

No sooner had the term come into use than people began to argue about it. Was Motown soul, for example? Or was its formula too strict to qualify? Could white people sing soul? (It was eventually decided that they could, with the result that the term blue-eyed soul was invented to describe records by artists like the Righteous Brothers, Dusty Springfield, Len Barry and the Box Tops.) And what was the dividing line between Ray Charles' records in the late '50s, when he was classed as R&B, and his early '60s sides, which were often described as soul?

The jury is still out on most of those questions — plus the others which came up later, when the disco beat imposed a new set of rules on black music. No one doubts the soul credentials of the music that came out of several strong regional scenes in the '60s, however. Southern soul — not just a geographical term, but a distinct sound — had a more rural, earthy feel, tied to blues and country, than its rival, uptown soul, which merged pop and jazz influences into a more sophisticated, urban sound.

Certain labels, cities and recording studios dominated the '60s soul scene. Outside of Motown and the other Detroit companies, the most important labels were Stax/Volt and Atlantic — who, appropriately enough, were linked together via a joint distribution deal in Britain. Stax was based in Memphis, but held many of its sessions outside the city, either at Muscle Shoals, Alabama or Atlantic's base in New York. Its leading light was Otis Redding ('Pain In My Heart', London, £15), while Sam & Dave ('No More Pain', King, £8), Joe Tex (*The New Boss*, Atlantic, £25), Booker T & the MGs ('Green Onions', London, £8) and William Bell ('Never Like This Before', Atlantic, £5) also cut plenty of hits for the label — often written by Isaac Hayes. Atlantic shared sessions, studios and sometimes artists with Stax, as in the case of Percy Sledge ('When A Man Loves A Woman', Atlantic, £5) and Wilson Pickett ('Let Me Be Your Boy', MGM, £35), but it also gathered up a fine collection of New York and California artists.

Besides Stax, the Southern states spawned scores of specialist soul labels — many of which have been excavated for reissues on labels like Ace and Charly. Though the golden era of Southern soul finished in the early '70s, the style still survives, often known as deep soul, to distinguish it from the lighter, pop-orientated output of Motown and New York.

Chicago had its own self-contained soul scene in the '60s, dominated by the work of the Impressions' Curtis Mayfield ('If There's A Hell Below We're All Going To Go', Buddah, £5) the in-house singer/writer/producer at Okeh (also home of Major Lance and Larry Williams). His delicate, lyrical style — owing much to doo-wop, but later taking on a more uptown feel — sparked many hits by his own group, the Impressions, and by singers like Jerry Butler and Major Lance.

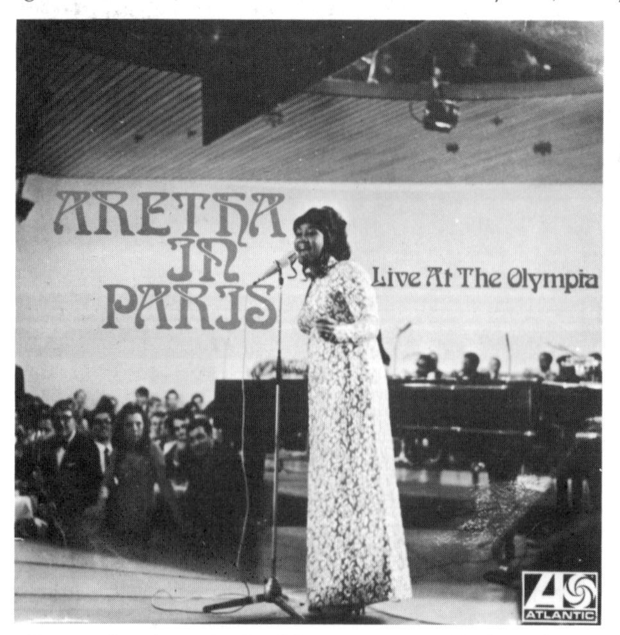

Queen of soul, Aretha Franklin, was captured in her prime on this 1968 Atlantic album, "Live At The Olympia, Paris".

Although best remembered for his '70s soundtrack, "Shaft", Isaac Hayes' career began in 1962.

Collecting notes: While 1950s R&B artists like James Brown ('This Old Heart', Fontana, £25) and Ray Charles ('Rockhouse Pts 1&2', London, £20) had a major impact on black music in the '60s — with Brown in particular taking dance music almost directly from blues to funk, via a remarkable series of mid-'60s singles — the collecting scene is dominated by more obscure names like Garnet Mimms ('I'll Take Good Care Of You', United Artists, £50), Gene McDaniels ('Walk With A Winner', Liberty, £50) and Ray Pollard ('The Drifter', United Artists, £100). In such cases, the records were originally flops, but have been belatedly recognised as classics — the result being intense competition for the relatively few surviving copies.

The British market has always tended to concentrate on Northern soul, and big labels like Atlantic, Stax and Motown, though there is strong specialist interest in Southern soul releases, right up to the 'real soul' work of artists like Z.Z. Hill ('Have Mercy Someone', R&B MRB, £20) and labels like Malaco, keeping the tradition of the '60s alive into the '80s.

MOTOWN

Golden era: **1963-1971**
Top U.K. rarity: **VALADIERS' 'I Found A Girl'**
(7", Oriole CBA 1809, 1963) **£500**

When Detroit songwriters Berry Gordy and Smokey Robinson formed their first record label in 1959, neither of them can have realised that they were creating what would become black America's most successful corporation within a decade.

Over the next few years, Gordy's labels — like Tamla, Motown, Gordy, Miracle, Soul and V.I.P. — would foster an incredible range of soul performers, linked by an instantly recognisable 'Motown sound'. Critics have accused him of using production-line methods, but no-one can argue with the results — an almost unbroken run of hit records in the '60s and early '70s by major artists like Diana Ross & the Supremes (*We Remember Sam Cooke*, Motown, £40), Smokey Robinson & the Miracles (*Hi! We're The Miracles*, Oriole, £100), the Temptations (*Meet The Temptations*, Tamla Motown, £60) Marvin Gaye ('Stubborn Kind Of Fellow', Oriole, £65), the Four Tops ('Ask The Lonely', Tamla Motown, £30) and Stevie Wonder ('Workout, Stevie, Workout', Stateside £30).

The Miracles with Smokey Robinson (far right), who scored a hit with "Tears Of A Clown".

Gordy's secret weapon was his rich seam of backroom talent. He threw teams of writers and producers into fevered competition with each other, holding weekly meetings where the entire staff would vote to decide whose songs most deserved release. These tactics compelled writers like Holland/Dozier/Holland, Whitfield/Strong and Smokey Robinson to keep to a strict hit formula — a straitjacket which produced some of the most memorable pop and soul hits of the era.

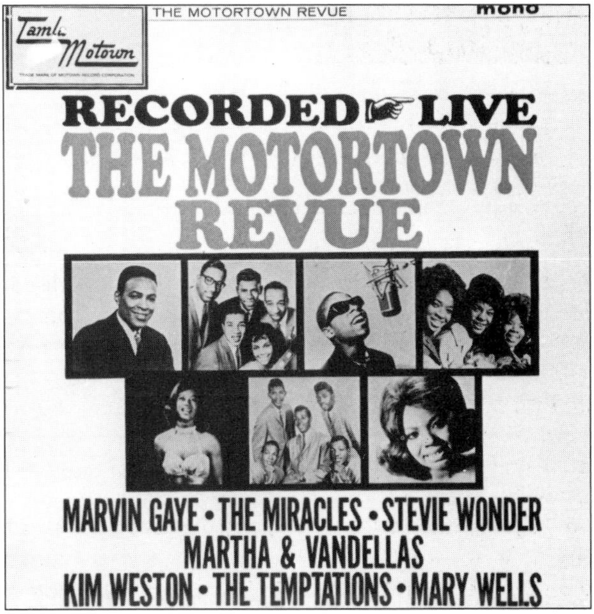

What Gordy's methods didn't do, though, was encourage the individual talents of his artists, and from the late Sixties onwards, a constant stream of performers and writers jumped ship — particularly after Gordy switched Motown's headquarters from Detroit to Hollywood in 1972. Some artists, like Stevie Wonder and Marvin Gaye, even managed to persuade Gordy to let them control their own records. But despite the emergence of the Jackson 5 and the Commodores, Motown's 1970s releases failed to match the artistic or commercial impact of their Sixties output. By the 1980s, Motown was simply another black music label, struggling to find its niche in the market.

"The Motortown Revue" live album from 1964 featured world-famous artists like Marvin Gaye and Stevie Wonder.

Collecting notes: Despite the classic nature of many of Motown's post-1968 recordings, almost all the collectable records date from its early years. Like many major labels, Motown has always attracted completists — people who want to own every release on the label. Most British collectors are more interested in the U.K. releases of Motown product on other labels like London, Fontana, Oriole, Stateside and Tamla Motown, than they are in U.S. pressings on Gordy's own labels. Pre-1964 releases in Britain are particularly collectable, as they failed to attract anything more than a cult following — mostly from Mods. Ironically, one of the rarest U.K. Motown album is a spoken-word record — a collection of speeches by civil rights leader Martin Luther King.

American releases from the Motown stable are infinitely more complex, as they include a number of early singles which received only limited distribution around the Detroit area, plus several records on Gordy-owned labels which only survived for a matter of months — like Weed, Melody, Inferno and Workshop Jazz (home of an extremely rare Four Tops LP).

U.S. hits on Gordy's various labels can often be found for a couple of pounds, and releases from 1964 onwards are rarely worth as much as their U.K. counterparts. Once they had established themselves as a hitmaking force, Motown enjoyed excellent distribution across America — unlike the many Detroit labels who sprang up in their wake, who often issued blatant imitations of the Motown sound. Many of these cash-in releases, which failed to match Motown's sales or chart success, are now eagerly collected on the Northern Soul scene.

NORTHERN SOUL

Golden era: **1963-1968**
Top U.K. rarity: **DARRELL BANKS' 'Open The Door To Your Heart'**
(7", demo-only, London HL 10070, 1966) **£200**

The rarest Northern Soul singles were released between 1963 and 1968. But none of the artists who made those records would have known what you were talking about if you'd said they were Northern Soul stars. Although the vast majority of the music was American, the concept of Northern Soul was a British invention — coined by soul journalist Dave Godin, to reflect what was happening in the soul clubs in the North of England.

"Solid Soul Sensations", a sought-after 1974 compilation bringing together 16 classic Northern Soul obscurities.

Just as the London Mod scene had built Jamaican ska, American soul and R&B into an underground cult, so the soul clubs across the North and Midlands developed their own twilight scene in the late '60s. Their requirements were simple — American soul records, or tracks which sounded as if they came from America, which were highly danceable (usually uptempo, but with the occasional smoocher for that end-of-the-night experience) and, most important of all, obscure.

The enthusiasts of the Northern scene thrived on the idea of exclusivity. Not for them the mainstream Motown hits which could be heard on Radio 1 or *Top Of The Pops*: they wanted music that couldn't be heard elsewhere. The more obscure it was, the better, to the extent that DJs who discovered a little-known dancefloor classic from Chicago or Detroit sometimes 'covered up' the original label with plain white paper, so that rival DJs couldn't poach their ideas.

The music which filled the Northern dancefloors was often inspired by Motown's big productions, or by the Chicago soul of the Impressions. Given the penchant for obscurities, however, it's not surprising that few major names in soul history crop up in lists of Northern rarities. Likewise, the preference for releases on small, local labels tends to mean that Northern favourites lack the production sheen of their Motown counterparts.

In the early '70s, there were a series of hit singles by artists like the Fascinations and the Tams, which were reissued when record company executives noted their popularity on the Northern scene. And over the last two decades, there have been scores of excellent compilations — notably on Ace's Kent subsidiary, which managed to fill over 100 LPs with genuine Northern dance numbers.

Collecting notes: It's still original singles that fetch the big money — with top prices going to U.S. originals like Frank Wilson's 'Do I Love You' (£8,000!) and Dennis Edwards' 'Johnny On The Spot' (£3,000+). Coming closer to home, demo copies of Darrell Banks' 'Open The Door To Your Heart' (£200) on London remain the ultimate U.K. prize, while there is also much interest in soul-styled recordings by British artists like Tony Middleton ('Don't Ever Leave Me', Polydor, £225), Dennis D'Ell ('It Breaks My Heart In Two', CBS, £175) and Chapter Five ('Anything That You Do', CBS, £175).

Some artists accidentally managed to record one single that appealed to Northern Soul fans — like Helen Shapiro, for instance. At £50, 'Stop And You'll Become Aware' is worth almost ten times more than any of her other 45s.

In recent years, the supply of classic uptempo soul releases has finally begun to run out, and collectors have started to take on board slower material. Prices on the Northern scene can fluctuate alarmingly, soaring as a particular record sweeps the clubs, and then dropping away as the dancers get tired of it. But Northern Soul remains one area of collecting where it's still possible to pick up a single for a few pence and discover that it's worth several hundred pounds. After all, it's estimated that there are around 30,000 obscure danceable soul singles from the '60s

FOLK & SINGER-SONGWRITERS

Golden ages: **1962-1965, 1968-1972**
Top U.K. rarity: **MELLOW CANDLE's *Swaddling Songs***
(Deram SDL 7, 1972)
£300

Almost every singer-songwriter who plays an acoustic guitar has been described as a folk performer at one time or another, but in fact the two areas often have nothing more in common than a shared use of acoustic instruments.

As soon as it became possible to record music, early in this century, collectors of folk songs went out of their way to document for posterity the traditional ballads that had been passed down the ages from one rural generation to the next. In fact, research in more recent times has revealed that many so-called 'traditional' songs were actually written in the Victorian age, and aren't any more authentic than music-hall ditties from the same period.

But many of the 'trad' songs that can still be heard in British folk-clubs today were originally composed many centuries ago. The

With songs like "By The Time I Get To Phoenix" to his name, Jimmy Webb is recognised as one of the songwriting greats.

same process occurred in America, though the situation there was complicated by the fact that some songs were transplanted from Europe to North America by the early pilgrims.

Since the Second World War, the folk scenes in Britain and America have been divided by the clash between 'traditionalists', who insisted that only the ancient songs should be sung, and 'modernists', who were open to new songs composed in the old tradition. In both countries, there was a folk boom in the late '50s and early '60s, which was sparked by musicians who had been inspired by the old songs, and wanted to write their own material in the same vein. Particularly in America, this coincided with the first wave of student and youth disenchantment with the political establishment, resulting in what became known as the 'protest' era.

Folk singer Donovan, famous for '60s hits like "Mellow Yellow" and "Jennifer Juniper".

Joni Mitchell's songs have been covered by everyone from Bob Dylan to Johnny Cash.

Bob Dylan, whose most famous collectable is the picture sleeve edition of 'Leopard-Skin Pill-Box Hat' (CBS, £35), was adopted as the figurehead of this movement, though he turned his back on protest material as early as 1964. Greenwich Village in New York became the centre of the scene, and Dylan's friends and foes — like Phil Ochs (*All The News That's Fit To Sing*, Elektra, £18), Dave Van Ronk (*Inside*, Stateside, £10) and Eric Andersen (*Today Is The Highway*, Fontana, £16) — gathered there to sing new material, and standards from the repertoires of '30s, '40s and '50s pioneers like Huddie 'Leadbelly' Ledbetter, Woody Guthrie and Pete Seeger.

In Britain, the link between politics and folk wasn't so strong, though performers like Bert Jansch did join the two. More typical, though, was Martin Carthy, who has always based his repertoire around traditional material. But it was Donovan who broke through to the pop market, overtly basing his style on early Bob Dylan. After that, folk took a commercial backseat, until Fairport Convention and Steeleye Span won a large audience for a mix of traditional songs and rock arrangements in the late '60s — a style known as folk-rock, though it's often quite different to the American music of the same name.

Bob Dylan's move to rock music in 1965 effectively killed off the American folk scene as a major commercial force. After Dylan, a generation of folkies formed rock bands, like the Byrds, the Lovin' Spoonful and the Youngbloods. Their successors also moved out of the rock clubs, but worked as soloists, with or without additional accompaniment. Taking elements from folk, blues and rock, they treated their music as a vehicle for writing about their own most intimate feelings — and the singer-songwriter tradition was born.

Not surprisingly, much of the singer-songwriter output proved to be embarrassingly self-indulgent, but the finest exponents of the genre — Joni Mitchell, Paul Simon, James Taylor, Tim Hardin, Tim Buckley, Leonard Cohen and the individual members of Crosby, Stills, Nash & Young — captured the imagination of a worldwide audience with their confessional songs. So, indeed, did British acts who embraced the singer-songwriter ethos like Cat Stevens, Kevin Coyne, David Bowie (on 1971's *Hunky Dory*) and even Elton John. They were adopted as patron saints by the Woodstock generation, and then just as heartily rejected when punk came along in 1977.

But the singer-songwriter tradition survived against the odds, and flowered again in America in the late '80s and early '90s, thanks to the success of artists like Tracy Chapman, Marc Cohn and Mary-Chapin Carpenter. These days, the dividing lines between rock singer-songwriters, country singers and folkies are often hard to identify, and someone like Carpenter is accepted in all three camps. In Britain, meanwhile, punk did such a thorough job of clearing away the past that both singer-songwriters and folkies are still regarded with much suspicion, unless they reshaped their music into a post-punk form, like Elvis Costello and Billy Bragg.

Collecting notes: Both the folk and singer-songwriter genres are dominated by albums, so it's no surprise that collectors tend to concentrate on this format. Although there is interest in singles — particularly if they include non-album B-sides or come in a rare picture sleeve — they don't tend to achieve the high prices you associate with some other genres.

The rarest British folk albums are those issued on private labels in the '60s and '70s, often by artists who regarded themselves as occupying the furthest fringe of the progressive rock movement. Keep your eyes peeled for names like Agincourt, whose *Fly Away* is worth £700, and the eponymously-titled *Caedmon*, which sells for £400. Otherwise, there's much specialist interest in the collections of '50s and early '60s folk recordings issued by labels like Topic and Transatlantic — who also released early LPs by many of the most important British folkies of the post-war era, like Bert Jansch and Martin Carthy. Of the later artists, original releases by Fairport Convention, Steeleye Span, John Martyn and Sandy Denny are particularly sought-after — particularly those on the 'pink' Island label.

The majority of important singer-songwriter releases (certainly by the major names) are currently available on CD, and only obscure items by long-forgotten artists like Jackson C. Frank (*Jackson C. Frank*, Columbia, £100) and Fred Neil (*Bleecker And MacDougal*, £25) fetch more than average prices. But there are a number of very rare Bob Dylan items, notably the withdrawn U.S. pressing of his *Freewheelin'* album (worth around £10,000) with four tracks that weren't featured on the later release. Mono versions of his pre-1967 albums are also highly collectable, as they can sound quite different to the familiar stereo mixes currently available on CD.

Continued on page 165

SYD BARRETT BOX SET

CD box sets like this Syd Barrett package have revolutionised the reissue business in the 90s.

PAUL WELLER BOX SET

Paul Weller's 1995 album "Stanley Road" was briefly available as a limited edition of singles, packaged with a book and an insert illustrating Peter Blake's original sketches for the sleeve design.

Paul Weller re-emerged as a major rock force in the mid-90s, two decades after he first performed as a member of the Jam.

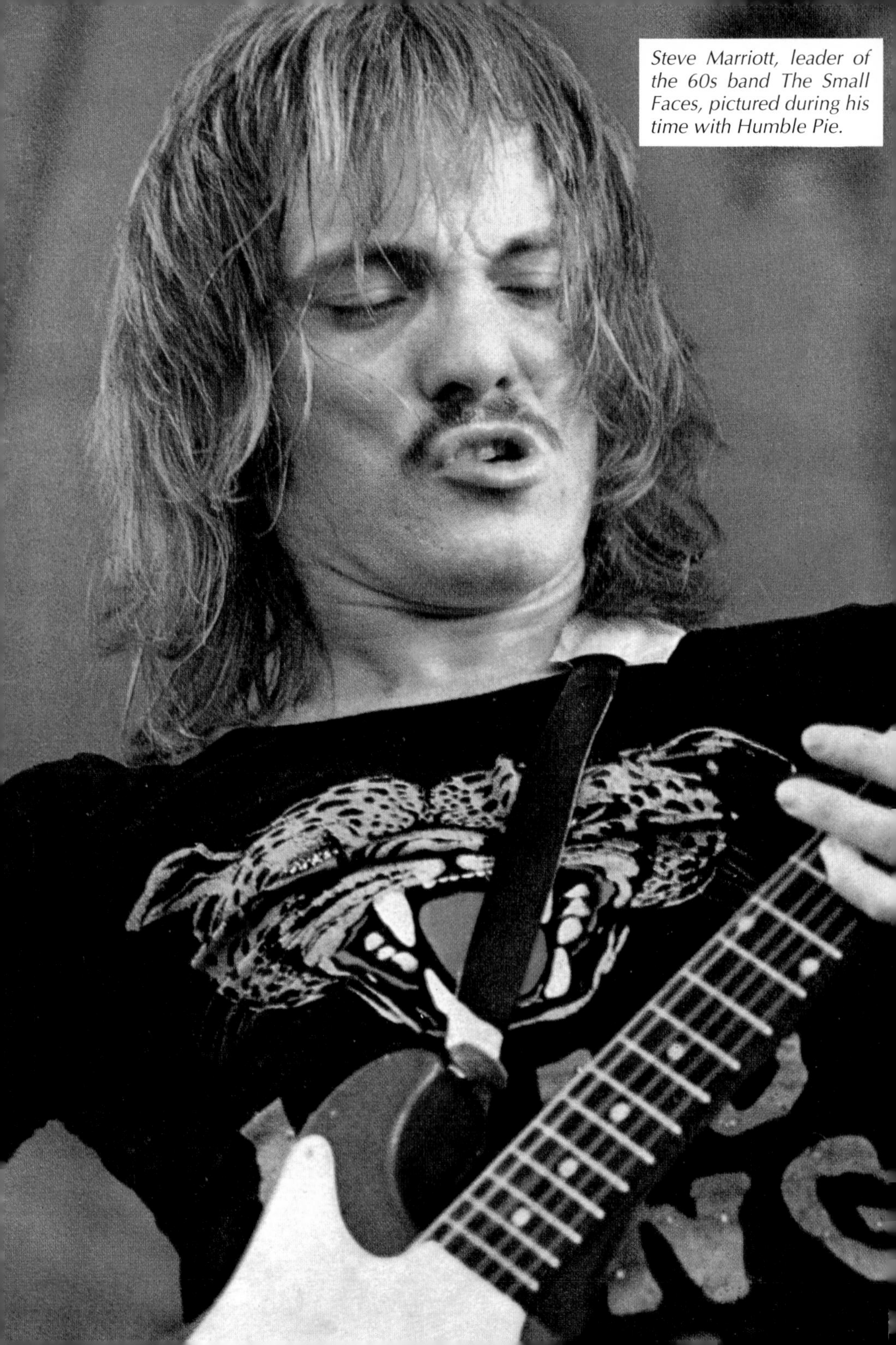

Steve Marriott, leader of the 60s band The Small Faces, pictured during his time with Humble Pie.

REGGAE, SKA AND BLUEBEAT

Golden Ages: **1962-1973, late '70s**
Top Rarity: **BOB MARLEY's 'Judge Not' 45**
(Island WI 088, 1963) **£120**

The British public were largely unaware of Jamaican music in the 1950s. However, that changed with the advent of ska in the early '60s. Ska had its roots in Jamaica, where enterprising DJs would tour with their own mobile sound systems, playing the latest imported American R&B discs. The offbeat New Orleans sound of Fats Domino was particularly popular, and inspired Jamaican musicians and producers to create their own hybrid of 'mento' — the island's own brand of calypso — and R&B. This they called 'ska'.

Several labels like Island and Blue Beat sprang up in Britain to cater for the rapidly growing interest in ska, which had became popular at black 'blues parties' and Mod clubs. The result was a short-lived ska craze in 1964, which spawned novelty hits like Millie's 'My Boy Lollipop' (Fontana, £5) and homegrown efforts from long-forgotten beat acts like the Migil Five, who debuted in 1964 with 'Mockingbird Hill' (Pye, £5).

In the mid-'60s, ska went underground, and although dozens of 45s and albums on labels like Ska Beat were issued over here, it took another couple of years before Jamaican music broke through to the U.K. pop charts again. By then, ska had evolved first into rocksteady (which had a slower rhythm) and, by the end of the decade, reggae.

In 1969, Desmond Dekker scored the first reggae No. 1 with 'Israelites' (Pyramid, £4), at a time when acts like the Ethiopians ('Live Good', Ska Beat, £12), Harry J. & the Allstars ('Liquidator', Harry J., £4), and the Skatalites ('Trip To Mars', Island, £15) were also enjoying hit singles. Reggae was big news, and the craze prompted a crop of new labels to add to more established outlets like Trojan.

Although artists like Jackie Edwards ('We're Gonna Love', Starlite, £10), Jimmy Cliff ('I'm Sorry', Blue Beat, £15) and Toots & the Maytals ('Hallelujah', Blue Beat, £15) became immensely popular in the early '70s, one artist — Bob Marley — completely dominated the reggae arena. A veteran of the Jamaican music scene since the early '60s, Marley's uncompromising politics slowed his progress towards the world stage. But, by the end of the '70s, he had attained his rightful position as an international star.

Bob Marley's 1975 show at the London Lyceum Theatre was recorded for this famous album, simply titled "Live!".

While Marley's star was in the ascendent, behind the scenes reggae was splintering into several distinct strands. The likes of Ken Boothe ('The Train Is Coming', Island, £12) were championing radio-friendly 'pop reggae', often relying on cover versions to reach the charts, while underground DJs were paving the way for rap by talking — or toasting— over instrumental tracks. Around the same time, reggae producers were beginning to experiment with dub, stripping songs down to their rhythm parts, which were then treated with reverb and echo.

When punk arrived in 1977, reggae underwent a renaissance in Britain, with punk bands like the Clash and the Police using reggae rhythms and experimenting with

Bob Marley, the inspirational reggae star who died in 1980. He was just 36.

instrument drop-out to give a dub effect.

For much of the '80s, reggae was conspicuous by its absence, though a smooth brand of reggae known as lover's rock spawned the occasional crossover hit. However, the start of the '90s saw the Jamaican sound enjoyed a resurgence, not only with ragga but the slowed-down ska rhythms of dance-hall, as championed by Shaggy.

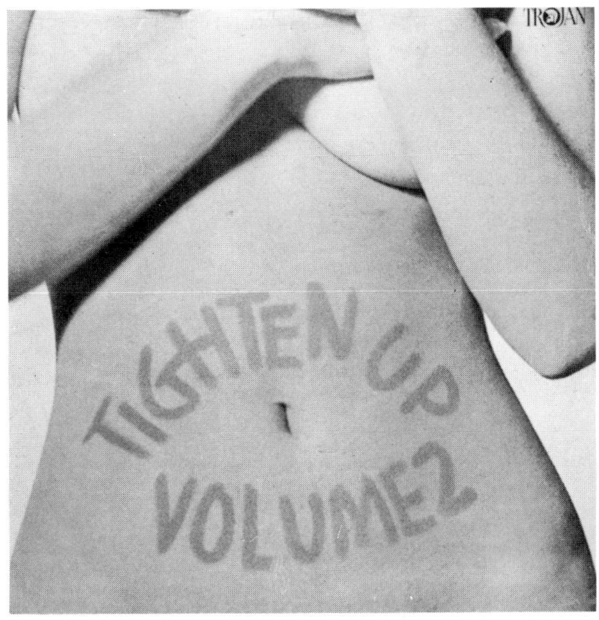

"Tighten Up Volume 2", the legendary ska and reggae compilation on the Trojan label, first appeared in 1969.

Collecting notes: There's a market for virtually every Jamaican record from 1960 to the mid-'70s. Most '60s singles are worth between £8 and £15, while LPs from the same period can sell for up to £200, though most change hands for £20-£30.

Jamaican releases by Bob Marley are particularly collectable, with several non-U.K. singles like 'Man To Man' selling for £70 or more. Also valuable are records issued on labels like Studio One (generally worth around £15) and those produced by respected producers like Coxsone Dodd and Lee 'Scratch' Perry.

Reggae and ska singles on the U.K. Bluebeat label tend to be worth £12-£15, while the LPs often sell for considerably more.

FUNK AND RARE GROOVE

Golden era: **1969-1975**
Top Rarity: **MARVA WHITNEY's *It's My Thing***
(LP, Polydor 583 767, 1969) **£125**

The end of the '60s saw one classic era in American soul come to an end, and another begin. The accessible, energetic sounds of Motown, Stax and Atlantic gave way to a more subtly rhythmic music, hinging around chunky, intricate bass lines and tight, shuffling drum patterns.

The inspiration for 'funk' came primarily from one man: James Brown. His 1970 hit 'Sex Machine' defines the genre: clipped, rhythmic horn riffs, staccato guitar chops and infectious drum beats that could stir the dead. Although soul was kept alive in the early '70s, especially in the southern states, it was funk that became Black America's rallying cry — not least because of its socially-aware lyrics.

Another funk landmark was Isaac Hayes' theme tune to *Shaft*. Taken from the ground-breaking movie of the same name, it had a lighter, more groovy feel, topped off by Steve Cropper's tight, wah-wah guitar. The film itself was a 'blaxploitation' flick — a term used to describe a style of early '70s action movies, set in, and around, the black ghettos of urban America. Many of the accompanying soundtracks were scored by respected black musicians like Quincy Jones.

Funk was earthier than soul, so it's not surprising that many of its big names hailed from the deep south rather than the big cities of the north. The Meters (*Rejuvenation*, Reprise, £25), featuring several of the Neville Brothers, epitomised the New Orleans sound, while the legendary Stax label in Memphis kept turning out blistering funk hits, like 'Mr. Big Stuff' by Jean Knight (*Mr. Big Stuff*, LP, Stax, £10).

Funkadelic's "Free Your Mind" album was produced by the band's spiritual mentor, the larger-than-life George Clinton.

James Brown wasn't funk's only hero. Sly & the Family Stone mixed funk and rock on 1968's 'Dance To The Music'. They spread the word at Woodstock in 1969 with their anthem, 'I Want To Take You Higher', and issued one of the genre's most politically aware albums, *There's A Riot Goin' On* (Epic, £15). George Clinton, an admirer of Sly Stone, created a monster mutha-ship out of two acts, Parliament and Funkadelic, who played a cosmic mixture of bass-heavy funk and glam rock, and issued LPs with titles like *Maggot Brain* (Westbound, £35) and *The Electric Spanking Of War Babies* (Warner Brothers, £15). Weird stuff!

As the 70s wore on, funk was superseded by the faster, more sophisticated sound of disco — a natural progression from the smooth and fluffy Philadelphia soul of the Three Degrees and the O'Jays. Disco went overground around 1977 with hits like Donna Summer's hypnotic 'I Feel Love', which owed as much to the formulaic, computer-driven sounds of, say, German synth act Kraftwerk, as funky black dance music.

By the mid-'80s, hip-hop was the predominant musical force in black America. To spice up its basic rap/beatbox sound, enterprising producers took advantage of recently developed samplers to steal drum breaks and refrains from old records. Ironically, this fuelled demand for the original tunes, rekindling interest in early '70s funk tracks by James Brown and, later, obscure funk soundtracks, late '60s Latin soul, early '70s jazz and Latin jazz.

Rare groove evolved as a catch-all phrase for any hard-to-find '70s jazz-funk track, though the term is also used more loosely to describe any late '70s club classics. There's a parallel here between rare groove and Northern Soul: ten years earlier, DJs had unearthed obscure soul 45s from the 60s, and turned them into in-demand dancefloor fillers, which became popular with collectors.

Over the last ten years, the market for vintage funk vinyl — and the general growth of interest in club culture — has grown to such an extent that there are now regular black music fairs, and specialist shops in London and other large cities. Today, people recognise as many sub-genres within '70s black music as they do in rock, including fusion (a blend of jazz and funk — but not jazz funk!) and garage (a term used both for a modern variation on soul, as well as a lilting style of late '70s and '80s soul).

Collecting notes: While '60s soul collectors compete for rare 45s, '70s funk fans tend to concentrate on albums. Many of the most important funk LPs weren't issued in Britain, so it's the American obscurities which attract most interest — and the highest prices. The market is definitely led by what happens in the clubs: if a DJ starts playing a particular tune, or it gets sampled, then demand for the original recording rockets overnight. Most blaxploitation soundtracks are popular, too, but beware: the club market is notoriously fickle, and an album can rise in value from nothing to £50 and drop back to £20 in the space of a few months. And few collectors are interested in the finer details of first pressings, so a vinyl reissue can kill the market stone dead.

And here he is . . . George Clinton, the king of black funk-rock, pictured in 1989.

PSYCHEDELIA & GARAGE ROCK

Golden Age: **1965-1969**
Top Rarity: **THE BACHS' *Out Of The Bachs***
(U.S. LP, Raio label, no cat. no., 1967) **£2,000**

In June 1967, the 'Summer Of Love' hit San Francisco and London, bringing with it 'flower power', long hair and love'n'peace. It was a time of beads and 'love-ins', free concerts and colourful clothes, political protests and social reform. And it was also the year that rock music took a giant leap forward in terms of imagination and creativity, with albums like the Beatles' *Sgt. Pepper* and Jimi Hendrix's *Are You Experienced?* redefining the parameters of pop and rock.

In many cases, artists were attributing their innovative sounds to their use of 'psychedelic' drugs like LSD (or 'acid'), which they claimed freed their minds and let them travel beyond the limits of conventional musical forms. As a result, the trippy, colourful music they made became known as psychedelia.

In many ways, the psychedelic era was the culmination of a decade of revolution which started with rock'n'roll and ended with the explosive rock groups like the Who, Cream and the Jimi Hendrix Experience, all of whom betrayed psychedelic influences. In America, psychedelia represented freedom and political activism — as well as hallucinogenic drugs and free love — and found a soundtrack in the music of West Coast acts like the Grateful Dead, who debuted in the U.K. with 1967's 'Born Cross-Eyed' (Warner Brothers, £12) and the Jefferson Airplane (*Surrealistic Pillow*, RCA Victor, £18). These hippie gurus took folk and blues, twisted them around, put them through an amplifier and turned out revolutionary sounds that owed as much to free-form jazz as to Chuck Berry.

A 'counter-culture' quickly emerged, rejecting the traditional values of the establishment. But as with punk in the late '70s, its idealism was quickly corrupted. By the time the hippie generation hosted their climactic love-in at the Woodstock festival in 1969, world peace and personal freedom were still distant dreams. As if to underline this fact, psychedelia also became distorted (quite literally!), having been hi-jacked by proto-

Pink Floyd during their psychedelic heyday in the late 1960s. Syd Barrett is second from right.

heavy metal, country rock and singer-songwriters.

Classic 'psych' can be broken down into several different types. 'Acid rock' is a term commonly used to describe American psychedelia. It generally implies a reliance on heavy guitars and extended solos (the latter a trademark of the Grateful Dead, for example), and contrasts with the 'pop-psych' of more whimsical groups like the Strawberry Alarm Clock, who scored a hit with the fabulous 'Incense And Peppermint' (Pye International, £15).

The Standells, one of a clutch of influential garage rock groups to emerge from America in the mid-1960s.

Another '60s Stateside innovation was 'garage punk'. Essentially, this described the mid-'60s teenage bands who tried to emulate the blistering British R&B of the Pretty Things, Them, the Who and the Yardbirds. Snotty, sneering and overflowing with attitude, they included groups like the Shadows Of Knight ('Gloria', Atlantic, £15), the Standells ('I'll Go Crazy', Liberty, £15) and the Count Five ('Psychotic Reaction', Pye International, £15), who used fuzz pedals and Farfisa organs to craft a string of punk anthems which occasionally broke through to the charts. Some of the best psychedelia happened when these louts gained access to drugs — then all hell broke loose.

In England, psychedelia blossomed in London's 'underground' clubs like the Middle Earth and the UFO. The leaders of the scene — the Pink Floyd, the Soft Machine, the Crazy World Of Arthur Brown and Tomorrow — decked themselves out in the latest Carnaby Street and Kings Road paisley designs and created a weird and wonderful mix of improvised instrumental passages and pure pop. While the Pink

"After Bathing At Baxters" by Jefferson Airplane epitomised the sound of American late '60s psychedelic rock.

Floyd's catchy 'See Emily Play' (Columbia, £20; with picture sleeve, £300) led to psych-by-numbers hits like the Status Quo's 'Picture Of Matchstick Men' (Pye, £7), the more experimental end of the underground evolved into an ambitious, sophisticated style called progressive rock. Psych also developed into 'space rock' — a kind of drug-inspired hippie-punk chiefly associated with free festival favourites Hawkwind.

Britain also had a garage punk scene. R&B bands seized upon the developing technology of amps and guitar effects to create what is known as 'freakbeat', the bridge between beat and psychedelia. An early example is the Who's 'Anyway, Anyhow, Anywhere' (Brunswick, £15), which adds an anarchic feedback middle-eight to its basic R&B format. Within a couple of years, guitarist Pete Townshend had created the fully-fledged psychedelia of 1967's 'I Can See For Miles' (Track, £6).

In the 1990s, the term psychedelia is far less specific than it was in the late '60s. Today, it's an all-embracing term which encompasses any late '60s music that's a bit odd or far out, or which boasts psychedelic trademarks like phasing, backwards guitars, wah-wah pedals and the use of Indian instruments like the sitar.

Arthur Brown scored a hit with "Fire!" in '68.

The term is also applied to any music that seems to have a dreamy, mind-expanding or hallucinogenic quality. For example, 1970s hippie progressive act Gong and '90s ambient house stars the Orb are sometimes described as psychedelic.

Collecting notes: There are hundreds of blistering U.S. garage 45s to check out, but because the originals are so expensive, they tend to be eschewed by British fans in favour of the wealth of psych compilations that appeared after the ground-breaking early '70s collection, *Nuggets* (Elektra, £35). The more sophisticated West Coast psych bands were always album-based, though there are several early U.K. singles and picture sleeve editions to look out for, such as like the Grateful Dead's 'Born Cross-Eyed' and Country Joe & the Fish's 'Not So Sweet Martha Lorraine' (Fontana, £10).

As far as U.K. bands are concerned, the highest prices are paid for obscurities by acts like Factory ('Try A Little Sunshine', CBS, £125), Mandrake Paddle Steamer ('Strange Walking Man', Parlophone, £60) and Fire ('Father's Name Is Dad', Decca, £100). These records often stray into 'freakbeat' territory, an area known for its avid collectors and sky-high prices. The value of some albums on the fringes of psch, like Apple's *An Apple A Day* (Page One, £600 with booklet) are similarly increased by demand from progressive rock fans.

PROGRESSIVE ROCK

Golden era: **1969-1974**
Top rarity: **DARK's *Dark Round The Edges*** *(LP, SIS 0102, private pressing, 12" with colour gatefold sleeve & booklet, 1972)* **£1,500**

Though at first it was synonymous with the late '60s psychedelic exploits of 'underground' acts like Tomorrow and the Soft Machine, progressive rock soon became a by-word for a style of rock which championed technical expertise and the notion of music-as-art. The fact that 'prog' musicians drew upon classical, jazz and folk influences added to the sense that what they were doing was serious, and had little in common with the frivolous pop music of the '60s.

Indeed, progressive rock was the antithesis of glam. While fans of Marc Bolan and David Bowie liked to dress outrageously and boogie the night away, 'prog' buffs preferred to sit cross-legged in darkened rooms and ruminate on the significance of the latest conceptual waxings by the likes of Colosseum (*Those Who Are About To Die*, Fontana, £15), Dr. Strangely Strange (*Kip Of The Serenes*, Island, £80) or Pink Floyd (*The Piper At The Gates Of Dawn*, Columbia, £45 in mono).

This idea was underlined by the progressive rock attitude to the 7" single, which was frowned upon once it was realised that the album, or better still, the double album, was far more suited to their long, complex instrumental arrangements and pseudo-classical suites. Although lyricists and singers were fêted for their poetical verses, it was the musicians who increasingly took over as the most vital group members — even drummers like Jon Hiseman (Colosseum) and Aynsley Dunbar (Retaliation) had their own bands, although the guitar, and to a lesser degree, the keyboard, remained the virtuoso's chief instrument.

Defining the moment when progressive rock started and ended is a thankless task. All the elements were in place by the time of the Beatles' *Sgt. Pepper* in mid-1967; and, while punk rock is generally regarded as killing prog off a decade later, acts like Pink Floyd, Sky (*Don't Hold Back*, RCA, £10) and the Alan Parsons Project ('Doctor Tarr And Professor Fether', Charisma, £4) continued to sell healthily for many years afterwards.

Original copies of progressive band Can's "Soundtracks" album from 1970 currently change hands for around £30.

In fact, the '80s saw a slow but certain return to progressive values, with many young bands like IQ and Marillion rejecting heavy rock in favour of more lofty musical pursuits. This

Rick Wakeman, one-time keyboardist and showman with progressive rockers Yes.

was coupled with renewed interest in the minor figures from progressive rock's past, who failed to achieve the success of giants like Yes, ELP and Genesis, yet in retrospect cut some stunning tracks.

Among the hidden treasures unearthed since are original albums by the likes of Leaf Hound, Fantasy (*Paint A Picture*, Polydor, £250) and folkies Mellow Candle (*Swaddling Songs*, Deram, £300), plus a multitude of 'private pressings' from obscure outfits who issued their albums in small runs, to sell at gigs and give to friends. Often, these contain third-rate folk-rock, but once in a while, a real gem surfaces, like the Dark's *Dark Round The Edges*.

Deep Purple, Led Zeppelin and Black Sabbath form the popular end of the U.K. hard rock/progressive crossover market, with their U.S. equivalents, like Grand Funk Railroad and Vanilla Fudge, falling in the same category. Also sometimes classed as prog are Jethro Tull, Fairport Convention, Mahavishnu Orchestra, Nucleus, the Allman Brothers and Johnny Winter, indicating just how wide the progressive catchment area was.

Some of the most influential progressive bands were European. Can, Faust, Tangerine Dream and Neu consistently enjoyed acclaim from critics and musicians alike, due to their mix of ambient soundscapes, rhythmic intensity and post-psychedelic experimentation.

Collecting notes: Because of the built-in scarcity factor, many private pressing albums command very high prices, which have been pushed up further in recent years by interest from European and Japanese collectors. Many prog fans concentrate on acquiring whole sets of releases on the leading progressive labels. Chief among these are Harvest and Vertigo (subsidiaries of EMI and Phonogram, respectively), which were set up specifically to cater for the early '70s prog market. Often housed in illustrated sleeves (creating another market for collectors — Roger Dean is a leading designer), these titles make little visual sense when shrunk down to CD size, and so demand for original LP sleeves, many of which were gatefold, remains high.

GLAM ROCK

Golden era: **1971-1975**
Top U.K. rarity: **T. REX's 'Ride A White Swan'**
(7", Octopus OCTO 1, unreleased, test pressings only, 1970) **£1,000**

For years it was regarded as one of pop's most embarrassing eras, but the '90s has seen glam rock — the launch pad for '70s stars like Marc Bolan, David Bowie, Gary Glitter and Suzi Quatro — finally saluted as one of our great national treasures.

Glam arrived in the spring of 1971, when Marc Bolan appeared on *Top Of The Pops* wearing glitter under his eyes and playing the updated rock'n'roll boogie of 'Hot Love'. In contrast to psychedelia and progressive rock, glam was simple, effective and — not surprisingly — glamorous. And it cheered up pop music no end.

Both veterans of the late '60s underground scene, Bowie and Bolan defined glam's image, with their androgynous looks and high-heeled boots providing an alternative for teenagers fed up with the rock uniform of jeans, T-shirt and sneakers. By the summer of '71, school kids everywhere were sporting corkscrew hairdos and orange feather-cuts, aping their idols in a mass outbreak of T. Rextasy and Ziggymania.

Marc Bolan invented glam rock when he wore glitter on 'Top Of The Pops' in 1971. This is T. Rex's "The Slider" album.

Inevitably, others artists quickly got in on the Glam act. Paul Gadd, one-time rock'n'roller and warm-up man for '60s TV show *Ready, Steady, Go!*, reinvented himself as Gary Glitter ('Papa Oom Mow Mow', Bell, £5), while Sweet ('Slow Motion', Fontana, £300) developed a poppy brand of bubble-glam and Slade ('Know Who You Are', Polydor, £70) re-cast themselves as the rockiest skinheads around.

All these groups sold singles in droves, which makes most glam rock 45s fairly easy to find. Only Bowie (*The Man Who Sold The World,* Mercury, with dress sleeve, £200) and, for a while, Marc Bolan and T. Rex ('Ride A White Swan', see above), saw extensive album sales. This gulf was widened further when Bowie and Bolan announced that glam was dead in 1973, leaving a new wave of weeny-bop idols to plug the gap. Although purists maintain that without Bowie and Bolan, the genre was extinct, history has tended to stick the glam tag on anyone who wore ridiculous costumes, had a simple backbeat and smiled inanely.

Historically speaking, the Osmonds, Roxy Music, Sparks, Roy Wood & Wizzard, Elton John, Alvin Stardust and, at a stretch, the Bay City Rollers, might fall within the

All dressed up for the "Ballroom Blitz" — the Sweet worrying a few parents in the early '70s.

glam arena, but the recent tendency to include mid-'70s acts like Abba, Baccara, the Brotherhood Of Man, and even Carl Douglas, is stretching things a bit. What it does reveal, though, is not only that image was glam's main trademark, but also that the term is now applied to anything from 20 years ago that was over-the-top and pop-inspired. After all, the gulf between Bolan's 'I Love To Boogie' and Baccara's 'Yes Sir, I Can Boogie' isn't that great.

Collecting notes: Glam coincided with one of pop's most buoyant periods, with record sales peaking and *Top Of The Pops* becoming the most important television programme. Because there are so few genuine rarities, the market for collectables has generally been restricted to the most successful artists' pre-glam work — and it's worth bearing in mind that most of the major glam figures had been loitering around the pop scene for several years before finally finding the right suit.

For instance, Bolan aficionados place a premium on the singer's mid-'60s singles, like Tyrannosaurus Rex's 'Debora' (£225 in a promo picture sleeve), which were generally as unsuccessful as David Bowie's early attempts at cracking the charts under a variety of guises. At £400, Davie Jones & the King Bees' 'Liza Jane' on Vocalion Pop is one of the top Bowie collectables, though its quaint R&B has little in common with the singer's glitzy early '70s swagger.

Sweet released a number of flop 45s during the late '60s, including 'Slow Motion' (Fontana TF 958; £300), as did Slade, who were responsible for several rare albums, like *Beginnings* (Fontana STL 5492; glossy sleeve, black label with silver print, £300).

Genuine glam collectables include the picture sleeve edition of Bowie's 'Starman' (£40) and 'Life On Mars' (£10), and the unissued version of *Diamond Dogs* with the dog's genitals visible on the cover. Also worth looking out for are T. Rex's 1,000-only foldout sleeve edition of *Zinc Alloy* (£150) and Suzi Quatro's debut 45, 'Rolling Stone' (£20).

HARD ROCK & HEAVY METAL

Golden eras: **1969-1975, early 1980s, late 1980s, early 1990s**
Top Rarity: **DEF LEPPARD's *Ride Into The Sun* EP** *(1st issue, Bludgeon Riffola SRT/CUS/232, in picture sleeve with lyric sheet, 1979)* **£300**

Depending on who you speak to, hard rock either started with Link Wray and his killer instrumental, 'Rumble', or with the Kinks' 'You Really Got Me'. But someone, somewhere, stumbled across the sheer thrill of playing loud, distorted guitar. It was then left to Jim Marshall to make the amplifiers that could make every guitarist's wish to make a satisfyingly loud noise come true.

The cover of "Led Zeppelin III", the group's third album, came in a sleeve housing a rotating cardboard wheel.

The term 'heavy metal' was probably picked up from the lyrics of American rockers Steppenwolf's late '60s biker anthem, 'Born To Be Wild'. The record itself was proto-heavy

The label which issued Iron Maiden's '79 debut was appropriately named Rock Hard Records.

metal itself, with powerful guitar riffs and a bellowing chorus, but it was the phrase which really stuck — though it didn't enter common parlance until the mid-'70s.

Before that, there were the late '60s 'power trios' of Cream (*Fresh Cream*, Reaction, £18 in mono) and the Jimi Hendrix Experience ('Hey Joe', Polydor, £8), the 'space rock' of Hawkwind ('Hurry On Sundown', Liberty, £60) and the 'blues rock' of Ten Years After (*Ten Years After*, Deram, £20) and Free ('Broad Daylight', Island, £25).

More important, though, were the giants of what was commonly labelled hard rock, who had an enormous influence on heavy metal — Led Zeppelin ('Communication Breakdown', Atlantic, £350 with promo-only picture sleeve), Deep Purple ('Hush!', Parlophone, £50 in promo p/s) and Black Sabbath ('Evil Woman', Fontana, £50), .

Zeppelin were the biggest of the three. Formed in 1968 by ex-Yardbird Jimmy Page and fronted by rock god Robert Plant (complete with bared chest and long, blond curly hair), they not only dominated '70s rock but conquered America with their first four landmark albums.

Let's not forget Status Quo, either. Having had a brief stab at psychedelic pop back in the late '60s, they built a lengthy career out of twelve-bar blues and attracted an army of denim-clad followers. Throughout the '70s, the British Isles threw up other big names like Judas Priest, U.F.O. and melodic Irish rockers Thin Lizzy, while America fostered the outrageously-dressed Kiss and bluesy Aerosmith. And Australia had the mighty AC/DC, famous for their school uniform-wearing axeman, Angus Young.

But the most successful heavy rockers of all were Queen, who inherited the title of biggest rock group when Led Zepp disbanded in 1980. Despite genuine stompers like 'We Will Rock You', 'Fat Bottomed Girls' and 'Hammer To Fall', Queen weren't strictly a heavy rock band, trading in a mix of styles ranging from symphonic pop to rock'n'roll.

Peddling a brand of crunching rock, Metallica are one of today's heavy metal successes.

Thin Lizzy started out on Parlophone in 1970 with the rare "The Farmer" single, worth £500.

rock'n'roll. However, their grandiose No. 1 hit, 'Bohemian Rhapsody' — a special blue vinyl edition of which sells for £1,000 — is a genuine rock classic.

In the late '70s, a fresh crop of bands mixed the power of heavy metal with the arrogance of punk. Under the banner of 'The New Wave Of British Heavy Metal', groups like Iron Maiden and Def Leppard rose to prominence and eventually achieved world stardom. Then there was Motorhead, who were far punkier than most punk bands. Fronted by ex-Hawkwind bassist Lemmy, they looked ugly, sounded ugly, and made a glorious heavy metal racket that endeared them to just about everyone.

At the opposite end of the spectrum there was a wave of mid '80s U.S. bands who looked as if they spent as much time in the hairdressers as rehearsing, though that didn't stop them turning out a string of rock anthems. Indeed, Bon Jovi and Europe harked back to the FM radio-friendly sounds of the late '70s, when Boston, Kansas, Toto and Journey plied what became known as AOR (adult-oriented rock), and sold millions of albums.

Heavy metal underwent something of a renaissance in the late '80s, with the arrival of Guns N'Roses and thrash metal acts like Metallica, Megadeth and Anthrax. Following in their wake was a crop of U.S. punk metal bands like Nirvana, Smashing Pumpkins, Hole and Pearl Jam, whose mix of Black Sabbath and the Sex Pistols earned them the tag 'grunge'. It was all a long way from 'You Really Got Me'.

Collecting notes: Since early '70s hard rock has been mostly album-based, so many of the early singles by Led Zeppelin, Deep Purple and Black Sabbath are very rare. Indeed, Led Zepp's first two singles — 'Communication Breakdown' and 'Whole Lotta Love' — were produced solely for promotional use, and the few copies that exist sell for around £350.

LPs by more obscure acts like Black Widow (*Black Widow III*, CBS, £25), Blue Cheer (*Outsideinside*, Philips, £20), May Blitz (*May Blitz*, Vertigo, £40) and Tear Gas (*Tear Gas*, Regal Zonophone, £100) are also very scarce. Look out for obscure independent releases from the late '70s and early '80s, because there is a small but keen market for 'New Wave Of British Heavy Metal' oddities like Iron Maiden's *The Soundhouse Tapes* EP (Rock Hard, £60), and Samson's 'Telephone' (Lightning £25).

There are also scores of picture discs and other limited edition singles to look out for, as these formats dominated the '80s heavy metal market, while important '90s rarities include early indie 45s by bands like Nirvana ('Blew' 12" on Tupelo, £18) and Therapy? ('Meat Abstract', Multifuckingnational, £25).

The picture disc of Whitesnake's "Standing In The Shadows" 45.

Continued on page 185

Madonna, the best-selling new artist of the 80s, has cleverly used her film career to publicise her music — and vice versa.

Actor Richard Harris teamed up with composer Jimmy Webb for this 1968 epic.

Lena Horne, on a rare 1957 live album recorded at New York's Waldorf Astoria.

Dean Martin paying his respects to a "Pretty Baby" on an album first issued in 1957.

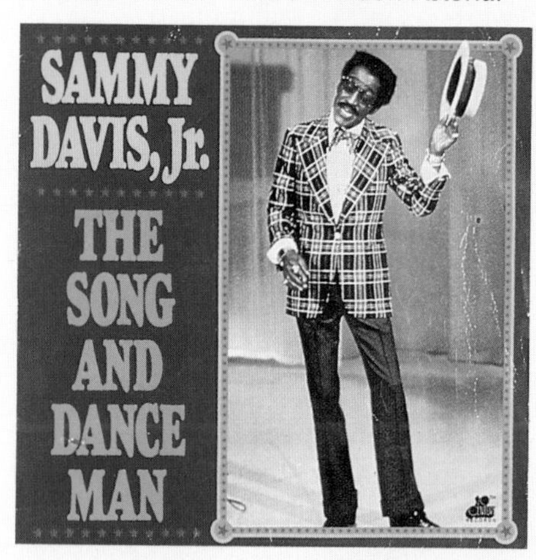

One track on this Sammy Davis Jnr album became a club favourite in 1995.

Frank Sinatra paid tribute to his old 40s bandleader on this lavishly-packaged LP.

Bobby Darin started out as a rock'n'roller, but soon switched to nightclub material.

Albums of psychiatric advice are prime fodder for the 90s exotica collector.

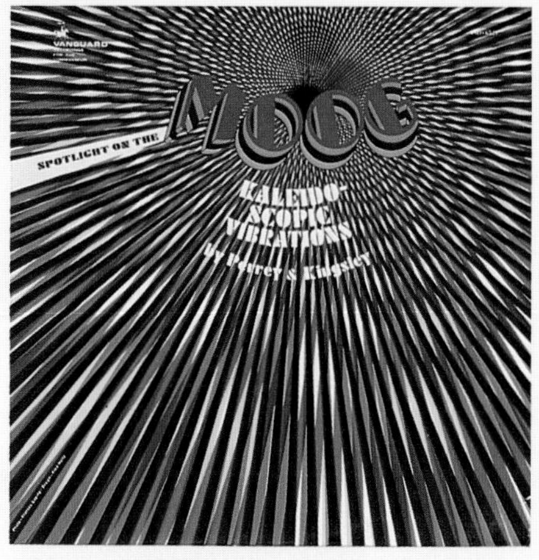

Exotica specialists are intrigued by any 60s or 70s album with psychedelic artwork.

TV themes, especially from the 60s, have a strong cult following among collectors.

Film themes, like those linked to James Bond, are another popular area of exotica.

Even the stoned hippie humour of Cheech & Chong is finding a new audience in the 90s.

The 'Star Trek' TV shows and films have spawned a large number of spin-off records.

k.d. lang, the Canadian country star who crossed into the mainstream pop market with her early 90s LP, "Ingenue".

PUNK

Golden era: **1976-1979**
Top U.K. rarity: **SEX PISTOLS' 'God Save The Queen'**
(7", A&M AMS 7284, withdrawn, 1977) **£1,000**

Aside from the rave and grunge explosions of the late '80s, punk was the last time the music business was turned upside down from the bottom, not the top. Led by the Sex Pistols, the movement was a direct reaction to the stagnant mid-'70s music scene. Its crunching rock'n'roll and war-cry for 'Anarchy In The U.K.' provided the perfect antidote to the slick noodlings of progressive groups like Yes and Genesis and the throwaway bubble-glam pop of the Bay City Rollers and Sweet.

By the time the Pistols headlined the infamous London Punk Festival in September 1976, many other misfits were mimicking their antagonistic, anti-establishment stance. Their chief partners in crime were the Clash (*Capital Radio* EP, CBS, £30), the Damned ('New Rose', Stiff, £8), the Stranglers ('Peaches', with 'blackmail' lettering sleeve, £200), the Buzzcocks (*Spiral Scratch* EP, New Hormones, £15) and the Jam ('In The City', Polydor, £7), all of whom took a very different approach to punk, both musically and politically. While the Clash and the Jam took politics very seriously, and borrowed from reggae and soul influences respectively, the Damned and Buzzcocks were heavily influenced by late '60s American garage punk bands like the Stooges, MC5 and the Velvet Underground.

By the spring of 1977, all but the Damned were signed to major labels, and arguments raged as to whether these bands were 'selling out' to corporate capitalism or not. However, no one questioned the energy and excitement of the music, and punk debuts like the Sex Pistols' *Never Mind The Bollocks*, the Jam's *In The City* and *The Clash* were hailed as — and remain today — classic rock albums.

In the wake of the initial punk explosion, scores of musicians cut their hair, tore off their flared trousers, and set about making their own new wave sounds, often releasing low-budget singles on small independent labels. Although the likes of Stiff Little Fingers, the Ruts and Sham 69 were keen to emulate the belligerent rock of the original punk groups, many others saw punk as a means of self-expression, and applied its anyone-can-do-it attitude to everything from electronic music (Ultravox, Human League, Tubeway Army) to art-rock (the Fall, XTC, Wire) and poetry (Patrik Fitzgerald, John Cooper Clarke).

"(I'm) Stranded", the 1977 debut LP by Australian punk band the Saints, which spawned a single of the same name.

West London rockers the Clash mixed punk and politics to devastating effect in the late 1970s.

By late 1978, punk had fragmented into scores of different musical strands, and its anti-establishment ideals were waning as more of its leading lights became wrapped up in the major label recording/touring treadmill. With the Sex Pistols having split, the Clash working with U.S. rock producer Sandy Pearlman on their second LP, *Give 'Em Enough Rope*, and the Jam rekindling the spirit of '60s pop bands like the Who, the Beatles and The Kinks, the world had to accept that punk had run its course.

Or had it? 1979 saw a second wave of punk-inspired acts breaking through, ranging from back-to-basics street-punks like the Cockney Rejects to intelligent pop bands like the Vapors, the Members and Elvis Costello & the Attractions. Add to this the burgeoning indie art-rock of Echo & the Bunnymen and Joy Division (signed to the Zoo label in Liverpool and Factory in Manchester, respectively) and the scene was set for one of the most diverse and invigorating years since the birth of rock'n'roll.

During the 1980s, punk went underground again with Crass, Discharge, Chron Gen and a whole host of other mohawked malcontents flying the flag of aggressive three-chord thrash. However, in recent years punk has enjoyed something of a renaissance, with American groups with their roots in 'U.S. hardcore' (an extreme version of punk) — like Green Day, the Lemonheads, Soul Asylum and the late, lamented Nirvana — attaining worldwide success. In Britain, interest in punk was also briefly rekindled by the 1994 'New Wave Of New Wave' movement, which spawned the likes of S*M*A*S*H, These Animal Men and Elastica.

Collecting notes: Although there are plenty of classic punk albums, many of the biggest collectables are 7" singles that were either released in limited numbers by independent labels like Chiswick, Stiff, Step Forward, New Hormones and Beggars Banquet, or else withdrawn or never released because they caused offence.

The latter was the case with the top punk rarity, the Sex Pistols' 'God Save The Queen' on A&M, worth around £1,000. Only a few exist because outraged record company bosses destroyed all but a handful of copies before it reached the shops. Another scarce single is 'Girl From The Snow Country', a solo recording by Stranglers bassist Jean-Jacques Burnel, which was scheduled for release by mistake. None reached the shops in this country, but there are still an estimated 20 copies in circulation — probably ones Burnel gave away to friends. Copies change hands for upwards of £250.

Other celebrated rarities include the Clash's *Capital Radio* EP, available by mail-order from the *NME* (£30); the Damned's 'Don't Cry Wolf' on Stiff, with a sleeve specially-made by Dave Vanian (£60); and the first D.I.Y. punk EP, the Buzzcocks' *Spiral Scratch* on New Hormones (£15).

"The Price Of Admission" was one of the last singles by Belfast's Stiff Little Fingers, and featured a pop-art sleeve.

INDUSTRIAL MUSIC

Golden era: **1977-1981**
Top U.K. rarity: **THROBBING GRISTLE's *24 Hours***
(box set of cassettes, Industrial IRC 1-24, 1981) **£200**

Originally coined as a musical term by Throbbing Gristle during the mid-'70s, 'industrial' is now used to describe all manner of weird and wonderful sounds, ranging from frenetic electro-dance to brutal-sounding punk and metal. Yet despite its broad span, there are several elements that are common to all industrial acts, including an inclination to use noise and atonal sounds in favour of pop melodies and established song structures.

As a rule, collectors are most interested in the first wave of industrialists, which included groups like Throbbing Gristle, Monte Cazazza, SPK and Whitehouse. All of these acts rejoiced in the oppressive power of sound, produced radical manifestos which offered critiques of so-called civilised society, and investigated the activities of outsiders and criminals, like Charles Manson, who operated at its fringes. The records often sounded like a working factory in full swing, but the industrial groups quickly won a following during the immediate post-punk era.

Unsurprisingly, this specialised area had close links to the punk avant-garde, with groups like Nurse With Wound (*To The Quiet Men From A Tiny Girl*, £70) and the Lemon Kittens (*Spoonfed And Writhing* EP, £15) helping to forge an Industrial/experimental crossover in the late '70s. Since then, this anti-rock alliance has broken down further, with electro groups such as Cabaret Voltaire, Front 242 and Front Line Assembly crossing wholeheartedly into the dance field, while the likes of Current 93, Sol Invictus and Death In June reject the modern world for mediaeval and occult mysticism.

Throbbing Gristle's Cosey Fanni Tutti adorned the cover of their album, "Greatest Hits — Entertainment Through Pain".

Many contemporary groups have been influenced by this once marginal style, not least some of the cream of America's underground rock, like Babes In Toyland, Nine Inch Nails, Ministry and Sonic Youth.

Collecting notes: In general, the more extreme the music, the more sought after it is. Original Industrial Records releases are highly prized, notably early copies of Throbbing Gristle's *Second Annual Report* (worth £70) and their blue vinyl *Heathen Earth* (£60). Almost anything on Nurse With Wound's United Dairies label is hot (the

Cabaret Voltaire's Stephen Mallinder, a pioneer of the contemporary industrial-dance crossover.

group's own *Chance Meeting On A Dissecting Table* changes hands for £100), as is everything issued on Whitehouse's Come Organisation imprint. Indeed, many Come Org. releases now command three-figure values, including Whitehouse's *Psychopathia Sexualis*, worth £120 on both clear and black vinyl.

DANCE POP

Golden Era: **1980s**
Top Rarity: **PRINCE's 'Gotta Stop (Messin' About)' 12"**
(Warner Bros LV 47, 1981) **£120**

Remember the new romantics of the early '80s, who pranced around their synthesisers wearing riding jodhpurs? Most journalists dismissed the scene as a bad joke, not realising that many of the bands were actually revolutionising British music. The dance-pop sounds of Depeche Mode and Duran Duran not only became the stadium music of the late '80s, but also paved the way for a rash of unusual synth-pop acts like Erasure and Pet Shop Boys, as well as Stock, Aitken & Waterman's 'hit factory' stable of stars.

Pet Shop Boys' famous single "West End Girls" was a flop when it was first released in 1984.

What Britain's top stars shared with American acts like Prince, Michael Jackson ('Bad' 12", red vinyl, Epic, £15) and Madonna ('Everybody', Sire, £40) was the ability to create pop music that worked on the dancefloor and in the home. Rock guitars were out — and in their place was digital technology, shifting the emphasis from the musicians to the producers and remixers.

The 12" of Prince & the Revolution's "Mountains" included an extended version of the track lasting nearly ten minutes.

Although groups like Spandau Ballet ('To Cut A Long Story Short', Reformation, £4) and ABC ('Tears Are Not Enough', Neutron, £3) flirted with dance music, there was still a definite divide between pop records intended for the charts and soul/disco dance records aimed primarily at the clubs. This gulf narrowed rapidly as the decade wore on, and by the end of the '80s, all manner of rock artists were getting the dance remix treatment, while indie rock enjoyed a brief affair with clubland in an indie-dance crossover.

Meanwhile, urban black music came out of its disco wilderness in the late '70s with rap — a hard-hitting reaction to the smooth sounds of modern soul-pop artists like Luther Vandross. Rap originated in the '70s with DJs talking over funk records but, by the early '80s, artists like Grandmaster Flash ('White Lines', £3) were spouting poetic images of life in the ghetto, setting the agenda for hip-hop, a slower, funkier rap style that Public Enemy ('Rebel Without A Pause' 12", Def Jam, £7) and NWA (*Straight Outta Compton*, £10) brought to the mainstream in 1988. Today, you'll find rap acts like Fun-Da-Mental alongside the latest indie sensations at most self-respecting festivals.

In 1983, Mancunian post-punk group New Order teamed up with U.S. dance producer Arthur Baker for the classic 'Confusion' (Factory, £3), and from that point on, British synth pop and cutting edge American dance music kept in touch. House music arrived from Chicago around 1986, and the subsequent impact on both British and American pop music began to rival those of Elvis, the Beatles and punk.

Collecting notes: The most expensive '80s dance pop items tend to be early singles, especially 12"s and CDs, recorded by the likes of Madonna, Prince and the Pet Shop Boys before they were famous. Indeed, all these artists' first singles are collectable: the 12" edition of Madonna's 'Everybody' is worth £55; Prince's 'I Wanna Be Your Lover' 12" sells for £18; and Pet Shop Boys' 'West End Girls' 12" on Epic changes hands for £45.

12" remixes are particularly popular, as indeed are other limited formats like picture discs, double packs and singles with freebies like posters. On the dance side, demand for rare hip-hop and house 12"s is huge, but it's a highly-specialised and mercurial market, primarily based around the latest imports and remixes.

INDIE

Golden era: **1980s**
Top U.K. Rarity: **THE MANIC STREET PREACHERS' 'Suicide Alley'**
(*7", picture sleeve, SBS 002, 1989)* **£80**

One of punk's greatest achievements was to convince groups that they didn't need to spend years trying to secure a record deal with a major label. Instead, they could put out their own releases for just a few hundred pounds — and make a profit.

The first truly 'independent' punk single, the Buzzcocks' *Spiral Scratch* EP (£15), was issued in January 1977 via the band's own New Hormones label. The record was paid for with a £250 loan from singer Pete Shelley's dad, plus smaller contributions from the band's friends, and all 1,000 copies quickly sold out. Brash, tinny and gloriously amateurish, it was was one of punk's defining moments, and inspired a revolutionary spirit among young musicians wanting to break the major's stranglehold.

Following the success of *Spiral Scratch*, scores of other groups including Warsaw (pre-Joy Division), the Drones and the Only Ones pressed up their own singles, unwittingly producing a string of rarities for today's punk and indie collectors. With most bands working on shoe-string budgets, production values were invariably low, and it was common for 45s to come in thin paper sleeves and contain primitive recordings. Even so, their charm was undeniable.

Although the number of genuinely self-funded records rocketed with punk, the independent scene was quickly dominated by large companies like Chiswick and Stiff (both of whom were active prior to punk); shops-turned-labels like Rough Trade, Small Wonder and Beggars Banquet; and outlets with major-label connections such as Step Forward and Safari.

With the Sex Pistols, the Clash, the Buzzcocks and the Jam signing to majors by mid-'77, the significance of being 'indie' — and whether that meant the same as anti-

Orange Juice in 1983. Edwyn Collins (far right) scored a 1995 solo hit with "Girl Like You".

establishment — was always unclear. Indeed, demand for many indie singles meant that the distribution for repressings was often handled by the very companies the indie scene was trying to undermine.

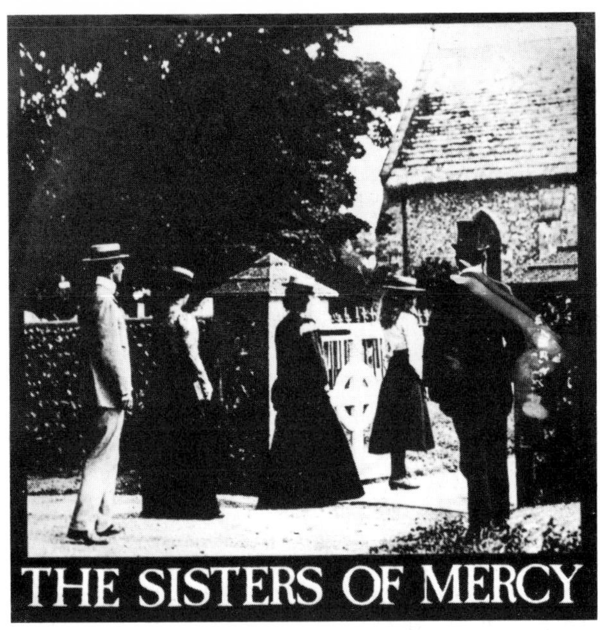

Only 1,000 copies of "The Damage Done", the first single by indie-Goth group the Sisters Of Mercy, were ever pressed.

Even so, the 'indie ethic' of the late '70s shaped the whole outlook of left-field guitar pop in the early '80s. As punk splintered into a kaleidoscope of styles, scores of smaller independent companies cropped up, issuing low-budget records in limited runs. Labels like Cherry Red, 4AD and Mute (London), Rabid and Factory (Manchester), Zoo (Liverpool), and Postcard (Edinburgh) all developed distinct identities, and between them they launched '80s stars like Depeche Mode ('Get The Right Balance' 12", £8), Echo & the Bunnymen ('Pictures On My Wall', £10), the Smiths ('Hand In Glove', £10), New Order ('Ceremony' 12", £8) and Aztec Camera ('Just Like Gold', £15).

There was never one 'indie' sound — though much of the music did share certain qualities. A fine example was Orange Juice's 1980 single, 'Falling And Laughing', which attempted to fuse '70s funk with the classic jangly guitar sound of the Byrds. The result was quirky and experimental, but also accessible and inventive; and with fewer than 1,000 copies in circulation, an original copy (with its foldaround picture sleeve, free flexidisc and postcard insert), will cost you £60.

Welsh punks the Manic Street Preachers released their first single, "Suicide Alley", on a small independent label, SBS.

1980s indies like Creation (London) and Subway (Bristol) fiercely maintained the original DIY spirit, and in 1986, the scene was pulled into focus with the *C-86* cassette, available through the *NME.* Since then, indie has thrown up blistering guitar-pop groups (on majors and independents) like the Wonder Stuff, That Petrol Emotion, Pop Will Eat Itself and the Wedding Present. After the 'indie-dance cross-over' of the late '80s, the list was swelled by the addition of the Stone Roses, the Charlatans, the Inspiral Carpets, Happy Mondays, Blur and Carter USM, all of whom achieved mainstream chart success.

The indie ethic is still widely championed by groups as diverse as Huggy Bear, Ash, the Bluetones, Oasis, Elastica and S*M*A*S*H.

Collecting notes: With many indie bands pressing up their early 45s in runs of 500 or 1,000, there are literally hundreds of genuine rarities to look out for. If a group charts, demand for their previous recordings tends to soar — and so do the prices. For example, recent indie faves like Elastica, Supergrass and the Bluetones have debut singles currently selling for upwards of £20.

Indie collecting is often label-orientated, too, with Factory, Postcard, Él and Creation ranking among the most popular targets. Don't fall into the trap of thinking that all indie releases are worth a fortune, though. Apart from punk and new wave obscurities from 1977-80, there is little interest in 95% of indie releases, and labels like Mute and Factory have kept many of their old releases on catalogue for years.

FILM SOUNDTRACKS AND TV THEMES

Golden era: **1960s**
Top U.K. rarity: **RAYMOND LEPPARD's *Alfred The Great***
(MGM MGM-CS 8112, 1969) **£200**

Collectors were first drawn to film soundtracks because of the involvement of rock and pop musicians. Elvis and the Beatles, the two biggest stars of the 1950s and '60s, were both lured into making movies, with the King starring in no fewer than 32 Hollywood films between 1956 and 1970, and the Fab Four romping through the British-made, low-budget delights of *A Hard Day's Night, Help!* and *Magical Mystery Tour.*

But dozens of other bands also dabbled in '60s cinema. Some, like the Dave Clark Five, followed in the Fabs' footsteps and featured in their own movies, though most only enjoyed cameo appearances, either as actors or, more importantly in hindsight, as performers.

However, the film soundtrack market isn't just about rock and pop at the movies. It also includes the specially-recorded incidental music used for TV and the big screen, which ranges from the sophisticated classic scores of the '50s Hollywood epics to the big band '60s James Bond themes, and the funky jazz and soul soundtracks to early '70s 'blaxploitation' movies.

Popular TV themes include everything from sedate late '50s muzak and wacky kids' TV favourites, like *The Banana Splits* and *Thunderbirds,* to tongue-in-cheek songs by actors like Dennis Waterman (*Minder*) and Nick Berry (*Heartbeat*).

Although most TV and film soundtracks from the '50s and '60s are collectable, some of them — like *The Sound Of Music* and *Dr. Zhivago* — sold in such enormous quantities that they're worth pence rather than pounds. At the other end of the price spectrum, rarities by highly-rated composers like John Barry (*Stringbeat,* Columbia, stereo £50), Jerry Fielding ('When I Grow Too Old To Dream', London, £18), Ennio Morricone (*A Fistful Of Dollars,* RCA, £15), Francis Lai (*Mayerling,* Philips, £60) and Jerry Goldsmith (*In Like Flint,* Stateside, £45) can fetch high prices. Many people single out particular composers in the same way that rock fans might concentrate on a particular band such as Led Zeppelin or the Stones.

Recently, the whole soundtrack market has been given an enormous shot in the arm by the club scene, which picked up on the jazzy vibes of many late '60s and early '70s albums by composers like Quincy Jones, Lalo Schifrin and Hugo Montenegro.

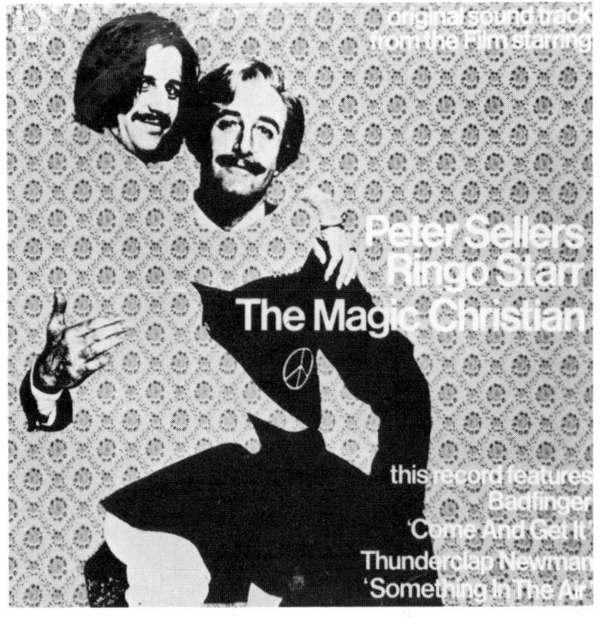

The collectable soundtrack LP for 'The Magic Christian', a 1970 comedy starring Peter Sellers and Ringo Starr.

With film music, the album is understandably the major format, though there are a few sought-after singles — like 'Carter' (Pye, £15 with p/s), a Roy Budd single from the *Get Carter* movie starring Michael Caine. TV themes tended to appear on 45s, with cult shows like *Danger Man, Dr. Who, Randall And Hopkirk* and *The Avengers* and American favourites like *Star Trek* spawning the most collectable items.

During the '70s and '80s, several companies were responsible for what are known as 'library' albums, which featured incidental music intended for use in the film and TV industries. De Wolfe and KPM (Keith Prowse Music) recorded hundreds of albums which provided the accompaniment to everything from chase scenes in *The Sweeney* to chewing gum adverts. These LPs are increasingly attracting interest, especially when they involve a major pop name — like ex-Shadow Brian Bennett, for example.

Those collector's shops which specialise in soundtracks often deal in studio cast LPs, too. These are recordings from stage shows, usually musicals based in the theatres of London or New York. Sometimes, you'll also find recordings of radio plays, though these are less common. Whereas the soundtrack and TV market is currently booming, demand for cast albums has waned, chiefly because there are very few younger fans showing much interest in this field.

Collecting notes: It's difficult for the novice to know a £200 soundtrack rarity from a worthless bargain bin filler — but here are a few handy tips. Always be on the lookout for name composers (like John Barry, Francie Lai and Quincy Jones), or any soundtrack which includes rock music or comes in an attractive psychedelic or 'swinging '60s' sleeve. And if the film itself has attracted cult interest, then it's a surefire bet that the soundtrack is worth picking up, too.

Throughout this book, song titles are printed in single quotation marks (for example: 'She Loves You', 'Anarchy In The U.K.', etc.).

Titles of LPs and albums are printed in italics (for example: *Sgt. Pepper, Automatic For The People*, etc.).

EASY AND EXOTIC

Golden Era: **1955-1975**
Top U.K. rarity: **PETER WYNGARDE's *Peter Wyngarde***
(LP, RCA Victor SF 8087, 1970) **£100**

Aficionados call it 'incredibly strange music'. Their parents probably knew it as 'easy listening' or 'leisure music'. Traditional rock fans prefer to call it rubbish. But there's no getting around the fact that the rehabilitation of the long-suffering 50p charity shop record has been one of the most exciting collecting phenomena of recent times.

Although they're closely related, because they have little or nothing to do with rock, there are clear differences between the exotic and easy categories. The quest for exotica first took root as an extension of the post-punk Industrial Music scene. Records with titles like *How To Strip For Your Husband* and *Songs Of Couch And Consultation* were championed for their sheer perversity; and the tropical island fantasy music of Martin Denny (the founding father of exotica) and the wayward Moog experiments of Perrey and Kingsley were hailed in the most unlikely quarters.

Since then, the area has grown to embrace almost anything that you won't find in your standard rock encyclopedia, whether that's comedian Arthur Mullard reviving the Beatles' 'Yesterday'; *Star Trek* actors William Shatner and Leonard Nimoy going psychedelic; or, most bizarre of all, Peter Wyngarde's record from 1970, performed in the manner of his debonair TV character, Jason King.

Best-known of all the 'personality' recording artists is Rolf Harris, whom many credit with making the first psychedelic record, 'Sunarise', back in 1962. That's the beauty of collecting exotica, and why contemporary mavericks like Stereolab and Japan's Pizzicato Five are drawn to the genre — because these records were conceived with little regard to convention, you can never be sure what to expect from that *Balsara & His Singing Sitars* album.

As long as you haven't paid out more than the price of a lottery ticket, there are surprisingly few disappointments to be found in bargain bins and at car boot sales.

While you'll be lucky to find more than one or two genuinely exotic recordings in your grandparents' garage, you'll probably be tripping over their easy listening collection — where names like Burt Bacharach, Ray Conniff, James Last, Percy Faith and Andy Williams will feature heavily.

Unlike most exotic

The 1960s 'Studio 2 Stereo' series of LPs is now collected by exotica fans. This LP is actually called "Exotica"!

The collectable Peter Wyngarde, who starred in the TV series 'Jason King' and 'Department S'.

titles, which weren't produced in great numbers, easy listening was as commercially successful as pop during the '60s, and you won't struggle to acquire a complete run of Conniff albums, for example.

'Easy' became the darling of London's club scene in 1994/95, and it was the mid-tempo material (as found on old film soundtracks, 'Studio 2' series titles and late '60s and early '70s 'made for stereo' recordings) which found most favour there.

Another aspect of easy collecting has been to recapture the days when pop hits were almost immediately covered by star names like Engelbert Humperdinck and Herb Alpert, or studio combos like Geoff Love & His Orchestra, the Wally Stott Chorale and Enoch Light & His Light Brigade.

Any album featuring versions of late '60s standards like 'Up, Up And Away', 'MacArthur Park', 'Aquarius' or 'Music To Watch Girls By' will no doubt be eagerly snapped up by the growing number of easy collectors.

Collecting Notes: Trust your eye. Exotica collectors are always drawn to the sleeve — the more bizarre, anarchic or archaic, the better. Phrases on the cover like 'A Study In High Fidelity Sound', 'Spectra-Sonic' or 'Visual Sound Stereo' are encouraging, as are shots of glamour girls peering through bamboo curtains or pseudo-psychedelic visual effects. And remember, if it's more than a quid, think again! Some Easy and Exotic purists argue that paying more than a nominal price for recordings that people used to throw away undermines the rationale behind collecting them — but even so, several Martin Denny albums now change hands for £40.

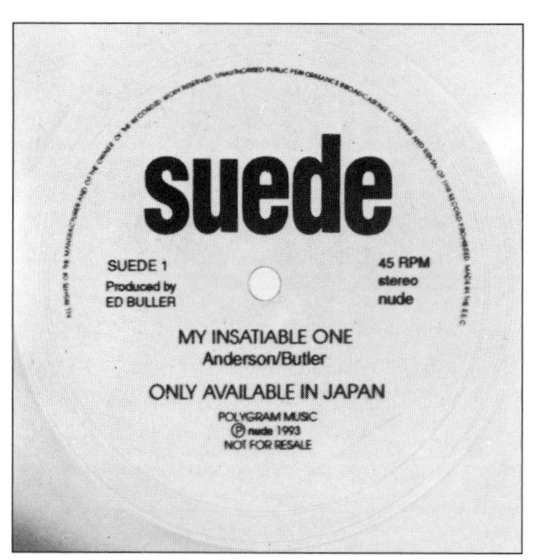

One of the most collectable recent flexis is Suede's gig freebie, "My Insatiable One".

The Scottish Postcard label began in 1980 with Orange Juice's "Falling And Laughing".

The Wonder Stuff put out the "Wonderful Day" EP on their own Far Out label in 1987.

1988's "Keep The Circle Around" signalled the start of the Inspiral Carpets' rise to fame.

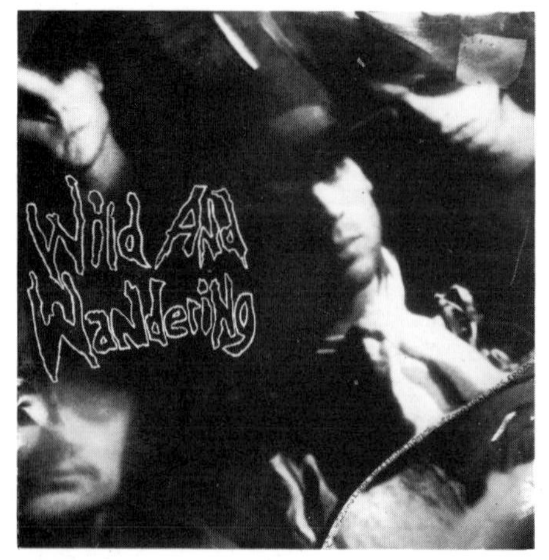

"2000 Light Ales From Home", from pre-Pop Will Eat Itself outfit, Wild And Wandering.

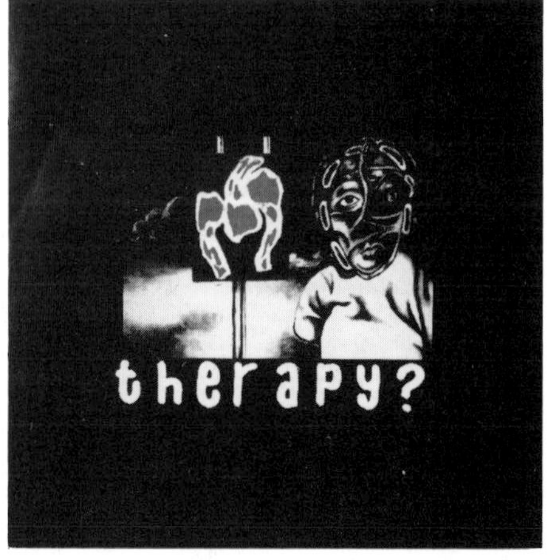

Issued on their self-financed MFN label, Therapy? debuted with "Meat Abstract".

THE TOP TEN COLLECTABLE ARTISTS

There are literally thousands — in fact, tens of thousands — of artists who have at least one collectable record to their name. But there are some performers who dominate the collecting scene, year after year.

Record Collector runs an annual readers' poll, to determine the Top 500 Collectable Artists. The results vary from one poll to the next, but the Top 10 names remain pretty constant. Over the next 25 pages, you'll find introductory guides to collecting those major performers, all of whom have sold millions of records. How can you tell which Beatles, Rolling Stones or R.E.M. releases are only worth a few pounds, and which might sell for a small fortune? The following pages will tell you.

THE BEATLES

TOP U.K. RARITY
THE QUARRY MEN's
'In Spite Of All The Danger'
(10", acetate, recorded by John, Paul and George's pre-Beatles skiffle group, 1958)

estimated value **£100,000**

Virtually everything the Beatles ever recorded is now available on CD. This includes all the material on their 13 original studio albums, 22 singles and 13 EPs, plus obscure recordings like the German-language renditions of 'She Loves You' and 'I Want To Hold Your Hand'.

But despite the fact that the Beatles' music is widely available, fans have never been so keen to get their hands on the group's original records. Because so much has been written about Beatles releases, collectors tend to centre their interest around the small details of their records — in fact, variations in label designs, artwork, and whether a recording is in mono and stereo, can sometimes make a difference in value of hundreds of pounds.

Despite the tremendous interest, we still don't know everything about Beatles records. Even today, 25 years after the group broke up, previously unknown items are still turning up for sale, and research is casting new light into poorly documented areas like export releases. New information is published in *Record Collector* magazine all the time, but here's a brief guide to the most popular areas of Beatles collecting.

Original U.K. pressings of the group's singles, EPs and albums are the obvious starting point. Due to the enormous numbers sold, most originals sell for just a few pounds each. The exceptions are the early red label copies of 'Love Me Do' (£30) and 'Please Please Me' (£35), and a 1960s black label re-pressing of 'Love Me Do', featuring a slightly different version of the song without Ringo on drums (£50). The original '60s picture sleeve editions of 'Strawberry Fields Forever' and 'Let It Be', at £18 and £8 respectively, are also worth looking out for.

No Beatles EP can be classified as really rare, although most are very difficult to find in pristine condition. Prices start at around £8 for *Twist And Shout*, and rise to £20 for 1966's scarce *Nowhere Man*.

Top of the range is the original 1963 gold-and-black label stereo version of *Please Please Me*, which sells for around £700. Early stereo and late mono albums are also sought after, though most fall into the relatively modest £20-£30 range.

Export albums are also pricey: for instance, in 1993, a U.K. export version of the 'White Album' sold for around £2,000 to a Japanese collector, though this price was over the odds. There are two distinct series — one based on the group's U.K. releases, the other on their U.S. catalogue. Most editions appear to have been re-pressed, spawning a host of label variations which can greatly affect the price. Rather fittingly, most Beatles export albums end up in the hands of overseas collectors, as most U.K. fans can't afford them!

Before signing to EMI, the Beatles recorded a handful of tracks with British singer Tony Sheridan for the Polydor label in Germany. All original issues of these recordings are valuable, some U.S. and Japanese editions fantastically so: for instance, 'My Bonnie' on U.S. Decca can fetch over £5,000.

Values for U.K. copies range from £40 for the orange label 'My Bonnie', to £80 for the rarely-seen 'Sweet Georgia Brown'. The Beatles' Polydor EP was a German record in a U.K. sleeve, and this now fetches around £50.

There are also many collectable Beatles reissues from the 1970s and 1980s, the most notable being coloured vinyls and picture discs. For example, late '70s white vinyl copies of the 'White Album', belatedly pressed by EMI U.K. for export around the world, now sell for £75, while the green vinyl of *Abbey Road* fetches around £65.

The sought-after Beatles' 1967 fan club flexidisc.

During the 60s, Paul McCartney 'gave away' hit songs to artists like Peter and Gordon, Billy J. Kramer and Mary Hopkin.

GATEFOLD SLEEVES

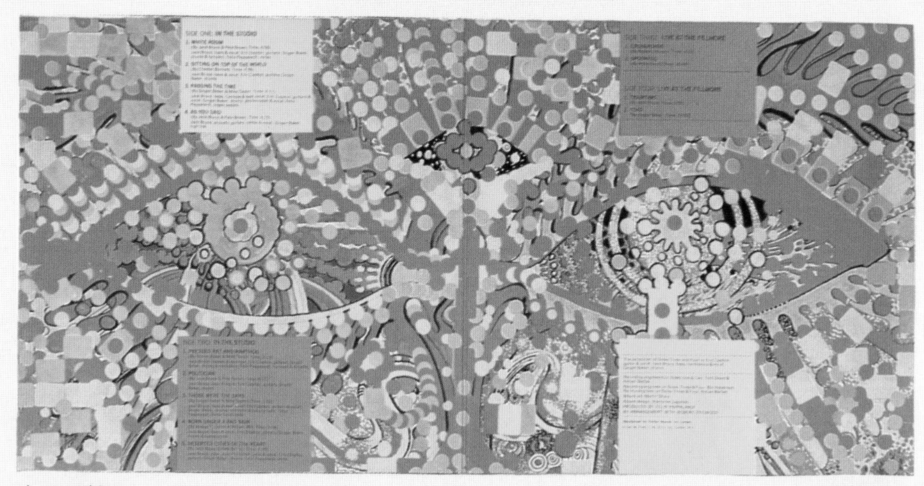

The inside gatefold for Cream's "Wheels Of Fire" reveals why this format was so popular.

This gatefold artwork only appeared on U.S. copies of Big Brother's "Cheap Thrills" LP.

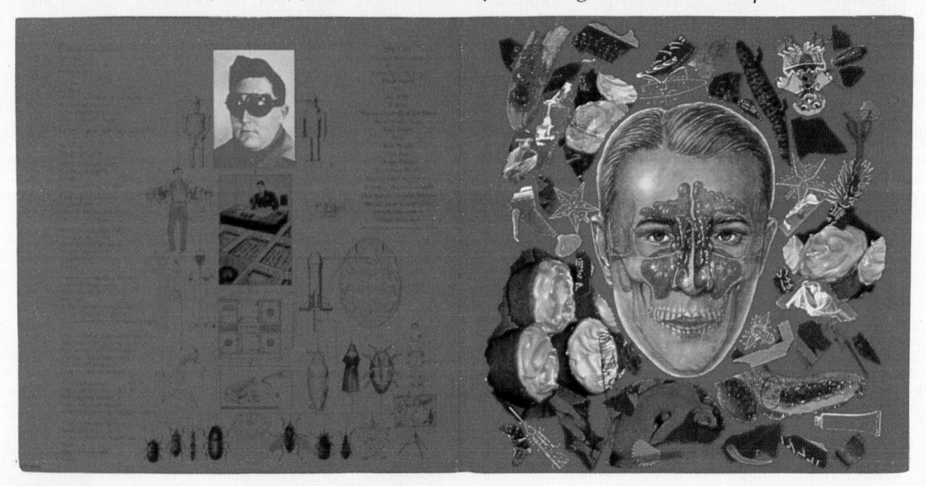

The sleeve of "Joe's Garage" allowed Frank Zappa room to show off his sense of humour.

LAVISH LATE 60s PACKAGING

Original copies of the Beatles' 1967 classic, "Sgt. Pepper's Lonely Hearts Club Band", came in a gatefold sleeve and included a cardboard insert.

Even more extravagant was the Small Faces' "Ogdens Nut Gone Flake", which was packaged like a tobacco tin. A later CD issue actually came in a tin!

Keith Richards of the Rolling Stones, who began his occasional solo career with a Christmas single in the late 70s.

The Beatles, pictured in September 1969, towards the end of their remarkable career.

Several picture discs issued to coincide with the 20th anniversary of the original singles are also now very collectable: 'She Loves You' is already an £18 rarity.

When it comes to overseas Beatles records, it's certain U.S. editions which are the most valuable. There can't be many collectors who haven't heard of the 'butcher cover' for the 1966 compilation album *'Yesterday' And Today*, which pictures the boys wearing white aprons and covered in dismembered dolls' limbs and slabs of meat.

There are, in fact, a variety of editions of this quickly withdrawn LP to sort through, including 'first state', 'second state', mono, stereo, still-sealed, etc. And, as with Beatles export albums, these differences can quite literally add an extra zero to the value.

In fact, trying to unravel the intricacies of the Beatles U.S. catalogue is always fraught with difficulties. The group's records appeared on a variety of labels before Capitol exercised their licensing option from EMI in the U.K. and decided to market the group. These pre-Beatlemania releases can now fetch hundreds, sometimes thousands, of pounds each, depending once again on label and sleeve variations.

RECOMMENDED LISTENING: It wouldn't be an exaggeration to list all the Beatles' recordings as essential listening, but *Please Please Me* catches the group in all their raw, primitive glory, while *Sgt. Pepper* is the obvious all-time classic (although many reckon that the early psychedelic pop of *Revolver* towers above it). The sprawling 'White Album' begins to reveal the Beatles as individual talents, and *Abbey Road* is an almost perfect climax to a riotous and breathtaking decade.

ROLLING STONES

> TOP U.K. RARITY
> **LITTLE BOY BLUE & THE BLUE BOYS**
> *(reel-to-reel tape, containing a pre-Stones recording by Mick Jagger, Keith Richards and friends, 1961)*
> **£50,000**

The Rolling Stones' thirty-year career has seen them grow from a stripling R&B covers group to the greatest, most famous rock'n'roll band in the world. True, it's arguable that they've been treading water since the rambling 1972 album, *Exile On Main Street*, but despite the fact that their fiftieth bithdays are now a receding memory, members Mick Jagger, Keith Richards, Charlie Watts and the recently departed Bill Wyman are still revered for their past glories and present prowess as a live act.

Because of the band's longevity, fans have an enormous back catalogue to get to grips with, and building up a set of Stones recordings presents a formidable task for the novice collector.

Acetates and other unreleased recordings represent a secret Stones treasure trove, and several important and highly expensive examples have turned up over the past few years. Nothing has come close to matching the impact of the Little Boy Blue & the Blue Boys' tape listed above, which features the earliest known recordings by Mick Jagger and Keith Richards. Intriguingly, it was apparently Jagger himself who bought this tape when it was auctioned at Christie's in 1995.

The most coveted U.K. Stones item is still without doubt the *Promotional Album*. Pressed in a limited run of 400, this LP was distributed among DJs and journalists on both sides of the Atlantic, and it now enjoys near-legendary status. Original copies (London RSD 1) are worth £600; but beware of an Australian edition, which is worth a considerably more modest £12.

Another popular area with Stones collectors is the rather confusing domain of their 'exports' — records manufactured in the U.K. for sale abroad. Examples like *Have You Seen Your Mother, Live* (LK/SKL 4838), *Flowers* (LK/SKL 4888) and *Out Of Our Heads* (LK/SKL 4725) are identified most easily by their catalogue numbers, since they could otherwise be mistaken for the ordinary U.K. editions. Early Stones export 45s mostly fall within the £30-£100 range, though a picture sleeve demo export 45 for 'Street Fighting Man' tops the lot at £125. And, speaking of picture sleeves, if you come across the withdrawn American cover for 'Street Fighting Man', only a handful of which are believed to exist, you could probably name your own price for it.

Early copies of the 1969 "Through The Past, Darkly (Big Hits Vol. 2)" collection came in an octagonal sleeve.

Unusual official U.K. releases are also highly-desirable, with the mono versions of *Their Satanic Majesties Request* (£40) and *Let It Bleed* (£35) being the hardest to find. Two cancelled releases, 'Poison Ivy' (Decca F 11742) and 'It's All Over Now'/'Paint It Black' (F 13517), are worth £400 and £100 respectively.

Demo and promo copies of the Stones '60s singles and albums are always in demand, although a special place is reserved for a small group of mid-'60s compilation albums featuring the group. *Thank Your Lucky Stars (Vol. 2), Ready, Steady, Go!, Saturday Club* and *Fourteen*, all of which contain just one Stones track, are all £25-£30 items. And *Today's Pop Symphony*, an album of orchestral versions of Rolling Stones songs, sells for £125.

For a basic collection of originals, you can expect to pay around £4-£7 apiece for the '60s singles, and between £15 and £35 for original '60s albums. Most '70s and '80s releases can still be purchased for a nominal price, including the 'zip' sleeve edition of *Sticky Fingers* (£10) and the original *Exile On Main Street* with its postcard inserts (£20).

RECOMMENDED LISTENING: *The Singles Collection* is a compact guide to the '60s singles; *The Rolling Stones* debut captures the group's original fiery brand of R&B, honed to sophistication on *Beggar's Banquet*; the double *Exile On Main Street* set offers a broader insight, while *Voodoo Lounge* is considered the best of their later output.

QUEEN

TOP U.K. RARITY
'Bohemian Rhapsody'
(7", blue vinyl, purple p/s, EMI EMI 2375, 1978)
£1,000

Freddie Mercury's untimely death in November 1991, and the spectacular Wembley Stadium tribute concert that followed soon after, inevitably focused public attention on Queen's flamboyant contributions to British rock. Not surprisingly, the value of the band's many rarities rose dramatically after Freddie's passing, as fans and dealers scrambled to scoop up everything in the group's back catalogue.

Strangely, it's Queen's best-known song that offers collectors the ultimate challenge. 'Bohemian Rhapsody' was the obvious choice for a celebratory limited edition when EMI won the Queen's Award For Export Achievement in 1978. The label manufactured 200 hand-numbered copies on royal blue vinyl, put them in purple picture sleeves and handed them out to selected employees. Those escaping onto the market currently change hands for over £1,000 each.

Also highly-prized by fans is a pre-Queen single from 1969. At that time, Freddie had yet to join the band, and Brian May, Roger Taylor and John Deacon went under the name Smile. Their only 45, 'Earth'/'Step On Me', appeared on the U.S. Mercury label and, if you manage to locate an original copy (and not one of the many counterfeits doing the rounds), then you can expect to shell out around £100 for it. Both sides also turned up on a 1983 Japanese mini-LP, *Getting Smile,* which itself can now fetch £25.

Another famous rarity is the one-off single made by Freddie Mercury when he was masquerading as glam-rock hero, Larry Lurex. EMI released this parody disc — which featured backing by the rest of Queen and assorted friends — several weeks before the group's debut album, but it sank without a trace. Today, you'll be lucky to find an original for under £50 but, again, beware of counterfeits.

A wild image adorned the "It's A Hard Life" 12" picture disc.

Incredibly, there is such a demand for Queen product that even the best-selling mid- and late '70s singles now sell for between £6 and £10 each. But in the main, collectors look abroad for the most interesting rarities. It goes without saying that overseas editions of the first few releases are much-coveted, including the Japanese edition of 'Keep Yourself Alive', the U.S. 'Liar' and 'Keep Yourself Alive', European picture sleeves for 'Now I'm Here', and a Japanese-language version of 'Teo Torriatte'.

Over the years, a variety of coloured vinyl editions of the group's albums have appeared, among them the Dutch white vinyl *A Night At The Opera* (£80), green vinyl copies of the French *News Of The World* (£100) and three versions of the French *Jazz* picture disc (£225-£500).

There is also considerable interest in the work of individual members, with solo releases by drummer/vocalist Roger Taylor currently proving the trickiest to find. Aside from two 1966 acetates by his '60s group the Reaction (valued at £1,000 and £6,000, respectively), look out for 7" copies of his first three singles, 'I Wanna Testify', 'Future Management' and 'My Country', which fetch £40, £8 and £12. His work with the Cross has also yielded some elusive limited edition CD singles, like 'Shove It' (£15).

RECOMMENDED LISTENING: The *Greatest Hits I & II* sets still provide a solid introduction, though you can try *Queen II* for their early power and *The Works* for their later pop majesty.

PINK FLOYD

TOP U.K. RARITY
'Arnold Layne'
(7", demo in promo-only picture sleeve, Columbia DB 8156, 1967)
£300

Although Pink Floyd are now famous for their 1970s concept albums, like *The Dark Side Of The Moon* and *The Wall*, it's their late '60s psychedelic recordings with cult figure Syd Barrett at the helm which tend to arouse most excitement among collectors.

The rarest records from that era are the promo-only picture sleeve editions of their first three singles, 'Arnold Layne', 'See Emily Play' and 'Apples And Oranges', worth £300 apiece. After quitting the group in 1968, Barrett issued a lone solo single, 'Octopus', which now sells for £60. Other late '60s collectables include the mono editions of Floyd's debut LP, *The Piper At The Gates Of Dawn* (£30), containing a radically different mix to the stereo version, and the elusive follow-up, *A Saucerful Of Secrets* (£40).

The remainder of the band's U.K. LPs are still relatively easy to come by in their original form, though quadrophonic editions of *Atom Heart Mother, The Dark Side Of The Moon* and *Wish You Were Here* are all priced around £25, chiefly because relatively few were bought at the time. After the Floyd's massive early '70s successes, exclusive items began appearing in the States, as EMI sought to break the band coast to coast. Consequently, a rash of U.S. promo singles appeared, with many of them — including 'One Of These Days', and later 'Learning To Fly' and 'Not Now John' — featuring the same song on both sides. These may still be picked up for between £15-£30.

More expensive are several U.S. promo LPs, often consisting of edited versions of complete albums — indeed, both *Animals* and *The Final Cut*, for example, were designed for radio play. But the most sought-after items in this field are a handful of radio albums featuring unreleased in-concert material. A double Westwood One set, capturing the group live at the start of the '70s, can fetch £100+.

Pink Floyd's 1967 hit "See Emily Play". Pick it up in a picture sleeve and you'll be in possession of a £300-rated rarity.

Up Close With Pink Floyd (£120) is currently the most in-demand Floyd-related U.S. radio show CD, though look out for *In The Studio* (£50) which features a mixture of music and chat.

All the band members past and present have made several solo recordings, but you should have little difficulty in tracking down most of Roger Waters, Dave Gilmour, Rick Wright and Nick Mason's output. However, there are a couple of interesting exceptions: prior to joining the Floyd, Gilmour

Syd Barrett, architect of the early Pink Floyd sound. He left the band early in 1968 to pursue a brief but much cherished solo career, releasing two brilliant and colourful albums.

was part of the Cambridge R&B outfit Joker's Wild, with whom he cut a single and a one-sided mini-LP, both limited to just 50 copies. Mint originals are extremely rare, with 'Don't Ask Me Why' worth an estimated £200, and *Joker's Wild* changing hands for £800.

RECOMMENDED LISTENING: *The Piper At The Gates Of Dawn, A Saucerful Of Secrets* and the Dutch-only *Masters Of Rock* are essential; *Ummagumma* and *Meddle* are sometimes slightly tarnished by indulgence, while *The Dark Side Of The Moon* and *The Wall* are simply too big to ignore. Also treat yourself to *Pulse,* the latest in-concert album, celebrating the band's mammoth '90s live experience, and Syd Barrett's two solo LPs, *The Madcap Laughs* and *Barrett.*

R.E.M.

TOP U.K. RARITY
'Radio Free Europe'
(7", IRS PFP 1017, 1983)
£35

If there's one thing that sets R.E.M. apart from many other stadium bands, it's their ability to quite happily splash about in the mainstream without ever getting their credentials soggy. From the start, they've always crafted pop tunes strictly on their own terms, and their current hypnotic brand of American music remains innovative and special enough to keep both the high-brow critics and their millions of fans happy.

Combining the directness of new wave with the melodic flair of the best '60s rock, their material has been an enormous influence on the U.S. rock scene over the past decade, first by leading a batallion of guitar bands in the early '80s, and subsequently by clearing the path for left-field acts like the Pixies, Throwing Muses and Nirvana.

R.E.M.'s first excursion onto vinyl was the 1981 single 'Radio Free Europe', which appeared on the U.S. indie label, Hibtone. The single didn't surface over

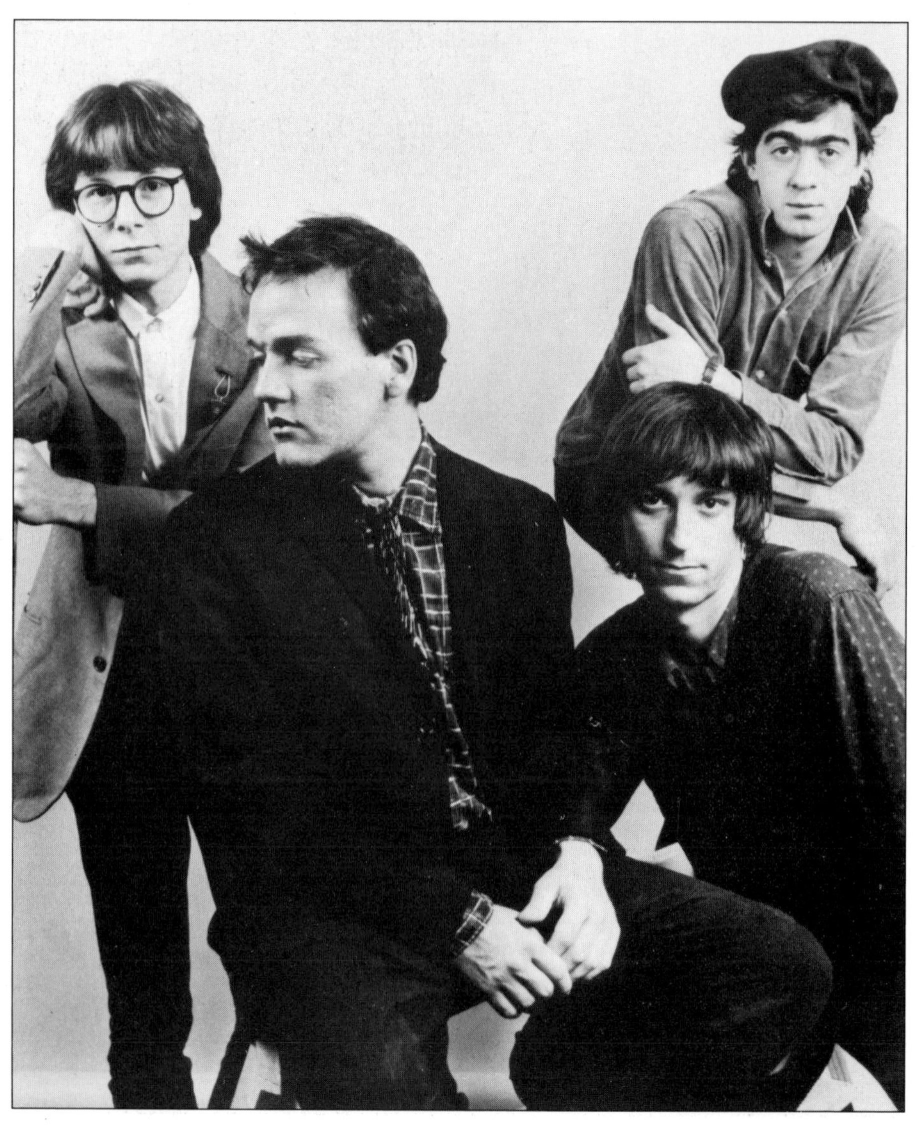

here until a year later, when a re-recorded version was lifted from their debut album, *Murmur*. Neither that LP nor any of its successors are hard to find, but the band's early U.K. 45s are scarce enough to have risen in price quite dramatically over the past decade.

Besides 'Radio Free Europe', the rarest U.K. singles are the 12" editions of 'Talk About The Passion' (£25), '(Don't Go Back To) Rockville' (£22) and 'Can't Get There From Here' (with a banner advertising unissued tracks, £20). All R.E.M.'s picture sleeve 45s on IRS are sought after, as are their U.S. and European equivalents, with the top prices being reserved for items with unusual A- and B-side couplings or different sleeve designs.

"Document", from 1987, one of the band's finest albums.

Other collectables include the series of Christmas records isued by the group's U.S. Fan Club, which now fetch anything up to £100 apiece, and several flexidiscs given away with magazines like *The Bob* and *Bucketfull Of Brains*. The band have managed to achieve megastardom without losing their 'small town' feel, and giving exclusive tracks to low-circulation fanzines has endeared them to their original fans.

Finally, watch out for records by offshoots like the Hindu Love Gods, plus guest appearances with artists like the Troggs.

"Stand", one of a string of highly-regarded R.E.M. 45s.

RECOMMENDED LISTENING: Aside from the hits packages on the market, try the initial blast of *Murmur*, the startling *Document*, and the mighty triumvirate of *Out Of Time*, *Automatic For The People* and *Monster*.

ELVIS PRESLEY

TOP U.K. RARITY
'A Mess Of Blues'
(78, RCA 1194, 1960)
£350

When Elvis Presley died in 1977, the BBC seriously considered announcing the news with the words "The king is dead". In the event, they modified the phrase to "The king of rock'n'roll is dead", but it was obvious from their deliberations just how deeply the singer from Memphis had touched a worldwide audience during his 42 years on the planet.

Elvis started out in 1954 on producer Sam Phillips' independent label, Sun, later the home of both Johnny Cash and Jerry Lee Lewis. Legend has it that, in Presley, Phillips had found the million-dollar formula he'd always dreamed of: a white boy who could sing like a black man. In the mid-'50s, Phillips' dream came true, and Elvis cut a string of rockabilly classics like 'That's Alright Mama' before manager Colonel Tom Parker took him to RCA Victor.

After a well-publicised national service stint in the U.S. Army, Elvis returned to action in the pop world and in Hollywood, where he starred in upwards of 30 films, which kept him insulated from developments in music (the Beatles, the advent of rock, etc.) for most of the '60s. Even so, he kept turning out million-selling records before re-casting himself in the early '70s as a gospel-tinged, rhinestone-studded Las Vegas attraction — a period which either signalled his artistic death or musical zenith, depending on your point of view. By the mid-'70s, booze and pills were taking their toll, and shortly after his comeback with the brilliant 'Way Down', he died.

The spectre of Elvis Presley still casts a forbidding shadow over the collector's market. As far as top-notch rock'n'roll artefacts go, there's little else to touch a pristine set of Presley's original U.S. 78s or 45s on Sun. Indeed, all five 45s together will cost you in the region of £1,000.

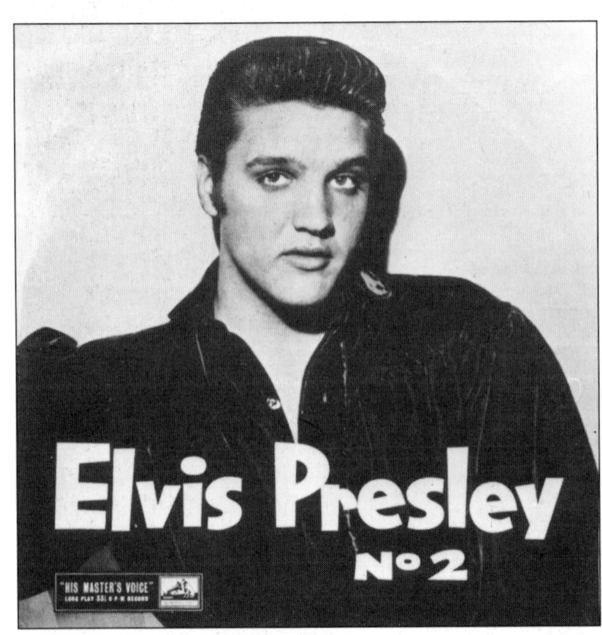

"Elvis Presley No. 2" was the King's second album for HMV. Expect to pay £200 for a copy in Mint condition.

In Britain, Presley's early recordings were issued by HMV, often both on 45 and 78. Of the 45s, it's the pressings with gold lettering on the label which are the rarest. In this form, 'Heartbreak Hotel', 'Blue Suede Shoes' and 'Rip It Up' are all worth upwards of £150. Even harder to find are HMV export 45s, with 'Mystery Train' (7MC 42) topping the pile at £225, while most silver lettering HMV 45s are scarce enough to hover around the £100 mark.

Early picture sleeve EPs fetch between £15 and £50, though *Love Me Tender* (£80) and *Good Rocking Tonight* (£90) fetch more.

Of Presley's '50s LPs, the heavyweights are the three HMV titles, *Rock'n'Roll* (£200), *Rock'n'Roll No. 2* (£200) and *The Best Of Elvis* (10", £160). Two other titles well worth bearing in mind are the famed *Elvis And Janis* South African 10" (£2,000) and the numbered edition of *The Legend* 3-CD 1984 box set (£180).

RECOMMENDED LISTENING: *The All-Time Greatest Hits* is the best guide to the 45s; *The Complete Sun Sessions* captures Presley at his primitive best; *Elvis,* from his '68 TV special, and *From Elvis In Memphis* recapture that early glory; while *That's The Way It Is* is the pick of the Vegas years.

LED ZEPPELIN

TOP U.K. RARITY
'Communication Breakdown'
(7", promo only, Atlantic 584 269, 1969)
£350

As the group who virtually defined heavy rock, you'd think that Led Zepp would have a back catalogue as blindingly extensive as Jimmy Page's best guitar solos. Sadly, the band's output originally stretched to just seven studio albums, and no 45s were ever commercially released in Britain.

However, fans shouldn't despair, as there's still a wealth of rarities and oddities to seek out, many stemming from the group's determination never to issue U.K. singles. For example, the tracks 'Communication Breakdown' and 'Whole Lotta Love' were both set to appear as 45s in 1969, though neither made the shops, making the promo copies in circulation now worth £350 each. With the support of singer Robert Plant, Atlantic tried again to push the band into the singles chart in 1973, when 'D'Yer Ma'Ker' was pressed up on 7" — but the rest of the band objected, and once again the 45 was shelved. The few copies that escaped fetch up to £100.

"Trampled Underfoot" is a highly-prized 7" U.K. promo.

In 1975, Zeppelin finally did make it onto a U.K. single, but only a promo. 'Trampled Underfoot' was sent out to encourage retailers to play and display Zeppelin product, and enough copies are in circulation to keep the price of copies at £15 each. Another single, 'Wearing And Tearing', is also rumoured to exist, though none has ever come onto the market. Intended for fans attending Zepp's 1979 U.K. shows, the single either never came to fruition, or else only a handful of copies were ever manufactured. If it does exist, 'Wearing And Tearing' would probably be worth well in excess of £500.

Atlantic attempted to promote the 1990 *Remasters* box set with a single, 'Stairway To Heaven'/'Whole Lotta Love'. Once again, promos were pressed, before the band intervened to stop them being distributed, and the few surviving copies now sell for £150 apiece.

Other prime collectables include Robert Plant's solo 45s, as well as the £125-rated 'You'd Better Run' single he made with Listen in 1967; overseas EPs and picture sleeve singles from the early '70s; and a host of mid-'60s beat/R&B singles featuring Jimmy Page on guitar, not least his superb £300-rated 1965 solo 45 for Fontana, 'She Just Satisfies'.

RECOMMENDED LISTENING: *Remasters* is the definitive boxed set, *Led Zeppelin II* the ultimate heavy metal assault; *III* profiles the band's mellower sound; while *Presence* is their grand mid-'70s statement.

NEIL YOUNG

TOP U.K. RARITY
'Buffalo Springfield'
(LP including 'Baby Don't Scold Me', 1967 Atlantic 587/588 080)
£35

More than thirty years after his first venture into a recording studio, Neil Young is more popular — and is getting better reviews — than ever. While most survivors of the 60s are regarded by the 90s rock press as tired dinosaurs, Young's career has been reborn since he returned to crazed electric guitar workouts at the end of the 80s. Since then, he's been feted as the 'godfather of grunge', and his collaborations with Pearl Jam have introduced him to an audience easily young enough to be his children.

That first Neil Young recording session took place in 1963, when he was the leader of a Canadian instrumental quartet called the Squires. Their one and only single, 'The Sultan'/'Aurora' (£1,000+) on the Winnipeg label V Records, has never been reissued, or even bootlegged. Apparently Neil doesn't own a Mint condition copy, either.

A brief spell with a Motown band, the Mynah Birds, didn't result in any vinyl, but Young recorded three albums with the Los Angeles band Buffalo Springfield between 1966 and 1968. Their self-titled debut LP was withdrawn at the start of '67, so their hit single 'For What It's Worth' (Atlantic, £5) could be added to the track listing. Collectors are keen to find original copies with the otherwise unavailable 'Baby Don't Scold Me'.

Since 1968, Young has maintained a solo career. But in the public eye, he's still linked with Crosby, Stills, Nash and Young, the late 60s super-group who were the stars of the 1969 Woodstock festival, and who seemed to sum up all the political passion and naivety of the era.

CSNY only recorded two studio albums, issued in 1970 and 1988, and their touring activity was effectively restricted to 1969/70 and 1974. The latter series of concerts spawned the ultimate CSNY rarity, a studio-enhanced live recording of Young's epic 'Pushed It Over The End'. This appeared on record just once, when it was included as a bonus 12" single in a multi-LP Young boxed set — in Italy (Reprise, £100).

Young inadvertently created a rarity or three with his first batch of solo sessions in 1968. His debut album, titled simply *Neil Young,* originally appeared in the States in a cover that didn't mention his name. These copies now fetch around £25 — twice the value of later U.S. copies, still boasting a gatefold sleeve, which added his name to the front of the package. These second issues also featured major remixes of several songs.

A tell-tale promo stamp in the top right-hand corner indicates that this copy of "Old Ways" was distributed as a promo.

Between 1968 and 1974, several of Young's singles featured tracks that weren't included on his albums. Particularly sought-after are the first promo issue of 'Everybody Knows This Is Nowhere', with an otherwise unissued 1968 take of the song; the vastly different version of 'Birds' which was slipped onto the flipside of the 1970 single 'Only Love Can Break Your Heart'; 1972's 'War Song', a political protest released all over the world apart from Britain; and 1973's 'Time Fades Away', which included a rare live recording of 'Last Trip To Tulsa' on the B-side (£6-£10 apiece).

Although none of Young's regular LPs is particularly rare, collectors are keen to make sure that their copies come with all the original inserts and special packaging. Young hand-scribbled his lyric sheets for albums like *After The Goldrush, Time Fades Away* and even his recent *Mirror Ball,* while *Tonight's The Night* came with an enigmatic four-page booklet printed in Dutch.

Like most current artists, Young's recent discography is full of special promo items — notably CDs like *The Complex Sessions,* with four live tracks, and various CD and 12" singles. Other non-LP cuts from recent years, like 'I'm Goin'' (the flipside of the U.S. single 'Ten Men Workin' ') and 'Don't Spook The Horse' (on the U.S. CD single 'Mansion On The Hill'), are also in demand from Young completists.

But the prize items in any collection would be the LPs he decided not to release. Acetates or test pressings exist for items like the original *Decade* (with a long version of 'Campaigner'), the first shot at *Trans* (with the unissued 'If You Got Love'), and the various steps towards getting the *Comes A Time* LP into the shops. Not surprisingly, the leftovers from these projects have been snapped up by the Young bootleg industry.

RECOMMENDED LISTENING: Young has adopted so many musical personas since 1963 that he's impossible to categorise. But any collection that begins with *Buffalo Springfield Again,* CSNY's *Deja Vu,* the 1970 solo LP *After The Goldrush,* 1979's *Rust Never Sleeps,* and a recent 'comeback' LP, like *Freedom* or *Ragged Glory,* wouldn't go far wrong. Aficionados, however, treasure the anguished mid-70s trilogy of *Time Fades Away, On The Beach* and *Tonight's The Night.*

DAVID BOWIE

TOP U.K. RARITY
'Station To Station'
(LP, with original colour proof sleeve, RCA APLI 1327,1976)
£500

It took several years for David Bowie to develop from art school R&B upstart into singer-songwriter genius, but by 1969 the transformation was complete. The *Ziggy Stardust* album and an impressive string of early '70s singles won Bowie acclaim from both sides of the rock/pop divide, and while many critics lament the passing of these golden years, the singer still commands a massive, fiercely loyal following.

Unsurprisingly, today's top rarities are records that no-one originally wanted to buy, and several are now three-figure items. Most evasive is the singer's debut single, 'Liza Jane', recorded as Davie Jones & the King Bees, which now has a price tag of around

The media's obsession with Courtney Love's status as the widow of Kurt Cobain has overshadowed her remarkable musical career with Hole.

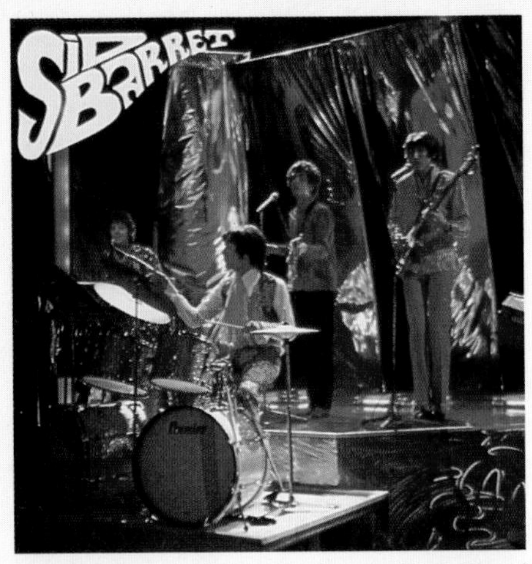

The existence of unissued early Pink Floyd tracks has sparked demand for bootleg LPs.

This bootleg of the Beach Boys' unissued "Smile" used the band's original artwork.

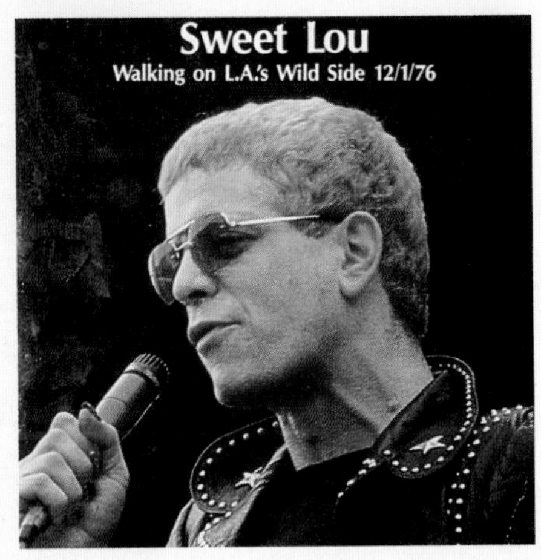

Bootlegs started out with plain sleeves, but colour photos were common by the late 70s.

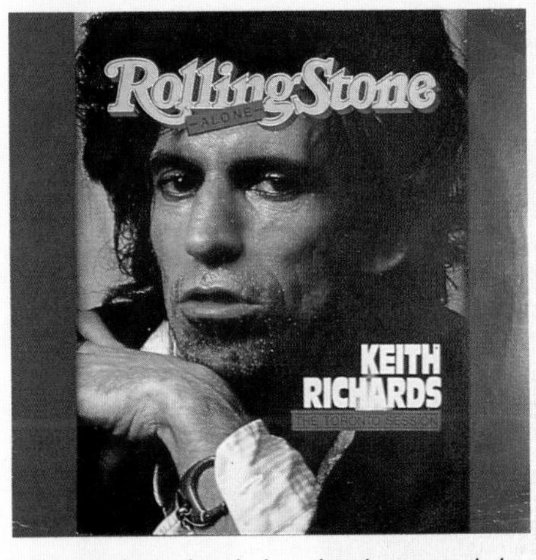

This Keith Richards bootleg borrowed the logo of 'Rolling Stone' magazine.

Beatles fans were stunned by the bootleg release of rehearsal tapes from 1960.

The U.S. edition of "The Beatles Christmas Album" has been heavily counterfeited.

Annie Lennox finally became a solo star in the 90s, after working for years as a member of bands like Eurythmics and the Tourists.

GRINdiNG HAlT
5
20p
the slits
THE THE
WALL
ATLETICO SPIZZ 20
WRECKLESS ERIC
5LA
COCKNEY REJECTS
16 =TONS=
THE ROCK MAGAZINE
ZIG ZAG
MEDIUM MEDIUM
KID CREOLE
THE CLASH
B·B KING
CRAMPS
CONGOS
BRIAN JAMES
CHRON GEN
PRESENTS
The Clash
SPA ROYA
SOUTH CLIFF RD., BRID
DAY 30th
THE ROCK MAGAZINE
GZAG
SIOUXSIE
THE FUTURE SHOCK
Linton Kwesi Johnson
Brixton Calling
SPECIAL OFFER
CLASH
NEVER MIND
THE BOLLOCKS
HERE'S THE
SEX PISTOLS
RIZLA
★ 'THE CLASH ★
SEX PISTOLS
NEW WAVE NEWS
SHAM 69
BUZZCOCKS
BLONDIE
OUT NOW

£400. Two more pre-David Bowie singles, 'You've Got A Habit Of Leaving Me' (as Davy Jones) and 'I Pity The Fool' (as the Manish Boys) comfortably sell for £250 each.

As far as Bowie's pre-RCA back catalogue goes — he signed to that label in 1971 — only his stray 'Space Oddity' hit single from 1969 can be found for under £10. His three 1966 Pye 45s are worth £80-£100 each; the trio of Deram singles £70-£90 apiece (though ensure 'The Laughing Gnome' has an inverted matrix number, unlike the later reissue); and his three 45s on Mercury £80 each.

Bowie's earliest 45s, like this 1965 flop, "You've Got A Habit Of Leaving", are among his most sought-after releases.

As for the early albums, a stereo edition of his self-titled Deram debut is, at £175, worth around £50 more than its mono counterpart. The similarly-titled Philips release is almost as rare, while a Mint copy of the famed 'dress' cover edition of *The Man Who Sold The World* sells for £200.

The massive sales and high profile associated with the RCA years means that the remainder of Bowie's official back catalogue is relatively easy to locate. But there are exceptions — notably the rare picture sleeve for 'Starman' (£40), the green vinyl pressing of 'DJ' (£20) and copies of *Changesonebowie* containing the 'sax' version of 'John I'm Only Dancing' (£25). Pride of place in any Bowie collection must be an original colour proof sleeve edition of *Station To Station* (later changed to black-and-white), which would now probably sell for a staggering £500 if it came onto the market.

The singer's strong visual appeal ensures that overseas picture sleeve singles are always in demand, too. If you find a European edition of any of the pre-RCA singles in a picture cover, with the possible exception of one or two of the 'Space Oddity' releases, the chances are that you'll have a £100+ item on your hands. Also particularly sought-after are Japanese and Italian copies of 'The Prettiest Star' (£300 and £400, respectively) and the Italian 'Space Oddity' (£350).

The final important sphere of Bowie collecting centres around the initial batch of CD reissue albums which appeared in the mid-'80s, but were hastily withdrawn. Because of their rarity — and certainly not for their aesthetic appeal — many of these shoddily-produced discs now sell for £20-£50, despite reappearing in remastered form in the wake of Bowie's EMI deal.

RECOMMENDED LISTENING: There's some great songwriting on Bowie's *Space Oddity* and *Hunky Dory* albums; *Diamond Dogs* and *Low* find Bowie at his most creative, and you certainly can't ignore *The Rise And Fall Of Ziggy Stardust*. 1980's *Scary Monsters (And Super Creeps)* is considered by some to be his last great album.

MADONNA

TOP U.K. RARITY
'Erotica'
(12", picture disc, withdrawn, Sire W 1038TP, 1992)
£300

Together with Prince and Michael Jackson, Madonna Ciccone brought the kind of glamour to '80s pop that we normally associate with the stars of '50s Hollywood. Starting off in a New York punk band the Breakfast Club, she found fame in 1984 when she teamed up with producer and DJ Jellybean Benitez for the dancefloor hit, 'Holiday'.

Her career quickly rollercoasted, and with 1985's 'Like A Virgin' casting her in the role of strong, sensuous and independent female icon, it wasn't long before she was a worldwide superstar, known as much for her outspoken opinions and risqué stage shows as her songs. Yet it was ultimately her music that maintained her profile — though appearances in movies like *Desperately Seeking Susan, Shanghai Surprise* and *Dick Tracy* certainly did her no harm — and albums like *True Blue, Like A Prayer* and *Erotica* were praised for their originality and innovation.

Since *Erotica* and her infamous book *Sex*, which pictured her in a variety of soft porn poses, Madonna's pace has slowed. But any new Madonna product will always be treated as a media event.

Madonna became a star overnight with 'Holiday', but it wasn't her first release. Two flops had preceded it, 'Everybody' and 'Lucky Star', both of which present today's collector with a challenge. Although 'Lucky Star' eventually became a hit when it was reissued, the original 12" edition in the 'sunglasses' picture sleeve is now so scarce copies change hands for £35, while the 12" of 'Everybody' sells for £55. And prices for the 7"s aren't far behind.

Since 'Holiday', every Madonna release has charted, leaving fans to concentrate on limited editions like the £65-rated shaped picture disc of 'Crazy For You' (backed with Sammy Hagar's 'I'll Fall In Love') and the *Royal Box* edition of the *Immaculate Collection* CD, with video, poster and postcards — a snip at £60. And while the picture disc editions of 'Borderline' and 'Who's That Girl' sell for upwards of £30, the biggest price is reserved for the withdrawn 'Erotica' 12" picture disc (£300), only 138 of which are thought to be in circulation.

Many special editions accompany each Madonna release, including this 'zipper' sleeve for "Express Yourself".

However, the vast majority of Madonna rarities come from overseas: Japan has spawned two ultra-rare promo-only CD compilations, *1983-1989* and *1983-1990*, both effectively greatest hits sets.

As you'd expect with an artist as visual as Madonna, packaging is as important as content, so any overseas picture sleeve different to its U.K. equivalent is automatically sought-after.

Madonna is proof that collecting flourishes among pop fans as well as rockers.

RECOMMENDED LISTENING: *Immaculate Collection* brings together the first six years of hits, while *Like A Prayer* and *Erotica* are the strongest and most mature of the individual albums.

THE WORLD'S RAREST RECORD

Not only are the Beatles by far the most collectable group in the world, they are also responsible for the two rarest and most valuable recordings of all time. One of them raised the highest price ever paid at a public auction for an archive tape; the other is a single which is safely in the collection of none other than Paul McCartney, but has been conservatively valued at no less than £100,000. Together, they represent the secret history of the early Beatles or, as they were known in the '50s, the Quarry Men.

LENNON BEFORE McCARTNEY

On 15th September 1994, EMI paid £78,500 at Sotheby's for a rough, two-song 1957 recording by the pre-Beatles outfit, the Quarry Men. For the first time in nearly 40 years, the world had the chance to hear how John Lennon sounded before he began working with Paul McCartney. On the evidence of 'Putting On The Style' (a snatch of which was played in the saleroom on the day of the auction), the ghostly quality of Lennon's piercing vocals proved that this cocky teenager was a star in the making.

With perfect timing, the tape captured the Quarry Men at the very start of their career. The band actually survived for around three years — from March 1957 to spring 1960 — but their roots stretched back as far as 1955. That summer, the 14-year-old Lennon dug out a harmonica he'd been given a few years earlier by his Uncle George, and took his first tentative steps towards playing Frankie Laine's 'Cool Water' and Johnnie Ray's 'Walking My Baby Back Home'.

Rock'n'roll arrived at Lennon's door in October 1955, when Bill Haley's 'Rock Around The Clock' reached No. 1. But it was Elvis Presley, with his sensual swagger and fiery youth, who embodied the essence of this wild new 'teenager's music'.

In addition to rock'n'roll, there was the skiffle craze, which captivated Britain's youth in 1956 and 1957. Pioneered by Lonnie Donegan, the banjo player in Chris Barber's Jazz Band, skiffle was an impromptu spin-off from the traditional jazz, folk and blues of America's southern states. Its appeal lay in the fact that almost anyone could play it. The song structures were simple, and so were the instruments: acoustic guitar, tea-chest bass and a glass washboard, which was played percussively with thimbles wedged over the ends of the fingers.

It was Donegan's 'Rock Island Line', a Top 10 hit in January 1956, which inspired Lennon to pick up a guitar. " 'Rock Island Line' was the record which set us all off," confirms Rod Davis, the Quarry Men's original banjo player. "It made us realise that you didn't need a 40-piece orchestra to play in a band. In fact, you didn't even need to know anything about music."

After stealing a guitar from a boy at school, only to return it when he discovered he couldn't play it, Lennon pestered both his Aunt Mimi and his mother, Julia, for an instrument of his own. He was finally rewarded with a £17 second-hand acoustic model, and struggled for the next year to learn his mother's four-string banjo chords — prompting Mimi to utter her immortal words, "The guitar's all very well John, but you'll never make a living out of it". When he finally felt comfortable with his strumming technique, John suggested to his best friend, Pete Shotton, that they should form a skiffle group — just for a laugh. Shotton was the first to admit his lack of musical skill, so he only agreed reluctantly, but he soon found himself rummaging through his parents'

The Quarry Men at the Woolton Church Fete in Liverpool on 6th July 1957 — the day Paul McCartney first set eyes on John Lennon. Paul would join the group in a matter of weeks.

garden shed looking for an old washboard, the easiest skiffle instrument to master.

They named their group the Black Jacks, after their new 'stage clothes' of black jeans and white shirts. They constructed a rudimentary bass from an old tea chest, a broom handle and a length of string, which they painted black and decorated with a white treble clef. This instrument can clearly be seen in a famous photograph of the Quarry Men performing on the back of a coal lorry in Liverpool's Rosebery Street.

BIRTH OF THE QUARRY MEN

Several of the other early Black Jacks came from the Liverpool Institute For Boys, like Paul McCartney and George Harrison. Ivan Vaughan and Nigel Whalley, who also came from the Institute, temporarily took over the broom-handle bass, although neither man survived beyond the band's air-raid shelter rehearsals. But Ivan later made Beatles history as the man who introduced Lennon to McCartney, while Nigel opted to become the Black Jacks' 'manager'.

By the time guitarist Eric Griffiths, drummer Colin Hanton and banjo player Rod Davis joined the ranks, the Black Jacks had become — at Shotton's suggestion — the Quarry Men. The name was an uncharacteristically affectionate reference to John and Pete's school, Quarry Bank High School For Boys, and its song, which (much to the teenagers' amusement) included the line, 'Quarry Men, strong before our birth'.

As well as playing at each other's houses, the Quarry Men — who now comprised

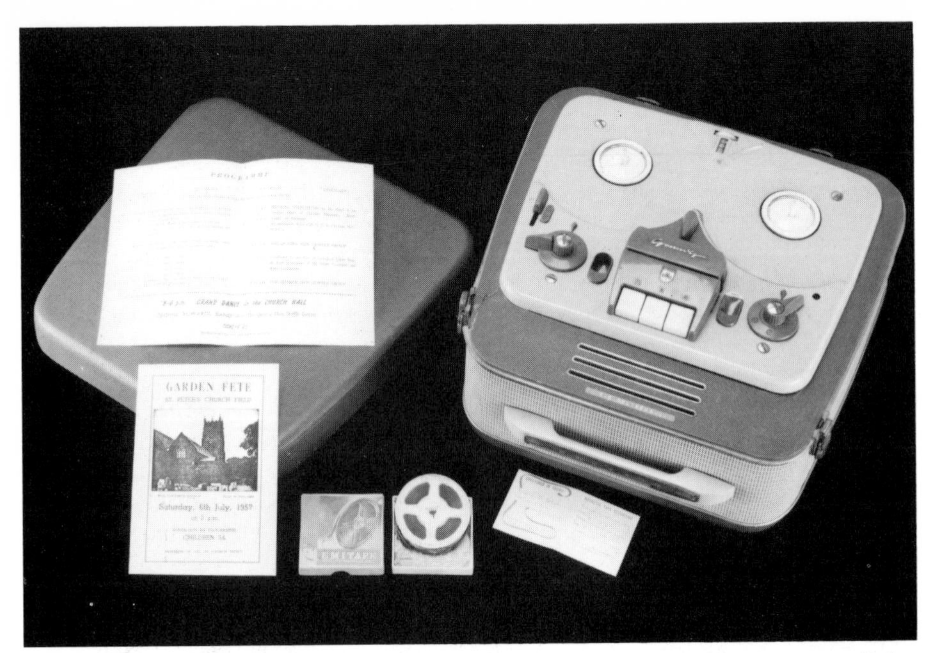

The recording of the Quarry Men at the Woolton Church Fete remained hidden for 27 years before being sold to EMI for £78,500 in 1994. Here it is complete with the machine on which it was made.

Lennon, Shotton, Davis, Eric Griffiths and Len Garry — began to perform in public. On 6th July 1957, the Quarry Men delivered three sets at the St. Peter's Church Fete, Woolton — John's local parish. It was here that Lennon first met Paul McCartney and also that Bob Molyneux, a teenager from John's youth club, set up his weighty Grundig TK 8 tape recorder to capture the band's rowdy evening performance. Two songs from this momentous recording — versions of Lonnie Donegan's 'Putting On The Style' and Elvis's 'Baby Let's Play House' — survived the years, although Molyneux admits he erased the remainder of the band's performance shortly afterwards. But that didn't seem to matter in 1994, when the tape eventually surfaced, and was sold at Sotheby's in London for £78,500. That price easily outstripped anything ever paid for a record or tape at any of the frequent memorabilia auctions held around the world.

THE FIRST BEATLES RECORD

A week or two after Lennon and McCartney's first meeting, Pete Shotton spotted Paul cycling through Woolton and invited him on John's behalf to join the Quarry Men. Paul's arrival more or less coincided with the decline of the skiffle craze, as up and down the country British groups graduated to rock'n'roll. McCartney's first gig with the Quarry Men took place that October — he'd missed the band's debut at the Cavern Club in August, because he'd been camping with the Boy Scouts. The following February, Paul introduced the band to the 14-year old George Harrison, yet another Liverpool Institute schoolboy, famous among his classmates for his fluorescent shirts and luminous socks. Slowly but surely, George too became a Quarry Man.

On the surface, 1958 was a quiet year for the group; although they did acquire a pianist in John Duff Lowe, a friend of McCartney's, and yet another recruit from the Institute. More importantly, they made a record, a 10" 78rpm acetate, which featured a version of the Crickets' 'That'll Be The Day' and a unique McCartney/Harrison composition, 'In Spite Of All The Danger'.

The man who 'produced' the recordings was Percy Francis Phillips, who ran an electrical shop from the front room of his Victorian terraced house at 38 Kensington, in the L7 district of Liverpool. A lifelong country-and-western fan, he didn't begin recording until he was well into his sixties. In 1955, spurred on by the local boom in C&W music, he boarded a train for London, where he took a course in electrical recording. He returned to Merseyside staggering under the weight of a tape recorder, an amplifier, microphones, a four-way mixer and an M.S.S. portable disc cutter — £400 worth of equipment in all. In his living room, Percy constructed a makeshift studio, hanging blankets at the windows and over the doors to muffle the sounds of the buses and trams rumbling along the busy A57 outside. It was on the M.S.S. machine that he cut the first professional recordings of the group who became the Beatles.

The sole copy of the Quarry Men's acetate now belongs to Paul McCartney, who acquired it for an undisclosed sum from John Duff Lowe in 1981. Having had the acetate in his possession for over twenty years before that, Lowe seemed the ideal person to reveal its secrets. But when we contacted him, he politely refused to discuss the acetate, citing a 1981 legal agreement with Paul McCartney. That not only gave Paul official possession of the record, but also ruled that Lowe must not reproduce the song or its lyrics, perform it live or even *talk about it publicly* for the next 15 years!

HEARING THE WORLD'S RAREST RECORD

Before his agreement with McCartney, Lowe had made attempts to sell the acetate on the lucrative collector's market, and had contacted one Beatles dealer in particular. Back in 1981, this dealer had been unable to offer Lowe enough money, and suggested instead that he should put the disc into Sotheby's inaugural rock'n'roll memorabilia auction. It was the pre-publicity for this sale which alerted the attention of Paul McCartney — and his lawyers.

The dealer in question, who is no longer active on the collector's circuit, clearly recalls his brief association with what is surely the world's rarest record. "I remember when John Lowe first got in touch with me," he says. "It didn't click who he was, at first. He said he had a really rare record for sale — haven't they all? — but when he told me what it was, and who he was, I nearly fell off my chair. I travelled up to his place like a shot, and sat there glued to the speakers as he played both sides of this scratchy old 78. These were early days as far as Beatles collecting was concerned, but I knew this was something very special."

Describing the recordings in detail, the dealer went on: "John Lowe wouldn't let me tape the record, although he did let me hear it over and over again. Both tracks were obviously cut straight to disc. Lowe said that they'd been laid down in one take — you could even hear John Lennon miss an intro on 'In Spite Of All The Danger'!

" 'That'll Be The Day' was fairly faithful to Buddy Holly's original," he continued, "with Lennon doing a pretty good copy of Holly's hiccup vocals. This version's on every bootleg going now, of course, since McCartney played an excerpt of it on his Buddy Holly TV documentary in the '80s, but at the time it was definitely a thrill to hear it.

"I was keener to hear 'In Spite Of All The Danger'," maintained the dealer, "especially when Lowe told me it was an unreleased McCartney-Harrison song. I never knew they'd written together. Being a bit of an Elvis fan as well, the first thing which struck me was how similar the song was to Elvis's 'Trying To Get To You'. I think McCartney said as much in an interview once, although I don't think he said which song it was. It opened with George's guitar intro. I'm sure Lennon sang lead vocal with McCartney and Harrison singing 'wah-wah' harmonies in the background. You could hear Lowe's piano quite clearly. I'd say it was a mid-tempo ballad-type song, and more sophisticated than their other early original songs, like 'Hello Little Girl' or 'Love Of The Loved'.

"Another thing which was unusual about that song," he concludes, "was its length. It's a very long recording for the time — it must have been at least four minutes long. I remember Lowe saying that the old guy who owned the studio started waving his arms in the air for them to wrap it up as the cutting stylus was getting near to the centre of the record."

The Quarry Men paid 17/6d (about 90p) to cut the acetate, and left Percy Phillips' studio with just the one copy. Each member of the band was entitled to 'a borrow' of it for a while, to play it to family and friends, and was then obliged to pass it on. For a week in 1958, it even fell into the hands of a worker from the Littlewoods factory in Crosby (possibly a friend of drummer Colin Hanton) and was apparently played over the building's Tannoy system. Shortly after John Duff Lowe had his turn with the disc, his association with the Quarry Men came to an end. As a pianist, he couldn't take his instrument with him to gigs, and if a venue had its own piano, it was often out-of-tune or nowhere near the stage. As luck would have it, in late 1958, Lowe found himself without any Quarry Men to give the acetate to, and it remained in his possession until Paul McCartney opened his cheque-book in 1981.

THE SECRET REISSUE

After Lowe left, the Quarry Men — reduced to Lennon, McCartney, Harrison and Colin Hanton — picked up a further two members. The first of these was a bassist called Kenneth Brown, who'd played in the Les Stewart Quartet skiffle group with George Harrison. He left in 1959 following an argument over 15 shillings' performance fee at Pete Best's Casbah club. The final Quarry Man was Stuart Sutcliffe, whom John Lennon met when he enrolled at the Liverpool College of Art after leaving Quarry Bank. With Sutcliffe's arrival, the Quarry Men — after a series of moonlight appearances as Johnny and the Moondogs — went through a series of name changes: first to the Beatals, then to the Silver Beats, the Silver Beetles (or the Silver Beatles), and finally, as the austere 1950s swung into the sensational Sixties, the Beatles.

All that was left of the Quarry Men was their one solitary acetate disc. Putting a price on 'In Spite Of All The Danger' is difficult. It belongs to Paul McCartney, and it's hard to imagine him putting it up for sale. But using the sale of Bob Molyneux's 1957 Quarry Men tape as a guide, a conservative valuation of at least £100,000 seems quite possible.

Remarkably enough, although the original acetate is so rare it's virtually a national treasure, there is a second pressing of this legendary record in existence. Paul McCartney buying the disc in 1981 was not the end of the story. In fact, that same year, Paul had both sides of the acetate remastered, and then privately pressed on replica 78rpm and 45rpm singles!

The remastering took place in Abbey Road's Room 13, a small studio at the back of the famous EMI complex where the Beatles made all their albums. The disc reportedly sounded as if it had been 'played with a six-inch nail'. Once it was safely positioned on a top-of-the-range turntable at Abbey Road, every trick in the book was used to try and get the best possible reproduction onto tape. It was even played backwards in an effort to secure a clearer signal from the wall of the groove with the least wear. Channelling it through de-clicking and noise-reduction systems only seemed to interfere with the sound quality, and it was eventually remastered in its original state, with just a little 'EQ' thrown in to balance the sound between the two songs ('In Spite Of All The Danger' was longer — and therefore quieter — than 'That'll Be The Day').

Paul apparently asked that the disc should be produced to match the original as closely as possible. From Abbey Road, the new master tape was taken over to the Orlake pressing plant in Dagenham, Essex. Orlake ceased production of shellac in the early '60s, but it did have a small batch of a substitute material in stock. New copies of 'That'll Be The Day'/'In Spite Of All The Danger' were run off until the material was exhausted, a total of two-dozen or so discs in all. At the same time, a similar number of vinyl 7" 45rpm singles were manufactured. The labels were photographic reproductions of the handwritten originals — so none of them mentioned the words 'Quarry Men'. Meanwhile, the tatty Parlophone sleeve into which Percy Phillips slipped the original disc back in 1958 had also been reproduced. On the 7" version, the speed on the sleeve was changed to '45rpm', but otherwise the appearance was authentic.

One side of the only Quarry Men record known to exist featured a cover of Buddy Holly's "That'll Be The Day".

All the metalwork was removed from the site as soon as the job was completed, any imperfect copies were destroyed, and McCartney took delivery of up to 50 copies. Apparently, he gave some away as Christmas presents to his closest friends, while the rest were locked away in a vault.

No tale about a hitherto unknown Beatles private pressing would be complete without a valuation. U.S. fans are willing to pay up to £12,000 for what they reckon is the ultimate Beatles rarity: sealed stereo copies of the 'Butcher Cover'. Paul's Quarry Men 'reissues' are certainly rarer than that, and if one ever came on the market, it would surely fetch an even higher price than that!

"In Spite Of All The Danger" is the only song known to bear a Paul McCartney-George Harrison composing credit.

TERMS & EXPRESSIONS USED IN COLLECTING

ACETATE — Soft lacquer disc with metal core, used in recording studios.

ART SLEEVE — Picture cover with design or cartoon, rather than photo.

ARTWORK — Original design for sleeves or labels.

AUCTION — Sale of records, usually via mail-order, to the highest bidder.

AUDIOPHILE RECORD — High quality pressing.

BOOTLEG — Illegal record or CD of material not intended for official release.

BOXED SET — Multi-LP or CD set in presentation box.

BUDGET RELEASE — New pressing retailing below full-price.

CARTRIDGE — Eight-Track Cartridge. Also term for stylus holder on turntable.

CASSETTE — Standard tape format, with two spools enclosed in a plastic case.

CASSINGLE — Abbreviation for cassette single.

CATALOGUE NUMBER — Identifying number on labels and sleeves.

CDi — Interactive variation of CD-ROM, containing remixes and visuals.

CD PLUS — Recent multi-media innovation, similar to CDi.

CDR — Recordable CDs, the digital equivalent of acetates. Occasionally used as promos.

CD-ROM — Audio/visual computer-compatible CD.

CD VIDEO (CDV) — CD single spin-off, featuring audio and audio/visual tracks.

COLOURED VINYL — Records pressed in any colour other than black.

COMPACT DISC — Standard commercial digital format.

COMPANY SLEEVE — Cover with company logo.

COMPILATION — Collection of tracks from various sources.

COUNTERFEIT — Illegal reproduction of an official release.

CUE SHEET — Printed supplement included with interview and radio albums.

CUT-OUT — U.S. term for deleted record, so called because of clipped cover.

DAT — Digital Audio Tape.

DCC — Digital Compact Cassette.

DELETED — No longer available from record company or distributor.

DEMO — Record pressed as demonstration disc, usually as review copy. Also term for early, rough-draft recording.

DIE-CUT SLEEVE — Sleeve with circular hole cut on one or both sides.

DIGIPAK — Patented name for gatefold CD sleeve with plastic inner tray.

DISCO SINGLE — Late 1970s term for 12" singles intended for DJs.

DJ RELEASE — Term for promos intended for club or radio DJs.

DOUBLE/TRIPLE ALBUM — Two or three LPs packaged and sold together.

DOUBLE-GROOVE — Record with two grooves on the same side.

DOUBLE-PACK — Two singles sold as one package.

DUOPHONIC — Short-lived stage between mono and stereo, developed in America in the early 1960s.

EDGE WARP — Warp restricted to record's perimeter.

EIGHT-TRACK CARTRIDGE — Tape format popular in the 1970s.

ENVELOPE SLEEVE — Thick cardboard sleeve with envelope-style foldover flap.

EPHEMERA — Collectable letters, photos, press releases, concert tickets, etc.

E.P.K. (Electronic Press Kit) — Promo device, including CD and video.

EXPORT — Record manufactured in U.K. for sale abroad.

EXTENDED PLAYS (EPs) — 7" discs with four tracks and picture cover.

FACTORY CUSTOM PRESSING — Unofficial record pressed after hours, usually in small numbers.

FLEXIDISC — Thin plastic record, usually issued free with magazine, etc.

FLIPBACK SLEEVE — Laminated LP or EP cover with front flaps folded over back sleeve. Also known as fold-over sleeve.

FOLDOUT SLEEVE — Open-out cover, sometimes folding out into a poster.

45rpm — Standard speed in revolutions per minute (rpm) for 7" single.

FREEBIE — Record given away free with record, magazine, etc.

GATEFOLD SLEEVE — Record cover which opens like a book.

GOLD/SILVER/PLATINUM DISC — Framed presentation disc used as sales award.

GRADING — Method of establishing a record's condition.

HALF-SPEED MASTER — Optimum quality disc remastered at half speed from original tapes.

HIP-POCKET RECORDS — Miniature American flexidiscs from the 1960s, intended for special toy players.

IMPORT — New record or CD manufactured overseas but sold in the U.K.

INNER SLEEVE — Protective sleeve inside main cover.

INSERT — Postcard, press release or lyric sheet included in packaging.

INTERVIEW ALBUM — Spoken word record or CD, often used as promo device.

JEWEL CASE — Standard clear plastic box for CDs and cassettes.

JUKEBOX SINGLE — Special 7" pressed for use in jukeboxes.

LABEL — Central area of record on which artist and track information is printed.

LAMINATED SLEEVE — Cover with high gloss finish.

LAND — Area of vinyl between grooves and label.

LASERDISC — 12" audio/visual video disc.

LIMITED EDITION — Release manufactured in limited quantities.

LONG BOX — Tall rectangular cardboard packaging for American CD albums.

LONG PLAYER (LP) — 12" 33rpm disc, the standard album format prior to CD.

LYRIC SHEET — Song-word insert.

MASTER — Finished recording used to manufacture record.

MATRIX NUMBER — Sequence of numbers and letters used by record companies to identify recordings, usually printed on label (near catalogue no.) and on 'land'.

MAXI-SINGLE — 1970s 7" successor to the EP.

MEGAMIX — Medley of different tracks, often linked by dance beats.

MEMORABILIA — Collectable items like posters, instruments or clothing.

MID-PRICE RELEASE — Record retailing at a discount price.

MINI-ALBUM — Mid-price album usually with half-length playing time.

MINI-DISC — Miniature CD.

MISPRESSING — LP or CD pressed with incorrect material.

MONO — Sound recorded for playback through one channel.

NON-ALBUM B-SIDE — A track on a single not included on any album.

NUMBERED — Individually numbered limited edition release.

ONE-SIDED DISC — Record with one side left blank.

PICTURE DISC — Novelty record with picture sealed within clear vinyl.

PICTURE SLEEVE — Single or EP cover with artist photo, etc.

PIRATE — Illegal reproduction of recording, often differing from official release.

POSTCARD FLEXIDISC — Playable postcards, popular in Eastern Europe.

POSTER SLEEVE — Poster folded to form picture sleeve.

PREMIUM — Record available via special offer with breakfast cereal, etc.

PRESS KIT — Information pack with photos and biography, used by record company to promote new release.

PRIVATE PRESSING — Record issued by an individual, rather than a professional record company.

PROMO — Promotional record.

PUSH-OUT CENTRE — Removable centre of a 7" single.

QUADROPHONIC — Four-channelled playback system.

RADIO ALBUM/RADIO SHOW — U.S. radio broadcast pressed for distribution throughout network of stations.

READY RECKONER — *Record Collector*'s system for valuing records.

RECORD FAIR — Indoor trade market for secondhand records, CDs, etc.

REEL-TO-REEL TAPE — Standard commercial format superseded by cassette.

REISSUE — Re-release of deleted disc.

REMIX — Variation of an existing track.

RE-PRESSING — A second run of records, identical to the first pressing.

REPROCESSED STEREO — Mono recordings electronically treated to give stereo effect.

RUN-OFF GROOVE — Continuous groove in 'land' between playing area and label.

SAMPLER — Compilation of tracks showcasing a label or artist.

SEALED/SHRINKWRAPPED — Machine-wrapped in cellophane.

SET SALE — *Record Collector* term for mail-order sale at a fixed price.

7" — Standard size for singles and EPs.

78rpm — Standard speed for pre-1960s singles.

SHAPED DISC — Any non-circular record.

SHELLAC — Brittle material used for 78s.

SLIP CASE — Small cardboard cover used for CD singles.

STEREO —Sound recorded for playback through two channels.

STICKERED — Release with sticker on packaging.

33rpm — Standard speed for vinyl LPs.

TEST-PRESSING — Record pressed by manufacturer for quality control.

TRANSCRIPTION DISC — Album made by the BBC's Transcription Service.

TRI-CENTRE — Triangular push-out centre common on 1950s 45s and EPs.

TRI-FOLD — Triple foldout sleeve.

VIDEO — Audio/visual cassette tape.

VIDEO CD — CD equivalent of laserdisc.

VIDEO DISC — Short-lived 12" audio/visual laserdisc launched in mid-1980s.

VINYL — Material from which records are made.

WARP — Buckle caused by heat.

WAX — American slang for vinyl.

WHITE LABEL — Term for demo, promo or test pressing with white labels.

WITHDRAWN — Record deliberately removed from sale.

ABBREVIATIONS

AS	Art Sleeve
B	Bad Condition
B&W	Black-And-White
CO	Cut-out
COV	Cover
DBL	Double
DEMO	Demonstration Copy
DJ	Disc Jockey Copy
D/LP	Double LP
EDN	Edition
EP	Extended Play
EW	Edge Warp
EX	Excellent Condition
F	Fair Condition
G	Good Condition
G/F	Gatefold Sleeve
IMO	International Money Order
IMP	Import
IRC	International Reply Coupon
LP	Long Player
M	Mint Condition
M	Mono
MAG	Magazine
MB	Minimum Bid
M/S	Mono/Stereo
NAP	Not Affecting Play
NC	No Cover
NM	Near Mint
NOC	No Original Centre
NO'D	Numbered
OFFS	Offers Required
P	Poor Condition
PC	Picture Cover
PD	Picture Disc
PR	Promotional
PS	Picture Sleeve
R&B	Rhythm And Blues
RI	Reissue/Rock Instrumentals
R&R	Rock'n'Roll
SAE	Stamped Address Envelope
SL.	Sleeve
SOC	Sticker On Cover
SOL	Sticker On Label
SS	Still Sealed/Surface Scratches
ST	Stereo
STC	State Total Cost
STKR	Sticker
TOC	Tear On Cover
TOL	Tear On Label
TOS	Tear On Sleeve
T/P	Test Pressing
TRI	Triangular Centre
VERS.	Version
VG	Very Good Condition
W/L	White Label
WLTP	White Label Test-Pressing
WOC	Writing On Cover
WOL	Writing On Label
WOS	Writing On Sleeve
2x45	Double Pack
2-LP	Double Album
3-CD	Triple Compact Disc

Throughout this book, song titles are printed in single quotation marks (for example: 'She Loves You', 'Anarchy In The U.K.', etc.).

Titles of LPs and albums are printed in italics (for example: *Sgt. Pepper, Automatic For The People*, etc.).

INDEX